EXPANDING YOUR VOCABULARY
A Skill-Based Approach

Kathleen T. McWhorter
Niagara County Community College

Brette McWhorter Sember

PEARSON
Longman

New York San Francisco Boston
London Toronto Sydney Tokyo Singapore Madrid
Mexico City Munich Paris Cape Town Hong Kong Montreal

Acquisitions Editor: Kate Edwards
Development Editor: Gillian Cook
Senior Supplements Editor: Donna Campion
Marketing Manager: Thomas DeMarco
Production Manager: Ellen MacElree
Project Coordination, Text Design, and Electronic Page Makeup: Nesbitt Graphics, Inc.
Cover Design Manager: John Callahan
Cover Designer: Kay Petronio
Photo Researcher: Jody Potter
Senior Manufacturing Buyer: Dennis J. Para
Printer and Binder: Quad/Graphics, Dubuque
Cover Printer: Phoenix Color Corporation

For permission to use copyrighted material, grateful acknowledgment is made to the copyright holders on pp. 243–244, which are hereby made part of this copyright page.

Library of Congress Cataloging-in-Publication Data
McWhorter, Kathleen T.
  Expanding your vocabulary : a skill-based approach / Kathleen T. McWhorter, Brette McWhorter Sember. —
1st ed.
    p. cm.
  Includes bibliographical references and index.
  ISBN-13: 978-0-205-64586-2 (student ed. : alk. paper)
  ISBN-10: 0-205-64586-0 (student ed. : alk. paper)
  1. Vocabulary—Problems, exercises, etc. 2. Universities and colleges—Curricula—Terminology—Problems,
exercises, etc. 3. Learning and scholarship—Terminology—Problems, exercises, etc. I. Sember, Brette
McWhorter, 1968– II. Title.
  PE1449.M397 2008
  428.1—dc22
                    2008037450

Visit us at www.pearsonhighered.com

ISBN-13: 978-0-205-64586-2 (Student Edition)
ISBN-10:   0-205-64586-0 (Student Edition)

ISBN-13: 978-0-205-64587-9 (Instructor's Edition)
ISBN-10:   0-205-64587-9 (Instructor's Edition)

3 4 5 6 7 8 9 10—V042—14 13 12 11

BRIEF contents

DETAILED **contents**

3 Dictionaries: Worthwhile Investments   44

4 Using Word Parts to Expand Your Vocabulary   71

5   Vocabulary on the Move!   113

PART two Discipline-Specific Vocabulary

PREFACE

Strong vocabulary skills are essential for success in college and in the workplace. They are the keys to comprehending what you read, understanding what you hear, and expressing yourself effectively through speech and writing. In one concise text, *Expanding Your Vocabulary* teaches students at all levels the skills they can use to decipher and learn new vocabulary in any setting.

Overview and Rationale

Most competing texts use a word-list learning approach: students learn approximately 250 to 300 words per book by using them repeatedly in a variety of exercises. Estimates of the average adult vocabulary range widely, from 50,000 words to well beyond 200,000 words. Using the conservative estimate of 50,000 words, if a vocabulary book that uses the word-list approach teaches students a total of 250 words, it improves a students' vocabulary by a mere 0.5 percent. This outcome is negligible for the effort put forth by both instructor and student. In contrast, *Expanding Your Vocabulary: A Skill-Based Approach* will enable students to increase their vocabulary exponentially, through effective use of context, word parts, and dictionary usage. For instance, a set of 30 high-utility prefixes, roots, and suffixes can unlock the meaning of over 20,000 words. This book also addresses discipline-specific vocabulary in ten academic fields, providing lists of high-utility words and content readings students can use to practice and apply the skills they have learned in the text.

Content Summary

> ➤ **Introduction to Vocabulary: College and Workplace Success.** The introduction explains the importance of learning vocabulary for success at work and in college.

> ➤ **Part 1: General and Academic Vocabulary.** Five chapters teach students specific skills for deciphering, learning, and remembering new vocabulary (how to learn and remember new words, using context clues, using word parts, using a dictionary and thesaurus, learning foreign words and phrases, understanding euphemisms, analogies, and figurative language, and how to deal with commonly confused words).

> ➤ **Part 2: Discipline-Specific Vocabulary.** Ten chapters are devoted to vocabulary specific to the disciplines of computer and information systems, law and criminal justice, allied health and medicine, education, business, biology, psychology and sociology, politics and government, literature, and the arts. Each opens with a list of 20 high-utility words, followed by three sets of exercises and a content reading with exercises designed to allow students to practice the skills they learned in Part I.

Special Features

> ➤ **Mastery Tests:** At the end of each of Chapters 1–5, Mastery Test 1: Applying and Integrating Your Skills provides vocabulary practice using one or more short passages, and Mastery Test 2: Applying and Integrating Your Skills (in a specific discipline) allows students to apply their skills to a full-length reading from an academic source.

- **Exercises:** Skills are learned through application and practice. Within each chapter, exercises provide small-step practice on sentences and paragraphs. Types of exercises include multiple-choice, fill-in-the-blanks, matching, write-in-definitions, and longer-answer questions. End-of-chapter mastery tests provide skill application on longer reading selections.

- **Readings:** Each of the ten chapters in Part II ends with a full-length, discipline-specific reading followed by two sets of exercises: the first deals with context clues and word parts, and the second asks students to apply the skills they have learned to decipher the meaning of a range of vocabulary words.

- **Exploring Language:** These boxes, often illustrated, are designed to provoke students' interest in language and introduce them to unique features of language. Topics include new meanings for old words, eponyms, acronyms, and ghost words.

- **Word Notes:** These appear throughout Chapters 1–5 and consist of boxed text and photos that introduce the content in an interesting or humorous way.

- **Learn More About . . . :** This feature directs students to Web sites to obtain further information or practice on the skills presented in the chapter.

- **Full-Color Design:** Each chapter opens with a photograph related to content, and color is used throughout to differentiate among heads, exercises, and readings, making the text engaging and easy to use.

Text-Specific Supplements

- **Annotated Instructor's Edition:** This is an exact replica of the student text, with answers provided for the instructor's convenience.

- **Test Bank:** The Test Bank offers a series of skill building exercises and quizzes for each chapter, formatted for ease of copying and distribution.

Acknowledgments

The editorial staff of Longman Publishers deserve special recognition and thanks for the guidance, support, and direction they have provided during the development of this text. In particular we wish to thank Gillian Cook, our development editor, for her valuable advice and assistance, and Kate Edwards, acquisitions editor, for her creative ideas and enthusiastic support. Thanks also to the following reviewers for their valuable comments and suggestions:

Nancy Bertoglio, American River College
Ana Fillingim, Salt Lake City College
JoAnn Foriest, Prairie State College
Linda Gilmore, Carroll Community College
Cathy Harvey, Grossmont College
James Jasmin, Eastern New Mexico University–Roswell
Judith I. Johnson, John Tyler Community College
Almarie J. Jones, Gloucester County College
Sandra G. Jones, Community College of Baltimore–Catonsville
Alison Kuehner, Ohlone College
Robert Mathews, Miami-Dade Community College, North Campus
Yuanzhong Zhang, Miami-Dade Community College, North Campus

Kathleen T. McWhorter
Brette McWhorter Sember

Introduction to Vocabulary: College and Workplace Success

Boy meets girl. Teacher meets student. Employer meets job applicant. Then what happens?

When people meet for the first time, they size each other up and form first impressions. New acquaintances may size you up by how you look—your clothing, hairstyle, shoes, jewelry, and so forth. They may also size you up by what you say and how you say it. People may notice an accent, the use of slang, the loudness or softness or pitch of your voice, and so forth. They also notice your vocabulary. Every time you begin speaking or as soon as someone reads a sentence you have written, you are revealing something about yourself:

➤ **You may reveal many personal characteristics.** You may reveal that you are a native or nonnative speaker of the language, for example. You may reveal where you live or grew up, based on your accent. Your use of slang may suggest what reference group or age group you belong to. Your use of technical words may reveal your occupation. (Don't physicians often tell you what's wrong with you in language you can't understand? Can't you always tell who is a computer techie as soon as the conversation turns to computers?) Your language, and specifically your vocabulary, may reveal your level of education, too. Professors and employers often can easily pick out those who are college educated from among the individuals in a group. College graduates often speak and write differently, perhaps because they think differently as well.

► **Your vocabulary also reveals whether accurate and clear expression is important to you.** If you lack the words to express an idea, you are revealing that effective communication is not a priority. Both in the classroom and in most careers, communication is essential. If you show no interest in communicating effectively, your professor may think you are not a serious student, and an employer may not be interested in hiring you.

► **By observing whether you are speaking and writing in the language of the subject matter you are studying, your professors can assess how interested and involved you are with a course.** If, in a biology class, you are still calling amoebas "those little things swimming around" and, in a chemistry class, you are still calling a beaker a "glass," you are revealing lack of interest in and seriousness about the course.

► **By listening to whether you can describe your prior employment experiences clearly without struggling for words, an employer can learn whether you can focus and organize information.** You also reveal, however, whether you have the words readily at your command to communicate what you know about your job history.

► **Most importantly, through your speaking or writing you reveal your thinking.** It is through language that you share information, express your ideas and feelings, solve problems, and present arguments. Your vocabulary—individual words that you know and use—are the building blocks of language. In both speech and writing, you string them together to express meaning.

So, you can see that vocabulary is important, and probably more revealing than you thought.

Vocabulary and College Success

WORD **notes**

Think about the following questions:

► Why do professors assign papers and give essay exams?

► Why do professors expect you to answer questions in class?

► Why might a professor require you to make a speech or participate in a class discussion?

Let's be practical. There's more to getting good grades than just studying hard. Grades in college depend on tests and exams, papers, oral reports, lab reports, and class participation. Each is a form of self-expression. You not only have to learn the material being tested or reported, you have to demonstrate that you have learned it, either through speech or writing. If you completely understand the theory of cognitive dissonance in psychology, for example, but cannot explain it clearly in your own words on an essay exam, what kind of grade can you expect?

Vocabulary and Workplace Success

WORD **notes**

Question: What do corporations look for in prospective employees?

Answer: The DeVry Institute of Technology conducted a survey to find out which skills and aptitudes corporations value most highly.[1] Of the top ten employee capabilities listed, can you guess what skill was ranked first? Excellent verbal and written skills were the most highly rated. Critical thinking ranked fifth; creative thinking ranked sixth. Both verbal and written skills depend in part on vocabulary, as does critical and creative thinking.

Can you imagine engineers, although technically competent, being unable to explain what they are working on, being unable to describe their role in a project, and being unable to relate their tasks to what others are doing? This lack of communication skills is a problem often cited by employers of engineers.[2] Many employers in a variety of fields report similar problems. Writing in the "Job Market" column that appears regularly in the *New York Times*, Sabra Chartrand reports that even in technical fields, communication skills are highly valued.[3]

Here are two research findings that point to the connection between a strong vocabulary and success in the workplace:

➤ A study conducted by the U.S. Department of Education concludes that literacy level, which includes knowledge of word meaning, is positively associated with higher annual earnings.[4] In other words, those with stronger literacy skills earned higher salaries.

➤ A study conducted by the Johnson O'Connor Research Foundation reports that successful executives have better vocabularies than nonexecutives of the same age group.[5]

To get and keep a good job, then, you will need excellent vocabulary skills.

Endnotes

1. From "Survival of the Fittest" from *Directions* newsletter, 1997. Used by permission of DeVry Institute of Technology, a division of DeVry University.
2. From "English and Your Career," by Nancy Saffer, *Occupational Outlook Quarterly* 43, no. 2 (Summer 1999).
3. From "A World Where Language and 'Soft Skills' Are Key" by Sabra Chartrand, *New York Times*, April 6, 1997.
4. U.S. Department of Education, National Center for Education Statistics, National Adult Literacy Survey, 1992.
5. From *American Demographics* 17, no. 4:13 (April 1995).

PART one

General and Academic Vocabulary

There are many ways to improve your vocabulary, some more effective than others and some more time consuming than others. This section of the book presents the most effective and efficient ways to learn new words and make them part of your working vocabulary. No one technique will work every time. The word itself and the situation in which you encounter it will often dictate your choice of method. If you learn all of the techniques taught in this part, you will be well-equipped to handle any new word you meet.

Strategies: Learning New Words

Remember the weekly spelling and vocabulary lists you used to get in school? The list was distributed on Monday; the test was on Friday. (Why are tests always on Friday?) After passing the test you forgot the words, right? Memorization is obviously the wrong way to learn new vocabulary. This section will show you two better ways.

In all of your college courses, and later in your career, you will be expected to learn new terminology. In fact, success in many college courses hinges on your ability to read, write, speak, and understand the language of the discipline. Likewise, in careers you are expected to "talk the talk." While learning new words is important, learning them the right way is also important. In this chapter, you will learn several effective systems for learning and remembering new words, including a system of word study called word mapping.

How to Learn New Words

Visualize It! Using Word Mapping

Word mapping is a visual method of expanding your vocabulary. It involves examining a word in detail by considering its meanings, synonyms (words similar in meaning), antonyms (words opposite in meaning), part(s) of speech, word parts, and usages. A word map is a form of word study. By the time you have completed the map, you will find that you have learned the word and are ready to use it in your speech and writing.

Figure 1-1 shows a sample map for the word *intercept*:

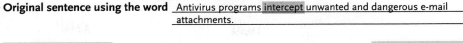

Word Map

Original sentence using the word Antivirus programs intercept unwanted and dangerous e-mail attachments.

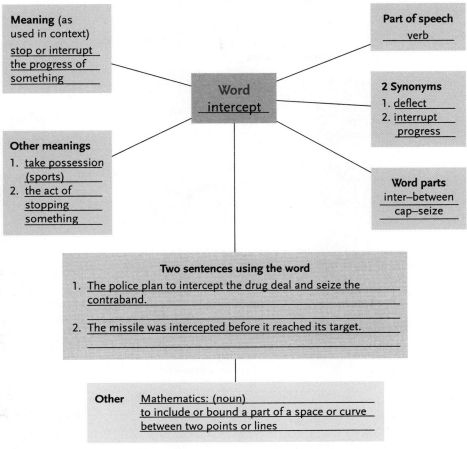

Meaning (as used in context)
stop or interrupt the progress of something

Part of speech
verb

2 Synonyms
1. deflect
2. interrupt progress

Word
intercept

Other meanings
1. take possession (sports)
2. the act of stopping something

Word parts
inter–between
cap–seize

Two sentences using the word
1. The police plan to intercept the drug deal and seize the contraband.

2. The missile was intercepted before it reached its target.

Other   Mathematics: (noun)
to include or bound a part of a space or curve between two points or lines

Figure 1-1   Sample word map.

Use the following steps in completing a word map:

1. **Write the sentence containing the word at the top of the map.**

2. **Look the word up in your dictionary.** Figure out which meaning fits the context of the sentence and write it in the box labeled "Meaning (as used in context)."

3. **In the "Part of speech" box, write in the word's part(s) of speech as used in context.**

4. **Study the dictionary entry to discover other meanings of the word.** Write them on the map in the box labeled "Other meanings."

5. **Find or think of two synonyms (words similar in meaning), and write them in the "Synonyms" box.** You might need a thesaurus for this.

6. **Analyze the word's parts and identify any prefixes, roots, or suffixes.** Write each word part and its meaning in the space provided.

7. **At the bottom of the map write two sentences using the word.**

8. **In the box labeled "Other," include any other interesting information about the word.** You might include antonyms, restrictive meanings, or word history.

Directions: Create a word map for an unfamiliar word you have encountered in one of your courses that you feel it is important to learn. Use the blank map provided.

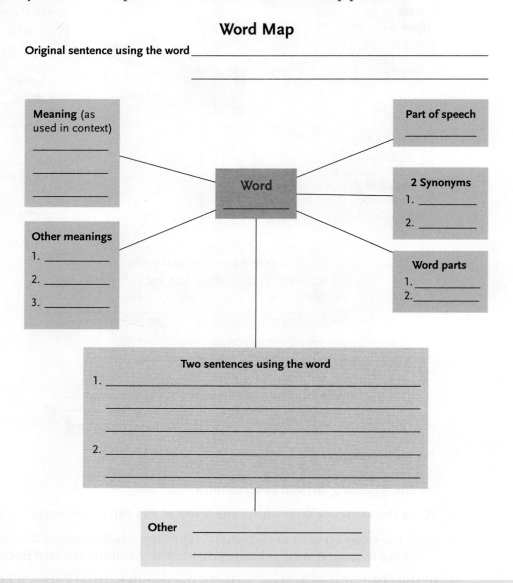

Word Map

Original sentence using the word _____

_____

Meaning (as used in context)
_____
_____
_____

Part of speech
_____

Word
_____

2 Synonyms
1. _____
2. _____

Other meanings
1. _____
2. _____
3. _____

Word parts
1. _____
2. _____

Two sentences using the word
1. _____
_____
_____
2. _____
_____

Other _____
_____

Write to Learn: Keeping a Vocabulary Log

A vocabulary log is a list of words you want to learn. They may be words that you find in textbooks, articles and essays, or magazines and newspapers. You might also record words you heard in class lectures. Be sure to record only useful words—those you want to learn. You can use a variety of formats. You can create a vocabulary log for each course you are taking, reserving a section in each of your notebooks in which you record lecture notes. You can keep a separate notebook and designate it as your vocabulary log. You can create a computer file or files.

In addition to recording words and their meanings, be sure to record each word's pronunciation if it is not familiar. Some students also record a sentence

Word	Meaning	Page
intraspecific aggression	attack by one animal upon another member of its species	310
orbitofrontal cortex	region of the brain that aids in recognition of situations that produce emotional responses	312
modulation	an attempt to minimize or exaggerate the expression of emotion	317
simulation	an attempt to display an emotion that one does not really feel	319

Figure 1-2 Sample vocabulary log for a psychology course.

using the word. Others include a text reference page number so they can locate where they first found the word. Experiment with different formats and different organizations until you find one that works for you. An excerpt from one student's vocabulary log for psychology is shown in Figure 1-2.

EXERCISE 1-2   Creating an Index Card/Vocabulary Log

Directions: Create an index card file or vocabulary log for one of your other courses. Update it weekly.

Use Spare Moments: The Index Card System

As you read textbook assignments and reference sources, and while listening to your instructors' class presentations, you are constantly exposed to new words. Unless you make a deliberate effort to remember and use these words, many of them will probably fade from your memory. One of the most practical and easy-to-use systems for expanding your vocabulary is the index card system. It works like this:

1. **Write down new words.** Whenever you hear or read a new word that you intend to learn, jot it down in the margin of your notes or mark it some way in the material you are reading.

2. **Later, write the word on the front of an index card.** Then look it up in a dictionary, and underneath the word, record the word's pronunciation and write in its part of speech. On the back of the card, write other forms the word may take and a sample sentence or example of how the word is used. If you are a visual learner, draw a diagram or picture to depict the word as well. Your cards should look like the ones in Figure 1-3, on page 10.

3. **Once a day, take a few minutes to go through your pack of index cards.** For each card, look at the word on the front and try to recall its meaning on the

inordinate
(in-or'de net)
(adjective)

beyond the proper limit,
excessive

The speaker made an inordinate
number of pronunciation errors.

FRONT

BACK

Figure 1-3 Sample index card.

back. Then check the back of the card to see whether you were correct. If you are unable to recall the meaning or if you confuse the word with another word, retest yourself. Shuffle the cards after each use.

4. **After you have gone through your pack of cards several times, sort the cards into two piles—words you know and words you have not learned.** Then, putting the known words aside, concentrate on the words still to be learned.

5. **Once you have learned the entire pack of words, review them often to refresh your memory.**

This index card system is effective for several reasons. First, it can be reviewed in the spare time that is often wasted waiting for a class to begin, riding a bus, and so on. Second, the system enables you to spend time learning what you do *not* know rather than wasting time studying what you already know. Finally, the system overcomes a major problem that exists in learning information that appears in list form. If the material to be learned is presented in a fixed order, you tend to learn it in that order and may be unable to recall individual items when they appear alone or out of order. By shuffling the cards, you scramble the order of the words and thus avoid this problem.

Use It or Lose It! Tips for Using the Words You Learn

WORD notes

The bad news: Forgetting happens! If you don't play a sport for several years, you forget some of the plays and moves and have to relearn them. If you don't perform a certain function on your computer for several months, you forget the commands to use. If you don't use a new word you just learned, you are likely to forget it.

The good news: You can prevent it.

Here are some suggestions for learning and retaining words. Depending on your learning style, some of the suggestions will work better than others.

➤ **Write the word immediately.** If you find the word in a textbook, you will have a better chance of remembering it if you write it rather than just highlight it. In fact, write it several times, once in the margin of the text, then again on an index card or in your vocabulary log. Write it again as you test yourself.

➤ **Write a sentence using the word.** Make the sentence personal, about you or your family or friends. The more meaningful the sentence is, the more likely you are to remember the word.

➤ **Try to visualize a situation involving the word.** For instance, for the word *restore* (to bring back to its original condition), visualize an antique car restored to its original condition.

➤ **Draw a picture or diagram that involves the word.** For example, for the word *squander* (to waste), draw a picture of yourself squandering money by throwing dollar bills out of an open car window.

➤ **Talk about the word.** With a classmate, try to hold a conversation in which each of you uses at least ten new words you have learned. Your conversation may become comical, but you will get practice using new words.

➤ **Try to use the word in your own academic speech or writing as soon as you have learned it.**

➤ **Give yourself vocabulary tests or, working with a friend, make up tests for each other.**

EXERCISE 1-3   Learning and Remembering New Words

Directions: For words in your index card file or vocabulary log, experiment with the above suggestions. List below two suggestions that seem to work well for you.

1. _____

2. _____

Once you have learned a new word, make sure you can spell it correctly. To learn the spelling of a word, use these four steps:

1. **Look for familiar or similar parts in a word.** For example, when you see the word *budgetary*, you can see the word *budget*. See if a word is spelled in a similar way to another word you already know? *Perceive* is spelled in a similar way to *receive*, for example. The more meaningful you can make the word's spelling, the easier it will be to remember it.

2. **Say the word aloud and copy it as you speak.** Copy it several more times.

3. **Try to write the word without looking at the original word.**

4. **Check to see if you spelled it correctly.** If not, repeat the above steps until you can spell it correctly.

Keep a list or log of words you have misspelled on papers or exams. Work on learning each word on the list. Periodically, test yourself to see if you can still spell each one correctly.

You Are What You Eat: A Daily Menu of New Words

WORD notes

What happens when you eat an orange popsicle? Your tongue turns orange! You are what you eat. To stay or become a healthy person, you have to pay attention to what you eat. A daily diet of new words will help you become a well-spoken individual and an effective writer.

Here are five easy ways to introduce new words into your diet:

➤ **Be alert for words that you know but do not use.** There are hundreds of words that you recognize when you read or hear them, but do not use yourself. Make a note of useful words that will sharpen your speech or writing. Add them to your index card file or vocabulary log.

➤ **Keep an eye out for precise words that will replace two to three smaller, less descriptive words.** For example, instead of *to take out,* consider words such as *remove* or *expunge.* Instead of *feeling sorry* about something, you could use the words *rue* or *regret, lament* or *bemoan* instead.

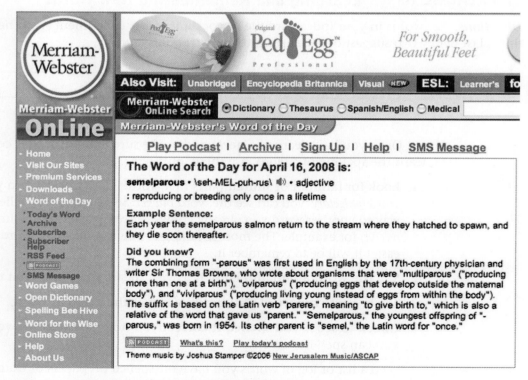

Figure 1-4 Merriam-Webster's word of the day.

From Merriam-Webster Online, www.Merriam-Webster.com. Copyright © 2004 Merriam-Webster, Inc. By permission.

► **Look for additional meanings for words you already know.** For example, you know that a *skirt* is an article of clothing, but you can also use it to mean to pass around or avoid, as in "The candidate *skirted* the controversial issue of gun control."

► **Play word games.** Various Web sites offer word games that heighten your word awareness and introduce new words. The Merriam-Webster Web site (http://www.merriam-webster.com) offers a word game that changes daily.

► **Learn a word each day.** No matter how busy you are, find a new word to learn each day. If you aren't studying or attending classes, find a word on the TV news or in the newspaper. The Merriam-Webster Web site also offers a "Word of the Day," as shown in Figure 1-4.

MASTERY test

Applying and Integrating Your Skills in Communications

Directions: Read the passage and answer the following questions.

Opening Lines

How do you strike up a conversation? How have people tried to open a conversation with you? Researchers investigating this question have found three basic types of opening lines:

Cute-flippant openers are humorous, indirect, and ambiguous as to whether or not the person opening the conversation really wants an extended encounter. Examples: "Is that really your hair?" "I bet the cherries jubilee isn't as sweet as you are."

Innocuous openers are highly ambiguous as to whether they are simple comments that might be made to just anyone or are in fact openers designed to initiate an extended encounter. Examples: "What do you think of the band?" "I haven't been here before. What's good on the menu?" "Could you show me how to work this machine?"

Direct openers clearly demonstrate the speaker's interest in meeting the other person. Examples: "I feel a little embarrassed about this, but I'd like to meet you." "Would you like to have a drink after dinner?" "Since we're both eating alone, would you like to join me?"

The opening lines most preferred by both men and women are generally those that are direct or innocuous. The lines least preferred by both men and women are those that are cute-flippant—and women dislike these openers even more than men.

—Adapted from DeVito, *Human Communication: The Basic Course*, Ninth Edition, p. 161.

1. Create word maps for the following words from the selection:

   a. innocuous

   b. flippant

2. Write a sentence using each of the following words. Relate the sentences to your life, as the more meaningful they are to you the more likely you are to remember the words.

   a. ambiguous _____

   _____

b. demonstrate _____

_____

c. extended _____

_____

d. initiate _____

_____

3. As a way to remember the word *encounter*, visualize a situation that involves the word.

4. Organize a vocabulary log using a notebook or a computer file that you can use for all of your courses this semester. Make a first entry using one of the words in this selection.

EXERCISE 1-5 Word Play

Directions: Play the word game of the day on the Merriam-Webster Web site (http://www.merriam-webster.com). Using the format of the game you played, create a new word game that would be useful for a classmate to play to improve his or her vocabulary.

Learn More about Building your Vocabulary by Visiting the Following Web Sites

1. **Vocabulary: An Ongoing Process**
   http://www.ucc.vt.edu/stdysk/vocabula.html

2. **Commonly Misused Words**
   http://www.cmu.edu/styleguide/trickywords.html#misused

3. **A Word A Day**
   http://www.wordsmith.org/awad/index.html

2

Using Context to Figure Out Words

What is the first thing you should do when you find a word you don't know?

➤ Look it up in a dictionary? No.

➤ Analyze its parts? No.

➤ Skip it? No.

➤ Keep reading and try to figure out what the word means by the way it is used in the sentence? RIGHT!

Making Educated Guesses About Word Meaning

This part of the text will show you how to figure out what words mean by understanding the way they are used in the sentence or paragraph in which they appear. Often there are clues to the meaning of a word built into the sentence or paragraph that give you enough information to make at least an educated guess about meaning. Does this method work? Yes! And you have good odds that your guess is right, too, if you pay attention to these clues, known as *context clues*.

Let's see how and why this method works. Many sentences have more information in them than a reader or listener really needs. This is called *language redundancy*. Because no one can maintain 100 percent attention on a task for very long, writers and speakers naturally build extra clues into their speech and writing to help keep their audience on track. Try this experiment. Read the following paragraph and supply the missing words; read it through completely before you write anything.

Research conducted _____ common foods such as orange juice, peach jelly, and strawberry sherbet shows that these foods were preferred when food coloring was added to _____ their natural colors. For example, _____ juice that was made to appear more orange _____ preferred over _____ orange juice. The _____ also found that the redder the _____ looked, the more appealing it was.

You did not have any trouble figuring out the missing words, right? From the words that were there, you knew what words were missing. How did you know? There were numerous clues. You could figure out some words from information that appeared earlier in the paragraph. Your knowledge of how English works helped, too. For example, you know that a noun (person, place, or thing) usually follows the word *the* (*the researchers*). You know that the word that comes before *juice* was an adjective (*orange*) that describes it. Just as you could figure out missing words in the above paragraph, you will be able to figure out what some (but not all) unfamiliar words mean when you meet them while reading.

Types of Context Clues

WORD **notes**

In this photo of a fruit bowl, you can tell a piece of fruit is missing by the presence of other fruit in the bowl, as well as by the blacked out shape. Similarly, you can figure out the meaning of an unknown word from clues in the rest of the sentence or surrounding paragraph. The words that surround a word are called its *context*. Information about the meaning of a word that is contained in the surrounding words is called a *context clue*.

Here are some quick tips for finding context clues:

> **Don't stop reading as soon as you meet an unfamiliar word.**

> **Finish reading the sentence containing the unknown word.** Many context clues follow the unknown word.

> **If you can't find a context clue in the sentence containing the word, read the next couple of sentences.** Context clues can appear anywhere in the paragraph.

> **Once you do figure out the meaning of a word from its context, circle or highlight the word and jot down its meaning in the margin.** Especially for textbooks that you are likely to review or reread, jotting down the meaning is especially important; you do not want to have to figure out a word's meaning all over again while reviewing.

> **If you cannot find a context clue but can understand the meaning of the sentence without the meaning of the unknown word, keep reading.** (You might want to mark the word with a question mark and check its meaning later.)

There are five types of context clues: (1) synonym, (2) definition, (3) example, (4) contrast, and (5) inference. You will learn how to use each in the following sections.

"THIS IS WHAT I GET FOR TRYING TO IMPROVE MY VOCABULARY"

Synonym Context Clues

A group of friends is talking. Someone says, "Joining the Marines was a mile-stone in my life." Another friend says, "A what . . .?" He replies, "You know, an important event." In speech, listeners can ask questions if they do not under-stand something. In writing, readers can't ask the writer questions, so writers must be careful to supply a clue, often a word or two, that suggests the meanings of words they think their readers might not know or may misunderstand. Often writers supply a *synonym*—a word or brief phrase that has a similar meaning. Here is an example. Can you tell what an *asterism* is from the underlined synonym?

An **asterism**, a cluster of stars, was visible last evening.

How to Spot Synonyms

Usually, the synonym immediately follows the word, as in the above example. Often it is set apart from the rest of the sentence by using a linking word or phrase or by punctuation such as a comma, a dash, or parentheses. Common linking words are *or, also known as,* and *also called.*

Using a linking word: **Taste receptor cells**, also called taste buds, can identify four basic tastes: salty, sweet, bitter, and sour.

Using commas: The amateur figure skater **surpassed**, or exceeded, the judges' expectations.

Using dashes: The sculptor usually created a **maquette**—<u>a small model</u>—before beginning work on the actual piece.

Using parentheses: Thick layers of **loess** (<u>wind-blown silt</u>) cover regions of the Mississippi River valley.

You may also find a synonym for a word later in the paragraph, not even in the same sentence. This is a less common type of clue, but writers do use it occasionally.

Later in paragraph: Many companies have transferred labor-intensive operations to **maquiladoras** located along the U.S.-Mexican border. These <u>factories that produce goods for export to the United States</u> have created new jobs and contributed to economic growth.

EXERCISE 2-1   Synonyms

Directions: In each of the following sentences, underline the synonym for each boldfaced word.

example   The debate involved two **discrete**, <u>separate</u> issues.

1. Melanoma most commonly occurs in the **epidermis**, or skin.

2. We blamed our **lethargic**, lazy behavior on the oppressive heat.

3. The patient suffered **angina pectoris**—severe chest pain—before being admitted to the hospital.

4. Quill usually makes it her policy to **eschew**, or avoid, dessert.

5. The hummus recipe calls for **chickpeas**, also known as garbanzo beans.

6. After his accident and subsequent physical therapy, Luis decided to go into **kinesiology** (the study of anatomy, physiology, and body movement).

7. The coral snake is **indigenous**, or native, to tropical America and the southern United States.

8. Did you know that certain flowers, such as violets, are **esculent** (edible)?

9. The fishermen carried a **creel**—a wicker basket—to hold the fish they planned to catch.

10. The **remora**, also known as the suckerfish, can attach itself to sharks, whales, sea turtles, or the hulls of ships.

EXERCISE 2-2   Synonym Context Clues

Directions: Revise each of the following sentences by adding a synonym context clue for the word in boldface. Use linking words, commas, dashes, and parentheses at least once in this exercise. Use a dictionary if necessary.

example   Jose listened to the **verbose** speaker discuss economic theories.

Jose listened to the **verbose**, talkative speaker discuss economic theories.

1. Ferdinand Magellan and his crew were the first people to **circumnavigate** the earth.

    _____

    _____

2. Jamil **prefaced** her speech with a poem by Derek Walcott.

    _____

3. Sheep typically **yean** in the spring.

    _____

4. The human **colon** is about 1.5 meters long.

    _____

5. The historical society raised money for an extensive **renovation** of the bank building.

    _____

6. Many creative people find **architectonics** a fascinating subject.

    _____

7. **Periwinkle** is an excellent ground cover for shaded areas.

    _____

8. The oldest **vertebrates** in the fossil record are fishlike fossils.

    _____

9. We tried not to laugh while Henry was **castigated** for his poor manners.

    _____

10. The **respiratory system** of premature babies is often underdeveloped.

    _____

Definition Context Clues

When writers are fairly certain their readers will not know a word they used, they include its definition. Definition context clues are especially common in textbooks where part of the author's purpose is to introduce and teach new terminology.

> A **tariff** can be defined as a special tax imposed by the government on imported goods to raise the price, thus protecting American businesses and workers from foreign competition.

How to Spot Definition Clues

When giving a definition, writers usually use linking words such as *is (are)*, *is called*, *means*, *refers to*, and *can be defined as*. A comma, dash, or parentheses rather than a linking word may be used if the definition is included as part of a sentence written for a purpose other than to simply define the term.

> *Using linking word*: **Advection** is the horizontal movement and transfer of air or substances caused by wind or ocean currents. [The sole purpose of this sentence is to define *advection*.]

Using comma: Children under the age of two cannot grasp the concept of **conservation**, <u>the idea that physical objects remain constant despite changes in appearance</u>. [The purpose of this sentence is to explain that children less than two years old do not understand conservation; the definition of *conservation* is included as well.]

Using a dash: **Relative humidity**—<u>a measure of the water content of the air</u>—is usually lower in warm afternoons and higher during cool evenings.

Using parentheses: Cholesterol level (<u>a measure of fatty substance in the blood</u>) has become a major health concern.

EXERCISE 2-3 Definition Clues

Directions: Underline the definition clue that provides the meaning of the word in boldface.

example **Hebephrenia**, <u>a mental disorder characterized by foolish mannerisms and senseless laughter</u>, may occur during adolescence.

1. **Telecommuting**, working at home at a computer terminal, has been linked to increased worker productivity.

2. **Genes**, the hereditary units that determine an organism's traits and characteristics, play an important role in biotechnology research.

3. **Dysphagia**—difficulty in swallowing—can be a symptom of strep throat.

4. Strangers often commented on the **sororal**, or sisterly, resemblance between the two girls.

5. **Acid precipitation**, usually defined as rain or snow with a pH below 5.6, is a result of fossil-fuel emissions.

6. Coran's parents were pleased to discover that he was truly **ambidextrous**, able to use both hands equally well.

7. **Dactylology**—more commonly known as sign language—relies on the use of a manual alphabet.

8. After James retired, he became a **docent**, or tour guide, at the state historical museum.

9. My grandmother's secret for her blue-ribbon fried chicken is **brining**—soaking the chicken in salt water—before frying.

10. The prosecutor accused the witness of giving **fallacious**, or deliberately misleading, testimony.

EXERCISE 2-4 Definition Context Clues

Directions: Revise each of the following sentences by adding a definition context clue for the word in boldface. Use linking words, commas, and dashes at least once in this exercise. Use a dictionary if necessary.

example The professor was in a **quandary** because she suspected some students had plagiarized, but she could not prove it.

The professor was in a quandary, or **predicament**, because she suspected some students had plagiarized, but she could not prove it.

1. Halfway up the mountain, the hikers were stopped by a huge **chasm**.

   _____

2. The **temblor** registered 5.2 on the Richter scale.

   _____

3. My music teacher taught me to look for terms such as **crescendo** and **rinforzando** in a piece of music.

   _____

   _____

4. The Manx cat can be described as **acaudate**, although it has an internal vestigial tail.

   _____

5. Gabriel lived in Paris long enough to become familiar with the city and its **environs**.

   _____

6. The televangelist preached passionately against all forms of **iconolatry**.

   _____

7. Dr. Galyon plans to take a **sabbatical** at the end of this semester.

   _____

8. Most word processing programs allow you to automatically **paginate** reports and other documents.

   _____

   _____

9. Parker was invited to sing the national anthem **a cappella** before the Braves game.

   _____

   _____

10. The candidate quickly became known for his **malapropisms** on the campaign trail.

    _____

Example Context Clues

One of the easiest ways to explain something is to give an example or two. You can easily explain the term _road rage_ by giving examples of angry driving behavior—cutting off other drivers, following at unsafe distances, honking the horn incessantly, and so forth. Examples often work better than definitions alone. Experienced writers know that many readers are pragmatic learners and need real, practical situations to help them understand an idea or concept. Often, then, if you are unfamiliar with a term, you can figure out what it means from the examples given.

Some forms of **nonverbal communication**, such as facial expressions, gestures, and posture, are universally understood.

In this sentence, the examples of nonverbal communication suggest that it means body language or communication without words.

How to Spot Example Clues

Writers may use linking words such as *for example* or *for instance*. At other times, the example is built into the paragraph without linking words.

> *Using linking words*: **Opiates**, such as opium, morphine, and methadone, often seriously affect the emotional state of the user.

> *Without linking words*: The speaker made a **gaffe** when he referred to the women in the audience as "little ladies."

EXERCISE 2-5   **Example Clues**

Directions: In the space provided, write the letter of the choice that best states the meaning of the boldfaced word as it is used in the sentence.

_____ 1. Rachel explained her interest in **genealogy** in personal terms; for instance, she described the thrill of discovering that each of her great-grandparents arrived at Ellis Island in 1903.

   a. nature   c. genes

   b. family history   d. timetables

_____ 2. The comedian proved himself **impervious** to the response of the audience when he continued to tell jokes despite loud groans and cries of "Get off the stage!"

   a. sensitive   c. disrespectful

   b. unaffected   d. amused

_____ 3. Children between the ages of three and six sometimes suffer from a form of **parasomnia**, as evidenced by sleepwalking, night terrors, and bed-wetting.

   a. excitement   c. sleep disorder

   b. anger   d. daydreaming

_____ 4. Among the **denizens** of the tiny town were two lawyers, a physician, a veterinarian, and a schoolteacher.

   a. residents   c. men

   b. critics   d. women

_____ 5. For the damage they caused at the school, the teenagers have been ordered by the court to make **reparations**—specifically, they must paint over the graffiti and pay for new windows.

   a. repairs   c. apologies

   b. plans   d. amends

_____ 6. The purchase contract for the house included several **provisos**; for example, the interior of the house was to be painted and the roof replaced by the current owners.

   a. warnings   c. agreements

   b. conditions   d. amends

_____ 7. The health drink was advertised as a **panacea**; it promised to improve memory, boost energy levels, and relieve sleeplessness.

a. dessert

c. cure-all

b. prescription

d. supplement

_____ 8. Many wills include at least one **codicil**, such as an instruction about the disbursement of assets to stepchildren.

a. addition

c. fee

b. error

d. request

_____ 9. The fire marshal cited the building's owner for several **infractions**; for example, the fire escape was blocked and none of the smoke alarms worked.

a. improvements

c. violations

b. signs

d. supplies

_____ 10. To qualify for the gifted program, students must undergo a **battery** of tests designed to measure intelligence, creativity, and aptitude.

a. series

c. connection

b. requirement

d. question

EXERCISE 2-6   Example Context Clues I

Directions: Read each sentence and write a definition or synonym for each boldfaced word or phrase. Use the example clue to help you determine the meaning.

example   **Histrionics**, such as wild laughter or excessive body movements, are usually inappropriate in business settings. <u>exaggerated emotional behavior performed for effect</u>

1. **Ethnic groups**, such as Chinese, Poles, and Italians, living in the United States have contributed much to its cultural diversity. _____

2. The school system recently received two **endowments**, one of $5,000 and one of $10,000, directed toward improvements in the art and music programs. _____

3. Jacob's appetite for books is **voracious**; for instance, no sooner had he finished the latest Harry Potter book than he began reading _The Chronicles of Narnia._ _____

4. The opposition was quick to **propagate** rumors about the candidate; for example, his routine visit to the doctor was soon broadcast as "serious health concerns" over the Internet. _____

5. Susan's father suffered a series of **debilitating** strokes, leaving him partially paralyzed and unable to care for himself. _____

6. The investigators accused the councilman of **obfuscating** the truth by destroying important records and threatening key witnesses. _____

7. Her workaholism and his infidelity were **precursors** to their divorce. _____

8. Even the positive aspects of a **sedentary** lifestyle, such as reading books and doing needlework, should be balanced with an appropriate level of physical activity. _____

9. The consultant proposed several **upgrades** to the current system, such as streamlined accounting procedures and automated inventory control. _____

10. The company has several **auxiliary** locations, including stores in Georgia, Tennessee, and North Carolina. _____

EXERCISE 2-7   Example Context Clues II

Directions: For each of the following words or phrases, write a sentence that provides an example context clue. Use a dictionary if necessary.

example   martial arts Martial arts, such as karate and judo, are growing in popularity. _____

1. sport utility vehicles _____

2. dignitaries _____

3. periodicals _____

4. pop music stars _____

5. flowering trees _____

6. comedians _____

7. fast foods _____

8. over-the-counter medications _____

9. spring break travel destinations _____

10. aggressive behavior _____

Contrast Context Clues

It is sometimes possible to determine the meaning of a word from a word or phrase in the context that has an opposite meaning. In the following sentence, notice how the meaning of *depressants* provides a clue to the meaning of *stimulants*.

> Unlike **stimulants**, depressants slow functioning in the central nervous system.

The word *unlike* tells us that depressants and stimulants are different. If depressants slow the functioning of the central nervous system, then stimulants speed up its functioning.

Basically, contrast clues require two steps. First you have to find a word that has the opposite meaning of the unknown word. Then you have to think of a word that has the opposite meaning of the context clue. Here are a few more examples.

> Despite his reputation for **parsimony**, the old man left a very generous tip for the waitress.

> In contrast to people with **myopia**, people with hyperopia cannot focus at short distances.

How to Spot Contrast Clues

In writing about two things or ideas that are different, writers often use linking words such as *but, although, on the other hand, yet, nevertheless, however, in contrast, while, unlike, even though, despite*, and so forth. These words signal that a contrasting, different idea is to follow.

EXERCISE 2-8   Contrast Context Clues I

Directions: In the space provided, write the letter of the choice that best states the meaning of the boldfaced word as it is used in the sentence.

——— 1. Despite her **penchant** for sweets, Maria was not tempted by any of the items on the dessert tray.

    a. fondness   c. diet

    b. distaste   d. intention

——— 2. In contrast to this year's drought in the southern United States, the upper northwest had its most **pluvious** summer on record.

    a. dry   c. rainy

    b. remarkable   d. unpredictable

——— 3. Although the composer intended it to be a happy, lighthearted piece of music, it sounded more like a **dirge** when it was performed by the choir.

    a. joyful tune   c. performance

    b. funeral hymn   d. recital

4. The starlet cultivated her image as a helpless and scatterbrained young woman, but in reality she was a **sagacious** businesswoman.

   a. independent

   b. shrewd

   c. unintelligent

   d. helpful

5. Every effort was made to ensure that the test was fair; nevertheless, several students complained that the questions were **skewed**.

   a. biased

   b. equal

   c. numerous

   d. too easy

6. In contrast to the former senator's long-winded, rambling speeches, his successor's comments were downright **pithy**.

   a. lengthy

   b. conservative

   c. unflattering

   d. brief

7. Unlike **perennial** plants, annuals complete their life cycle in a single season.

   a. tender

   b. winter-hardy

   c. blooming only once

   d. lasting more than one season, or recurring

8. While several aspects of the new charter school were open to discussion, the location of the new school was **immutable**.

   a. not subject to change

   b. unpleasant

   c. not decided

   d. debatable

9. This particular drug is often prescribed for its **soporific** effect; however, some patients have experienced sleeplessness upon taking it.

   a. stimulating

   b. sleep-inducing

   c. medical

   d. harmful

10. In dramatic contrast to the tropical temperatures of the Dominican Republic, Ramón found the climate in Iowa **hyperborean**.

    a. mild

    b. warm

    c. very cold

    d. similar

EXERCISE 2-9   Contrast Context Clues II

Directions: Read each sentence and write a definition or synonym for each boldfaced word or phrase. Use the contrast clue to help you determine the meaning.

example   Despite their seemingly **altruistic** actions, large corporations are self-interested institutions that exist to make profits. <u>unselfish or selfless</u>

1. City-dwellers often imagine that rural areas are peaceful at night, but the **cacophony** of insects and other night creatures can be deafening. _____

2. In contrast to the **levity** of the stockholders' meeting, the mood in the boardroom was sober.

_____

3. Although violence is **abhorrent** to most of us, certain forms of "street justice" have become somewhat acceptable in our society. _____

4. In contrast to **bradycardia**, tachycardia is a rapid heart rate of more than 100 beats per minute in an adult. _____

5. Although the store seemed to have a **plethora** of cowboy boots, there were none in his size.

_____

6. Walter gave up alcohol every Sunday, yet by 10:00 on Friday night he was again in a state of **inebriety**. _____

7. Although women are **enjoined** from serving as clergy in many mainstream churches, the Episcopal church is one that allows the ordination of female priests. _____

_____

8. The tycoon was found guilty of tax evasion, but his wife was declared **inculpable**.

_____

9. The lunchtime series has featured several entertaining speakers, although today's lecturer was much more **didactic**. _____

10. When our criminal justice class interviewed inmates at the city's holding center, some were **hostile**; others were friendly and talkative. _____

Inference Context Clues

Many times, you can infer the meaning of an unknown word from the general meaning of the paragraph or passage in which it appears. Unlike the other context clues previously discussed, this type of clue does not depend on a particular word or phrase. Instead, from the overall sense of the passage and your own background knowledge or experience with the topic, you can figure out what a particular word means.

> After the playoff game, a **fracas** broke out among the fans of the losing team.

In the above sentence, you can reason that a *fracas* is a disorderly fight, quarrel, or brawl. From your background knowledge you know that brawls can break out among fans, and you know that playoff games may be particularly emotional or intense. The passage indicates that the fracas broke out among the fans of the losing team and, again, you know that fans of losing teams are likely to be disgruntled or unhappy. Here is another example:

> After finding an **egregious error** on a recent statement, the auditor checked the company's accounts payable for the previous three years.

In this sentence, you can assume that an *egregious error* is a serious one if it caused the auditor to review three years' worth of accounts. *Serious* is close in meaning to the dictionary meaning of *egregious*, which is "conspicuously bad or offensive."

Directions: In the space provided, write the letter of the choice that best states the meaning of the boldfaced word as it is used in the sentence.

_____ 1. The arrival of the hurricane season was **heralded** by several small tropical storms in the Gulf of Mexico.

a. played

b. begun

c. announced

d. defined

_____ 2. Halfway through the horror movie, the fear in the audience was **palpable**.

a. obvious

b. terrifying

c. humorous

d. invisible

_____ 3. Many young people are leaving the state after graduation because of the **dearth** of good jobs in the area.

a. offers

b. abundance

c. scarcity

d. appearance

_____ 4. After her appearance in the highly successful low-budget film, the actress was **inundated** with offers.

a. pleased

b. swamped

c. confused

d. denied

_____ 5. Hugh finally decided that the **frenetic** pace of Wall Street wasn't for him and moved back to his family's farm in Vermont.

a. slow

b. financial

c. calm

d. frantic

_____ 6. Several factors **impeded** the progress of the new housing development, including zoning restrictions and opposition from landowners.

a. encouraged

b. allowed

c. promoted

d. obstructed

_____ 7. Her leopard-skin outfit at the humane society fund-raiser was the **antithesis** of good taste.

a. definition

b. opposite

c. design

d. appearance

_____ 8. Before the third graders got off the bus at the museum, their teacher urged them to conduct themselves with **decorum**.

a. politely

b. respectfully

c. quietly

d. cheerfully

_____ 9. The press reported that the leaders of the two countries had reached a critical **juncture** in their negotiations.

a. breakdown

b. topic

c. point

d. debate

———— 10. The prosecution presented a **cogent** argument, but the jury was not persuaded.

    a. convincing   c. deliberate

    b. unclear   d. weak

EXPLORING language

Eponyms—Making Words from the Names of People

An **eponym** is a word that formed from a person's name.

➤ Sandwiches are a popular lunch item. But did you know that the word comes from the Earl of Sandwich? According to legend, John Montagu, the fourth Earl of Sandwich, was an avid gambler. One evening in 1762 he was hungry but did not want to interrupt his game, so he asked for a slice of roast beef placed between two slices of bread. It was the first sandwich.

➤ Did you know that the term *teddy bear* came from the name of a U.S. president? President Theodore Roosevelt, nicknamed Teddy, was once shown in a cartoon sparing the life of a bear cub. From that cartoon, the words *teddy bear* evolved.

➤ A *munchkin* is a very small, elflike person. Did you know that the word comes from the Munchkins, characters in *The Wonderful Wizard of Oz*?

The Earl of Sandwich and his legacy

Use a dictionary to discover from whom each of the following words originated.

1. Prince Charming _____

2. cesarean section _____

3. leotard _____

4. diesel engine _____

5. Doberman _____

EXERCISE 2-11   Inference Context Clues II

Directions: Read each sentence and write a definition or synonym for each boldfaced word or phrase. Use the general sense of the passage context clues to help you determine the meaning.

example   She was the **archetypal** grandmother: she brought wonderful presents, she told exciting stories, and her house always smelled of cookies.

           <u>ideal example; model</u>

1. After an **auspicious** first novel, the writer turned out several books that were panned by the critics. _____

2. Because we had invited them to join us, we felt that the **onus** was on us to be sure that they had a good time. _____

3. Many Americans considered President Clinton's behavior **flagrant**, although he ultimately survived the scandal. _____

4. The **pungent** smell of something burning greeted us as we walked in the door.

   _____

5. To the police detective, the most **salient** aspect of the case was the suspect's lack of an alibi. _____

6. After playing in the yard all morning, the puppy was **inert** for the rest of the day.

   _____

7. As Maria organized her bookshelves, she **segregated** fiction and nonfiction.

   _____

8. I thought the television program was **innocuous** until I saw some children acting out an especially violent episode. _____

9. In an effort to **rectify** the situation, the manufacturer offered full refunds to dissatisfied customers. _____

10. The toddler's parents tried to **dissuade** him from climbing on furniture, but to no avail.

    _____

What to Do When Context Doesn't Work

WORD notes

Sometimes context does not work. What do you think this is a picture of? (Answer at bottom of following page.)

Now try to use context to figure out the meaning of the under-lined word in the following sentence.

The Italian director Federico Fellini was best known for his surrealistic films.

Give up? You should. There are no context clues to help you figure out what the picture is of or what *surrealistic* means.

Using context is a great technique, but it does not always work. Not all sentences or paragraphs contain context clues. When you cannot find a context clue, then you have to use other methods to figure out a word's meaning. Here are some suggestions:

➤ **Pronounce the word.** Hearing it aloud may help you recall hearing or using the word before. Or, you may hear a word or part of a word within the unknown word that will ring a bell in your memory. For example, by pronouncing the word *predecessor*, you may recall your history professor using it in reference to presidential succession. Or, by pronouncing the word *deregulatory*, you may recognize the word *regulate*.

➤ **If pronouncing the word does not help, analyze the word's parts.** This method is discussed in Chapter 4 of this text.

➤ **If analyzing word parts does not work, look up the word in your dictionary.**

After Context, Then What?

WORD notes

Here today, gone tomorrow! This is what will happen to words that you figured out from context, unless you take steps to remember them.

Let's say you have figured out seven or eight meanings of words using context while reading a sociology chapter. Let's assume you jotted down each meaning in the margin of your sociology text, too. Now what should you do? If you think the words are useful additions to your general vocabulary or if the words are important words in sociology, then you should take the following steps.

Checking Exact Meanings

The first step is to check the exact meaning for any words you are unsure of. For example, in the following sentence, you may infer that *precipitately* means *quickly*:

Investors reacted **precipitately** to the news that the company's stock had fallen.

But if you check a dictionary, you would discover that a more precise meaning is *hastily* or *rashly*. Once you find a more accurate meaning, jot it down in the margin of your textbook.

Answer to p. 31: a baseball

Directions: Use context to figure out the meaning of each of the words in boldface. In the space provided, write a brief definition or synonym. Then confirm or revise your definition by checking the word's meaning in your dictionary.

example   Mia arrived on time for her class despite **adverse** travel conditions.

Bad ( ) confirmed (X) need to revise (check one)

Revision: unfavorable

1. When a lecturer interjects **extraneous** information into the lecture, note taking becomes difficult.

_____ ( ) confirmed ( ) need to revise (check one)

Revision: _____

2. The computer we purchased in 2000 is well on its way to **obsolescence.**

_____ ( ) confirmed ( ) need to revise

Revision: _____

3. The scientist was able to **substantiate** her conclusions with the results of tests she performed.

_____ ( ) confirmed ( ) need to revise

Revision: _____

4. Because he had just become a father, Oscar was able to obtain a **deferment** of his military service.

_____ ( ) confirmed ( ) need to revise

Revision: _____

5. The storm was severe, but the damage to our house was **negligible.**

_____ ( ) confirmed ( ) need to revise

Revision: _____

6. With friends in both places, Faye **vacillated** between the job offer in Raleigh and the one in Des Moines.

_____ ( ) confirmed ( ) need to revise

Revision: _____

7. Dog-lovers have found that Newfoundlands make **stalwart** companions.

_____ ( ) confirmed ( ) need to revise

Revision: _____

8. A **cabal** of religious extremists was responsible for the assassination attempt on the prime minister.

_____ ( ) confirmed ( ) need to revise

Revision: _____

9. Her nephew gave her a **perfunctory** kiss on the cheek.

_____ ( ) confirmed ( ) need to revise

Revision: _____

10. The architect was known for his **minimalist** approach to design.

_____ ( ) confirmed ( ) need to revise

Revision: _____

Adding Words to Your Index Card File or Vocabulary Log

Definitions recorded only in the margin of your textbooks are not convenient for review or study. For each word that you want to learn, add it and its meaning to your vocabulary log file or index file (see p. 8 or p. 9). You might also want to include a brief note indicating the title and page of the book in which you originally encountered the word.

EXERCISE 2-13   **Using an Index Card File or Vocabulary Log**

Directions: Update your index card file or vocabulary log using words you have learned so far in this part of the book.

> **EXERCISE 2-14**   Applying Your Skills in American History

Directions: Read the following passage and use context clues to figure out the meaning of each boldfaced word or phrase. Write a synonym or definition for each in the space provided. Consult a dictionary if necessary.

Martin Van Buren

Martin Van Buren's brilliance as a political **manipulator**—the Red Fox, the Little Magician—has tended to **obscure** his statesmanlike qualities and his engaging personality. He made a powerful argument, for example, that political parties were a force for unity, not for **partisan** bickering. In addition, high office sobered him, and improved his judgment. He fought the Bank of the United States as a monopoly, but he also opposed irresponsible state banks. New York's Safety Fund System, requiring all banks to contribute to a fund, supervised by the state, to be used to **redeem** the notes of any member bank that failed, was established largely through his efforts. Van Buren believed in public construction of internal improvements, but he favored state rather than national programs, and he urged a **rational** approach: each project must stand on its own as a useful and profitable public utility.

He continued to **equivocate** spectacularly on the tariff—in his *Autobiography* he described two of his supporters walking home after listening to him talk on the tariff, each convinced that it had been a brilliant speech, but neither having obtained the slightest idea as to where Van Buren stood on the subject—but he was never in the pocket of any special interest group or tariff **lobbyist**. He **accounted** himself a good Jeffersonian, tending to prefer state action to federal, but he was by no means **doctrinaire**. Basically he approached most questions rationally and **pragmatically**.

—Adapted from Garraty and Carnes,
The American Nation, Tenth Edition, p. 267.

1. manipulator: _____

2. obscure: _____

3. partisan: _____

4. redeem: _____

5. rational: _____

6. equivocate: _____

7. lobbyist: _____

8. accounted: _____

9. doctrinaire: _____

10. pragmatically: _____

Directions: Read the following passage and use context clues to figure out the meaning of each boldfaced word or phrase. Write a synonym or definition for each in the space provided.

Advergaming

If you roar down the streets in the *Need for Speed Underground 2* video racing game, you'll pass a Best Buy store as well as billboards **hawking** Old Spice and Burger King. Chrysler devotes 10 percent of its overall marketing budget to **planting** Chrysler, Jeep, and Dodge cars in more than a dozen video games.[67] *America's Army*, produced by the U.S. government as a recruitment tool, is one of the most successful advergames. Twenty-eight percent of those who visit the *America's Army* Web page click through to the recruitment page.

As gaming goes mass market, marketers turn to **advergaming**, where online games merge with interactive advertisements that let companies target specific types of consumers. And, the **mushrooming** popularity of user-generated videos on YouTube and other sites creates a growing market for **linking** ads to these sources as well. At Starstyle.com, for example, you can buy the fashions you see on TV shows and in music videos. This strategy is growing so rapidly that there's even a new (trademarked) term for it.

Plinking™ is the act of **embedding** a product or service link in a video.

Why is this new medium so hot? For one thing, compared to a 30-second TV spot, advertisers can get viewers' attention for a much longer time: Players spend an average of 5 to 7 minutes on an advergame site. Also, they can **tailor** the nature of the game and the products in it to the **profiles** of different users. For example, they can direct **strategy games** to upscale, educated users, while at the same time gearing action games to younger users. In addition, the format gives advertisers great flexibility because gamemakers now are shipping PC video games with blank spaces in them to insert virtual ads. This allows advertisers to change ads **on the fly** and pay only for the number of game players that actually see them. Finally, there's great potential to track usage and conduct marketing research. For example, an inaudible audio signal coded into Activision's *Tony Hawk's Underground 2* skating game on PCs alerts a Nielsen monitoring system each time the test game players view Jeep product placements within the game.

1. hawking _____

2. planting _____

3. advergaming _____

4. mushrooming _____

5. plinking _____

6. embedding _____

7. tailor _____

8. profiles _____

9. strategy games _____

10. on the fly _____

Directions: Read the following passage and use context clues to figure out the meaning of each boldfaced word or phrase. Write a synonym or definition for each in the space provided.

The Toll of Contemporary Life

Many psychologists maintain that contemporary life takes its toll on the human **psyche** in economically developed industrial nations, particularly among children. These observers suggest that the human mind may be better adapted to life in less "advanced" survival-centered societies. Various people once labeled "primitive" by Europeans lived in a state of harmony with nature, spending perhaps ten to fifteen hours a week finding food. While they lacked the luxuries of the contemporary Western world, they never **craved** such luxuries. After securing food, shelter and clothing, these **indigenous** peoples had time for rituals, reflection, community events and leisure. Although we must avoid the temptation to **romanticize** these people (they experienced serious illnesses and dangerous conflict and generally died young), they seemed able to escape boredom and malaise.

With its scientific gadgetry and technological wonders, **modernist** civilization promotes a regulated, intransigent pattern of existence that **represses** creative impulses. Neither school nor work in our society offers many **avenues** for creative **endeavor**. Perhaps the most important difference between traditional and modernist cultures appears in the daily lives of children. In traditional societies children spent the day with their parents and other community members participating in the activities of the group or clan. Constantly engaged, these young people learned throughout each day. By contrast, **contemporary** children find themselves removed from everyday **commerce**, sitting by themselves or in disconnected and bored bunches that countenance psychological difficulties and **pathological** behavior.

—Kincheloe, Slattery, and Steinberg, *Contextualizing Teaching*, pp. 68–69.

1. psyche _____

2. craved _____

3. indigenous _____

4. romanticize _____

5. modernist _____

6. represses _____

7. avenues _____

8. endeavor _____

9. contemporary _____

10. commerce _____

11. pathological _____

This textbook excerpt was adapted from *Psychology: From Science to Practice* by Robert A. Baron and Michael J. Kalsher. Read the passage to learn about the importance of sleep. Then answer the questions that follow.

Sleep: The Pause That Refreshes

1 What single activity occupies more of your time than any other? Though you may be tempted to say "studying" or "working," think again. The correct answer is probably **sleep**—a process in which important physiological changes and slowing basic bodily functions are accompanied by major shifts in consciousness. In fact, most people spend fully one-third of their entire lives asleep (Dement, 1975; Webb, 1975). What is the nature of sleep? What functions does it serve? And what are dreams? These are key questions on which we'll focus. To get started, let's first consider the question of how psychologists study sleep.

The Basic Nature of Sleep

2 Everyone would agree that when we sleep, we are in a different state of consciousness than when we are awake. But what is sleep really like? To find out, psychologists carefully monitor changes in the electrical activity occurring in people's brains and muscles as they fall asleep. Recordings of electrical activity of the brain are known as the **electroencephalogram** (or EEG for short), while those for muscles are known as **electromyogram** (or EMG for short). Research using these methods indicates that as people fall asleep, they move through four distinct stages during which faster activity in the brain in gradually replaced by slower activity (**alpha waves** replace faster *beta waves*). Then, as we fall more deeply asleep, activity slows still further, and delta activity appears. This may represent a **synchronization** of neurons in the brain, so that an increasingly large number of neurons fire together, in unison. Such sleep in known as *slow-wave sleep.*

3 About ninety minutes after we begin to fall asleep, something quite dramatic often happens: We enter a very different phase of sleep known as **REM (rapid eye movement) sleep**. During this phase, the electrical activity of the brain quickly comes to resemble that shown when people are awake. Slow delta waves disappear, and fast, low-voltage activity returns. Sleepers' eyes begin to move about rapidly beneath their closed eyelids, and there is an almost total suppression of activity in body muscles (as measured by the EMG).

4   These shifts in brain activity and bodily processes are accompanied, in many cases, by one of the most dramatic aspects of sleep: *dreams.* Individuals awakened during REM sleep often report dreaming. In some cases, eye movements during such sleep seem to be related to the content of dreams (Dement, 1975). It is as if dreamers are following the action in their dreams with their eyes, but this relationship has not been clearly established.

Possible Function of Slow-Wave Sleep

5   Any activity that fills as much of our lives as sleep must serve important functions, but what, precisely, are these? Here, the most obvious possibility is that this kind of sleep serves mainly a **restorative** function, allowing us—and especially the brain—to rest and recover from the wear and tear of the day's activities. Several findings provide evidence for this suggestion. First, if sleep allows our brains to rest, then we would expect to see more delta (slow-wave) activity in portions of the brain that have experienced intense activity during the day. The findings of several studies suggest that this is so (e.g., Kattler, Djik, & Borbely, 1994). For instance, **PET scans** of the brain (which reveal the level of activity in various areas) indicate that portions of the brain that are most active during the day are indeed the ones showing most delta activity during the night. Slow-wave sleep may be, at least in part, a mechanism for allowing our brains to rest after intense periods of activity.

6   Slow-wave sleep emphasizes the relationship of sleep to circadian rhythms. According to this view, sleep is merely the neural mechanism that evolved to encourage various species, including our own, to remain inactive during those times of day when they do not usually engage in activities related to their survival. As one well-known sleep researcher (Webb, 1975) has put it, sleep is nature's way of keeping us quiet at night—a dangerous time for our ancestors, and for us, because we are not equipped with sensory capacities suited for nighttime activity.

Effects of Sleep Deprivation

7   Another way of discovering the functions of sleep is to see what happens when we are **deprived** of it. Everyone has had the experience of feeling completely miserable after a sleepless night, so it seems reasonable to focus on sleep deprivation as a possible source of information about the functions of sleep. So what *are* the effects of sleep deprivation? Among humans, even prolonged deprivation of sleep does not seem to produce large or clear-cut effects on behavior for many persons. For example, in one famous demonstration, seventeen-year-old Randy Gardner stayed awake for 264 hours and 12 minutes—eleven entire days! His **motivation** for doing so was simple: He wanted to earn a place in the *Guinness Book of Records,* and he did. Although Randy had some difficulty staying awake this long, he remained generally alert and active throughout the entire period. After completing his ordeal, he slept 14 hours on the first day, 10 hours on the second, and less than 9 on the third. Interestingly, his sleep on these nights slowed an **elevated** proportion of slow-wave (stages 3 and 4) sleep and REM sleep but did not show a rise in the early stages (1 and 2). So, it was as if his brain focused on making up

the deprivation in slow-wave and REM sleep but could get along fine without **compensating** for the losses in stages 1 and 2. Randy suffered no lasting physical or psychological harm from his long sleepless period, but please don't consider trying to beat Randy's record: There are potential risks in long-term sleep deprivation, including an increased chance of serious accidents and harm to personal health.

8   That long-term deprivation of sleep *can* be harmful to human beings, however, is suggested by several recent findings. First, growing evidence suggests that sleep deprivation is associated with **physiological changes** (e.g., lowered glucose tolerance, elevated activity in the sympathetic nervous system) that mark increased wear and tear on our bodies (e.g., Spiegel, Leproult, & Van Cauter, 1999). These findings suggest that sleep serves a restorative function.

9   A disorder known as fatal familial insomnia (e.g., Gallassi et al., 1996), suggests that sleep may truly be essential. In this disorder, individuals experience increasingly severe disturbances in sleep until, finally, slow-wave sleep totally disappears and only brief periods of REM sleep occur. The disease is fatal, but whether this is due to the sleep disturbances themselves or whether the sleep disturbances are simply a sign of other neurological problems, remains uncertain.

Sleep Disorders: No Rest for Some of the Weary

10   Do you ever have trouble falling or staying asleep? If so, you are in good company: Almost 40 percent of adults report that they sometimes have these problems, known, together, as **insomnia** (Bixler et al., 1979). Further, such problems seem to increase with age and are somewhat more common among women than men. Although many people report insomnia, it is not clear that the incidence of this problem is as high as these self-reports might suggest.

Disorders Associated with REM Sleep

11   Perhaps the most dramatic disturbance of REM sleep is **narcolepsy** a disorder in which sleep occurs at inappropriate—and often unexpected—times. Persons suffering from narcolepsy often have *sleep attacks* in which they experience an irresistible urge to sleep in the midst of waking activities. They sleep for from two to five minutes and then awake, refreshed. I once had a colleague who had sleep attacks in class. He would stop lecturing, put his head down on the desk, and— much to the amusement of his students who made many jokes about "putting himself under"—sleep.

12   Another symptom of narcolepsy is **cataplexy**, in which the individual falls down suddenly and without warning. Often, such persons will remain fully conscious, but their muscles are paralyzed, as during REM sleep. And sometimes they experience vivid dreams while in this state: in other words, they are dreaming while awake!

Disorders Associated with Slow-Wave Sleep

13   Perhaps the most dramatic disorder associated with slow-wave sleep is **somnambulism**—walking in one's sleep. This is less rare than you might guess; almost 25 percent of children experience at least one sleepwalking episode

(Empson, 1984). A second, related disorder is **night terrors.** Here, individuals, especially children, awaken from deep sleep with signs of intense arousal and powerful feelings of fear. Yet, they have no memory of any dream relating to these feelings. Night terrors seem to occur mainly during stage 4 sleep. In contrast, *nightmares* which most of us have experienced at some time, occur during REM sleep and can often be vividly recalled. Both somnambulism and night terrors are linked to disturbances in the functioning of the **autonomic system,** which plays a key role in regulating brain activity during sleep.

14   Another disturbing type of sleep disorder is apnea. Persons suffering from sleep apnea actually stop breathing when they are asleep. This causes them to wake up, and because the process can be repeated hundreds of times each night, apnea can seriously affect the health of persons suffering from it.

EXERCISE 2-17   Using Context Clues I

Directions: Use your knowledge of context clues to figure out the meaning of each of the following words as they are used in the reading. Then, for each word, create a context clue of your own that conveys the same meaning as the word has in the selection. Consult a dictionary if necessary.

1. **Sleep** (para. 1) is important for the body because it is a process that causes _____
   _____

2. The machine was used to perform an **electromyogram** (para. 2), a recording of _____

   _____

3. The drummers were highly skilled at **synchronization** (para. 2), and often played together

   _____

4. **PET scans** (para 5) allow scientists to study _____

5. Hungry and thirsty, the prisoner had been **deprived** (para. 7) of _____

   for many days.

6. Because one wheel of the shopping cart kept pulling to the left, the man was **compensating**

   (para. 7) by pushing the cart _____

7. She has a cat with **narcolepsy** (para. 11)—it will suddenly _____ without warning.

8. She was surprised to learn there was a medical diagnosis for her _____

   somnambulism (para. 13).

9. Symptoms of **night terrors** (para. 13) include _____

10. Although our bodies sleep, our brains do not, and the **autonomic system** (para. 13) continues

    to _____

Directions: Use your knowledge of context clues to determine the meaning of the following words or phrases used in the selection. Write the letters of the correct answers on the lines provided.

——— 1. An **electroencephalogram** (para. 2) records

    a. sleep amounts   c. muscle activity

    b. brain activity   d. volts of electricity

——— 2. The reader can determine that **alpha waves** (para. 2) are slow activity in the brain because they are contrasted with the faster

    a. beta waves   c. EEG

    b. EMG   d. delta activity

——— 3. The definition of **REM** sleep (para. 3) does not include

    a. fast, low-voltage brain activity   c. suppression of body muscle activity

    b. fast eye movements   d. slow delta waves

——— 4. **Restorative** sleep (para. 5) refers to

    a. slow-wave motion   c. wear and tear

    b. recovery activity   d. replacement behavior

——— 5. A context clue for **motivation** (para. 7) in this selection is

    a. Randy wanted to earn a place in the *Guinness Book of Records.*

    b. Randy remained generally alert.

    c. Randy had some difficulty staying awake this long.

    d. Randy Gardner stayed awake for 264 hours.

——— 6. A contrast clue for **elevated** (para. 7) is

    a. but did not show a rise   c. his sleep on these nights

    b. proportion of slow-wave   d. making up the deprivation

——— 7. What type of context clue provides information about the meaning of the term **physiological changes** (para. 8)?

    a. definition   c. contrast

    b. synonym   d. example

——— 8. Part of the definition of **insomnia** (para. 10) is

    a. experiencing nightmares.   c. problems getting to sleep.

    b. sleeping at inappropriate times.   d. difficulty waking up.

——— 9. **Cataplexy** (para. 12) is defined as a condition in which a person has

    a. difficulty breathing.   c. sudden collapses.

    b. sleepwalking episodes.   d. repetitive nightmares.

_____ 10. **Nightmares** (para. 13) are different from night terrors because nightmares

    a. are remembered.

    b. are not as frightening.

    c. cannot be prevented.

    d. occur mainly in children.

 Learn More about Vocabulary in Context by Visiting the Following Web Sites

1. **Vocabulary in Context Tutorial**
   http://www.cerritos.edu/reading/vocab.html
2. **Word Games**
   http://www.merriam-webster.com/game/index.htm
3. **Vocabulary Quizzes**
   http://grammar.ccc.commnet.edu/grammar/vocabulary.htm#quizzes

3

Dictionaries: Worthwhile Investments

Item	Estimated Cost
Large pizza (cheese and pepperoni)	$10.00
American Heritage Dictionary (paperback)	5.99
The New American Roget's College Thesaurus in Dictionary Form (paperback)	6.99

Now, which is the best investment? Certainly not the pizza!

To improve your vocabulary, you need the right tools. As you can see, both a paperback dictionary and a paperback thesaurus are great investments. Every college student should own a paperback dictionary, and many students find a thesaurus to be a worthwhile investment as well. In this section, you will learn how to use each to improve your vocabulary. You will also learn about another useful resource, a subject area dictionary.

A Dictionary: Which One to Use?

Collegiate Dictionaries

You should have at least one dictionary, and it should be a collegiate dictionary or the equivalent. Other dictionaries, such as student dictionaries and pocket dictionaries, are not as useful, since they are written for different audiences (high school students or office personnel, for example), and may not contain as many of the words or meanings you will need. A collegiate dictionary is written with college students in mind. Collegiate dictionaries are available in either hardback or paperback. Desk versions (hardback) contain many more words than do paperback versions and list many more meanings for most words.

The following are the most popular collegiate dictionaries:

New American Webster Handy College Dictionary

American Heritage Dictionary of the English Language

The Random House Dictionary of the English Language

Webster's New World Dictionary of the American Language

Merriam-Webster's Collegiate Dictionary

Unabridged Dictionaries

A dictionary that is unabridged is the most complete. The most complete unabridged dictionary of the English language is the *Oxford English Dictionary (OED)*. It is expensive—with a list price of $995.00—so it is available only in libraries. The second edition comprises 20 volumes and lists approximately 500,000 words, many more than even the most complete collegiate dictionary. In addition to many more words, it also contains more meanings for each word and information about word history and usage. You may need to refer to an unabridged dictionary to find an unusual word or an unusual meaning, to check a word's origin, or to check the various prefixes or suffixes that can be used with a particular word. You can visit the OED Web site (http://www.oed.com) for a visual tour of the dictionary.

Using an Online Dictionary

Many dictionaries of different types are available on the World Wide Web. Two of the most widely used English print dictionaries are:

► Merriam-Webster http://www.merriam-webster.com

► American Heritage http://www.bartleby.com/61

Online dictionaries are particularly helpful if you are not sure of the exact spelling of a word or if you mistype the word. At merriam-webster.com, if you type in a word with the incorrect spelling, several suggested words will be returned:

Both online dictionaries mentioned above feature an audio component that allows you to hear how a word is pronounced. When you hear the word, write it the way it sounds so you can remember its pronunciation.

These sites are useful for both quick lookups and also in-depth assistance. For example, while you are completing a reading assignment for class, keep an online dictionary open in your computer. Use it to find definitions for new words or to clarify unfamiliar shades of meaning. When writing a paper, use an online dictionary to help with spelling and proper usage. If there is a thesaurus (dictionary of synonyms) feature, use it to find more descriptive or more accurate words for your essays. (See the next section for more information about using a thesaurus.) The thesaurus feature at merriam-webster.com gives synonyms, related words, and near antonyms:

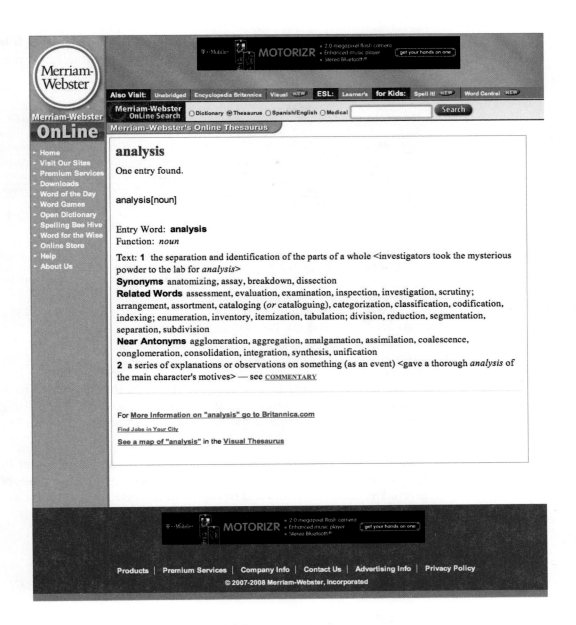

Be careful when clicking around the site to avoid getting distracted by ads and other unrelated material. Remember, do not take definitions word for word from an online dictionary and use them as your own. Be sure to paraphrase or quote and use proper citations to avoid plagiarism.

In addition to the standard English language dictionaries, there are specialized dictionaries in all fields available online. From medical terminology to foreign languages, Web searchers can find vocabulary and spelling help for almost all their needs. For example, go to www.law.com to see a legal dictionary.

Using a Dictionary

Since you will have hundreds of occasions to use a dictionary throughout your college career, you should learn to use it efficiently. A dictionary is a wonderful resource, and it contains much more than just word meanings. The first step in using a dictionary effectively is to become familiar with the kinds of information it provides. In the following sample entry, each kind of information is marked.

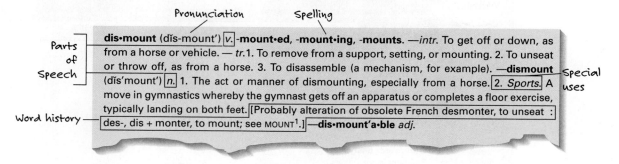

Pronunciation key and entries for "dismount," "dismiss," "familiar," "found 1," "found 2," and "oblique." Copyright © 2000 by Houghton Mifflin Company. Reproduced by permission from *The American Heritage Dictionary of the English Language,* Fourth Edition.

You can see that a dictionary entry includes information on a word's spelling, pronunciation, part of speech, history, and special uses.

Spelling

Dictionary entries give the correct spelling of words, including how to make them plural and how to add endings such as *-ed*, *-ing*, and so forth. They also give variant spellings (alternative acceptable spellings), as well as principal parts of verbs, and comparative and superlative forms of adjectives.

➤ **Plurals:** If the plural of a noun is irregular, the plural is given after the part of speech designation in the entry. If two plural spellings are acceptable, both will be given. For example, the plural of the word *criterion* will be shown as *pl. -teria or -terions.*

EXERCISE 3-1   Plurals

Directions: Locate the plural of each of the following words in a dictionary.

example   potato: <u>potatoes</u>

1. jockey: _____

2. robbery: _____

3. alumnus: _____

4. radix: _____

5. labellum: _____

➤ **Derivatives:** Words formed by adding beginnings (prefixes) or endings (suffixes) to a base word are called *derivatives*. The words *preread* and *reading* are derivatives of the base word *read.* If you cannot find a derivative listed as an entry, look under the base word. Derivatives of a base word are often listed at the end of the entry. For example, if you cannot find the word *decreasingly* as its own entry, look under the entry for *decrease.*

EXERCISE 3-2   Derivatives

Directions: List at least two derivatives of each of the following base words using a dictionary.

example   man: <u>mankind, manmade, manhunt, chairman</u>

1. earn: _____

2. cohere: _____

3. act: _____

4. potent: _____

5. spirit: _____

▶ **Variant spellings:** Entries may include alternative acceptable spellings of words. The more accepted spelling is given first. The alternative spelling is designated by the word *also*, in italics. For example, an entry for the word *medieval* would say "*also* mediaeval."

EXERCISE 3-3   Variant Spellings

Directions: Locate a variant spelling for each of the following words in a dictionary.

example   judgment: <u>judgement</u>

1. glamorize: _____

2. esophagus: _____

3. pilose: _____

4. lachrymal: _____

5. aerie: _____

▶ **Syllabication:** Each entry shows how the word is divided into syllables. This information is helpful in pronouncing words and when you must split and hyphenate a word that appears at the end of a printed line. (Hyphens are placed only between syllables.)

▶ **Principal parts of verbs:** For verbs, an entry may contain the verb's principal parts: past tense, past participle, present participle (if different from the past), and third person singular present tense. These parts use the endings, *-ed, -ing,* and *-es*. Some dictionaries list the principal parts of all verbs; others list the principal parts only if they are irregularly formed. The verb *write*, for example, is irregularly formed, and a dictionary entry would show the following parts: *wrote, written, writing, writes.*

EXERCISE 3-4   Principal Parts of Verbs

Directions: Locate the principal parts of each of the following verbs using a dictionary.

1. leave: _____

2. lie: _____

3. throw: _____

4. burst: _____

5. get: _____

Pronunciation

The pronunciation for each entry word in a dictionary is shown in parentheses following the word. This pronunciation key shows you how to pronounce a word by spelling it the way it sounds. Different symbols are used to indicate certain sounds. The first step to using the pronunciation information is to learn to use the key that shows what the symbols mean and how they sound. The key appears on each page of the dictionary. Here is a sample key from the *American Heritage Dictionary of the English Language.*

ă pat	oi boy
ā pay	ou out
âr care	o͝o took
ä father	o͞o boot
ĕ pet	ŭ cut
ē be	ûr urge
ĭ pit	th thin
ī pie	*th* this
îr pier	hw which
ŏ pot	zh vision
ō toe	ə about, item
ô paw	◆ regionalism

Stress marks: ′ (primary); ′ secondary, as in dictionary (dĭk′shə-nĕr′ē)

The key shows the sound the symbol stands for in a word you already know how to pronounce. For example, suppose you are trying to pronounce the word *helix* (hē′lĭks). The key shows that the letter *e* in the first part of the word sounds the same as the *e* in the word *be*. The *i* in *helix* is pronounced the same way as the *i* in *pit*. To pronounce a word correctly, you must also accent (or put stress on) the appropriate part of the word. In a dictionary phonetic respelling, an accent mark (′) usually follows the syllable, or part of the word, that is stressed most heavily.

Examples

audience	ô′dē-əns
football	fŏŏt′bôl′
homicide	hŏm′ĭ-sīd′
hurricane	hûr′ĭ-kān′

Some words have two accents—a primary stress and a secondary stress. The primary one is stressed more heavily and is printed in darker type than the secondary accent.

interstate	ĭn′tər-stāt′

The syllables with no accent marks are unstressed syllables. The vowel sounds in these unstressed syllables are often marked with a symbol that looks like an upside down letter *e*. It is called a schwa sound (ə). The schwa sound stands for sounds that can be spelled by any vowel or combination of vowels. The schwa stands for the blurred sound of "uh." Listen to it in each of the following words:

alone	ə-lon′
nickel	nik′əl
collect	kə-lect′

Try to pronounce each of the following dictionary respellings, using the pronunciation key:

dĭ-vûr′sə-fī′	bŏŏsh′əl
chăl′ənj	bär′bĭ-kyōō′

EXERCISE 3-5   Pronunciation

Directions: Use the pronunciation key on page 50, or one from your dictionary, to sound out each of the following words. Write the word, spelled correctly, in the space provided.

1. sfîr _____

2. wûr′kə-bəl _____

3. prĕj′ə-dĭs _____

4. nīt′mâr′ _____

5. dĭ-lĭsh′əs _____

Part(s) of Speech

The part of speech, which follows the entry word's pronunciation, is given as an italicized abbreviation (*n.* for noun, *pron.* for pronoun, *v.* for verb, *adj.* for adjective, *adv.* for adverb, *prep.* for preposition, *conj.* for conjunction, and *inter.* for interjection). Verbs may be identified as either transitive (*tr.*) or intransitive (*intr.v.*). Transitive verbs are action verbs that direct their action at someone or something and are followed by a direct object (She **wrote** the poem, He **lifts** weights).

Intransitive verbs do not need a person or thing to complete the meaning of the sentence in which they are used (He **lied**, She **cries**). Intransitive verbs do not take a direct object.

Many words can function as more than one part of speech. For example, *train* can be both a noun and a verb. When a word can be used as more than one part of speech, the meanings for each part are grouped together, as shown in the entry for the word *dismount* on page 48. It can function either as a transitive or intransitive verb.

EXERCISE 3-6   Parts of Speech

Directions: For each of the following words, indicate at least two parts of speech for which it can be used. Use a dictionary if necessary.

example   lapse: verb, noun _____

1. contract: _____

2. right: _____

3. pinch: _____

4. quarter: _____

5. each: _____

Definitions

Some dictionaries arrange word meanings in an entry chronologically, with the oldest meaning first. *Webster's Ninth Collegiate Dictionary*, for example, arranges meanings with the oldest known meaning first. (This dictionary is available online at http://www.merriam-webster.com/dictionary.htm). Other dictionaries, such as the *American Heritage Dictionary of the English Language,* arrange meanings in order of most common usage. The sample entry on page 48 arranges meanings by how commonly they are used.

Etymology

Many dictionaries include information on each word's etymology—the origin and development of a word, including its history traced back as far as possible to its earliest use, often in another language. The sample dictionary entry on the next page shows that the word *dismiss* was derived from Middle English.

EXERCISE 3-7   Word Etymology

Directions: Find the origin of each of the following words in a dictionary and write it in the space provided.

example   vanilla: Spanish _____

1. continue: _____

2. granite: _____

3. jaunty: _____

4. charisma: _____

5. sauna: _____

Subject Labels

Many dictionaries include subject labels that show how a word is being used for a specific topic or field of study. Often called restrictive meanings as well, they define a word as it is used in a particular academic discipline. The subject area in which the word is used is printed in italic type followed by the meaning of the word in that particular discipline. The following entry for *dismiss* shows the meaning of the word in law and in sports. If you found this word in a legal document, you would focus on the first subject label, while physical education majors would find the second subject label more useful.

> **dis·miss** (dĭs-mĭs′) *tr.v.* **-missed, -miss·ing, -miss·es. 1.** To end the employment or service of; discharge. **2.** To direct or allow to leave: *dismissed troops after the inspection; dismissed the student after reprimanding him.* **3.a.** To stop considering; rid one's mind of; dispel: *dismissed all thoughts of running for office.* **b.** To refuse to accept or recognize; reject: *dismissed the claim as highly improbable.* **4.** *Law.* To put (a claim or action) out of court without further hearing. **5.** *Sports.* To put out (a batter) in cricket. [Middle English *dismissen,* from Medieval Latin *dismittere, dismiss-,* variant of Latin *dīmittere : dī-, dis-,* apart: see DIS- + *mittere,* to send.] **—dis·miss′i·ble** *adj.* **—dis·mis′sion** (-mĭsh′ən) *n.*

EXPLORING language

Old Words, New Meanings

➤ **Bundling**
  Old: A form of courtship in bed in which lovers are tied up or bundled to prevent undue familiarities
  New: Selling elements of a computer system as a package to eliminate competition

➤ **SPAM**
  Old: A canned meat made from spiced ham
  New: Junk e-mail

➤ **Cookie**
  Old: A small Dutch cake served as a dessert
  New: A text file placed on a computer hard drive by an Internet server to track a user's habits and tastes

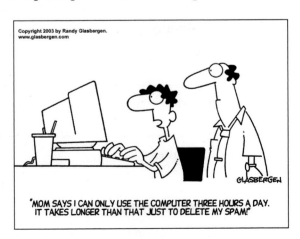

Source: "On Language" column by William Safire. "Bundling: Low-Tech Meanings Find High-Tech Meanings." *The New York Times Magazine,* June 11, 2000, pp. 26, 28.

Directions: For each of the following words, use a dictionary to find the definition for the subject area listed.

	Word	**Subject Areas**

example   band   Biology: <u>a chromatically, structurally, or functionally differentiated strip or stripe in or on an organism</u>

Anatomy: <u>a cordlike tissue that connects or holds structures together</u>

Computer science: <u>circular tracks on a storage device such as a disk</u>

1. family   Linguistics: _____

Mathematics: _____

Chemistry: _____

2. mode   Music: _____

Philosophy: _____

Mathematics: _____

3. tonic   Physiology: _____

Medicine: _____

Music: _____

4. nucleus   Botany: _____

Anatomy: _____

Astronomy: _____

5. charge   Law: _____

Physics: _____

Accounting: _____

Synonyms

Desk dictionary entries often list synonyms—words that have similar meanings—for entry words and explain the differences in meanings among the synonyms. The synonyms given in the entry below for the word *familiar* are followed by the shared meaning: "These adjectives describe relationships marked by intimacy." Then the different shades of meaning for each synonym are described: "Familiar implies . . .," "Close implies . . .," and so forth.

fa·mil·iar (fə-mĭl′yər) *adj. Abbr.* **fam. 1.** Often encountered or seen; common. **2.** Having fair knowledge; acquainted: *was familiar with those roads.* **3.** Of established friendship; intimate: *on familiar terms.* **4.** Natural and unstudied; informal: *lectured in a familiar style.* **5.** Taking undue liberties; presumptuous: *Students should not try to be familiar in their behavior toward an instructor.* **6.** Familial. **7.** Domesticated; tame. Used of animals. —**familiar** *n. Abbr.* **fam. 1.** A close friend or associate. **2.** An attendant spirit, often taking animal form. **3.** One who performs domestic service in the household of a high official. **4.** A person who frequents a place. [Middle English, from Old French *familier*, from Latin *familiāris*, domestic, from *familia*, family. See FAMILY.] —**fa·mil′iar·ly** *adv.*

SYNONYMS: *familiar, close, intimate, confidential, chummy.* These adjectives describe relationships marked by intimacy. *Familiar* implies an easy, often informal association based on frequent contact or shared interests: *a familiar song; a familiar guest. Close* implies strong emotional attachment: *close friendship; close to my brothers and sisters. Intimate* suggests bonds of affection or understanding resulting from the sharing of interests, problems, and experiences: *intimate friends; on an intimate footing. Confidential* suggests closeness founded on trust: *the prime minister's confidential secretary. Chummy* implies the comfortable, casual sociability shared by close friends: *The bartender was chummy with the regular customers.*

EXERCISE 3-9   Synonyms

Directions: For each of the pairs or sets of synonyms listed later, explain the difference in meaning between the words. Use a dictionary if necessary.

example   subject, topic: both denote the principal idea or point of a speech, a piece of writing, or an

artistic work; *subject* is the more general term, whereas *topic* is a subject of discussion,

argument, or conversation

1. form, figure, shape: _____

_____

_____

2. bright, brilliant, radiant: _____

_____

_____

3. offend, insult: _____

_____

_____

4. perform, accomplish, achieve: _____

_____

_____

_____

5. complex, complicated: _____

_____

_____

Homographs

Homographs are words that have the same spelling but different meanings and different origins. An example would be the words *prune* (as in *prune* juice) and *prune* (as in *prune* the fruit trees). Homographs are identified by raised numbers called *superscripts* following the entry.

The word *found* is a homograph. It has three distinct meanings, as shown below.

---

found[1] (found) *tr.v.* **found·ed, found·ing, founds. 1.** To establish or set up, especially with provision for continuing existence: *The college was founded in 1872.* **2.** To establish the foundation or basis of; base; *found a theory on firm evidence.* [Middle English *founden,* from Old French *fonder,* from Latin *fundāre,* from *fundus,* bottom.]

SYNONYMS: *found, create, establish, institute, organize.* The central meaning shared by these verbs is "to bring something into existence and set it in operation": *founded a colony; created a trust fund; establishing an advertising agency; instituted an annual ball to benefit the homeless; organizing the metal-trading division of a bank.*

found[2] (found) *tr.v.* **found·ed, found·ing, founds. 1.** To melt (metal) and pour into a mold. **2.** To make (objects) by pouring molten material into a mold. [Middle English *founden,* from Old French *fondre,* from Latin *fundere.* See **gheu-** in Appendix.]

found[3] (found) *v.* Past tense and past participle of **find.**

EXERCISE 3-10   Homographs

Directions: Explain the meaning of each of the following homographs. Use a dictionary if necessary.

example   former: <u>one that forms/occurring earlier in time</u>

1. gyro: _____

2. pink: _____

3. quail: _____

4. tender: _____

5. splat: _____

Abbreviations

All dictionaries provide a key to abbreviations used in the entry itself. Most often this key appears on the inside front cover or on the first few pages of the dictionary. Dictionaries also contain information on how to abbreviate common words and phrases. You can look up an abbreviation and find the word or phrase it stands for, or you can look up a word and find its abbreviation. Abbreviations are labeled "abbr." For example, the entry for the abbreviation *lb.* indicates that it is an abbreviation for *libra*, an ancient Roman weight, and for *pound*, a modern measurement of weight.

EXERCISE 3-11   Abbreviations I

Directions: For each of the following abbreviations, list the word or phrase it represents. Use a dictionary if necessary.

example   LDL: low-density lipoprotein _____

1. EPROM: _____

2. RDA: _____

3. POE: _____

4. MRI: _____

5. NATO: _____

EXERCISE 3-12   Abbreviations II

Directions: For each of the following words or phrases, locate its abbreviation using a dictionary.

example   Joint Chiefs of Staff: J.C.S. or JCS _____

1. educational television: _____

2. surface-to-air missile: _____

3. kilowatt: _____

4. horsepower: _____

5. Attorney General: _____

Other Useful Information

Many dictionaries, especially desk dictionaries, contain numerous types of information. You may find entries for geographic places (*Mexico City*), historical figures (*Napoleon Bonaparte*), events (the *Civil War*), famous authors, artists, and composers (*Chaucer, van Gogh,* and *Mozart*). You also may find entries for literary and mythological illusions (*albatross, Hercules*).

Directions: Use a dictionary to answer each of the following questions.

example   Where is Istanbul located? <u>Turkey</u>

1. What color are the flowers on an ocotillo? _____

2. For how many terms was Ulysses S. Grant president? _____

3. When did the Congo (Zaire) become independent? _____

4. Who was Amphitrite's husband in Greek mythology? _____

5. What kind of dog is a Dandie Dinmont? _____

How to Locate Words Quickly in a Print Dictionary

Most dictionaries use **guide words** to help you locate the page on which a particular word occurs. At the top of each dictionary page are two words in bold print, one on the left corner and one on the right. The guide word on the left is the first entry on that page; the one on the right is the last entry. All the words on that page come between the two guide words in alphabetical order. If the word you are looking for falls alphabetically between the two guide words on the page, scan that page to find the word. Suppose you are looking for the word *kinesics*. If your dictionary shows a page with the guide words *kindling* and *King of Prussia*, the word *kinesics* would be found there because, alphabetically, *kinesics* comes after *kindling* and before *King of Prussia*.

EXERCISE 3-14

Directions: Read each entry word and the pair of guide words that follows it. Decide whether the entry word would be found on the dictionary page with those guide words. Write *yes* or *no* in the space provided.

Word		Guide Words	
example	interstellar	interrogate—intervocalic	yes
1.	jaundice	jay—Jell-O	
2.	chutney	chute—cilium	
3.	ooze	ontogenesis—open	
4.	quart	quant—quarry	
5.	dragoman	dragonhead—drapery	
6.	shallop	Shaker Heights—shambles	

How to Find the Right Meaning

Most words have more than one meaning. When you look up the meaning of a new word, you must choose the meaning that fits the way the word is used in the sentence context. Here are a few suggestions for choosing the correct meaning from among those listed in an entry:

1. **If you are familiar with the parts of speech, try to use these to locate the correct meaning.** For instance, if you are looking up the meaning of a word that names a person, place, or thing, you can save time by reading only those entries given after *n.* (noun).

2. **In most types of academic reading, you can skip definitions that give slang and colloquial (abbreviated *colloq*.) meanings.** Colloquial meanings refer to informal or spoken language.

3. **If you are not sure of the part of speech, read each meaning until you find a definition that seems correct.** Skip over the subject labels that are inappropriate.

4. **Test your choice by substituting the meaning in the sentence with which you are working.** Substitute the definition for the word and see whether it makes sense in the context.

Suppose you are looking up the word *oblique* to find its meaning in this sentence:

> The suspect's **oblique** answers to the police officer's questions made her suspicious.

> **o·blique** (ō-blēk', ə-blēk') *adj. Abbr.* **obl. 1.a.** Having a slating or sloping direction, course, or position; inclined. **b.** *Mathematics.* Designating geometric lines or planes that are neither parallel nor perpendicular. **2.** *Botany.* Having sides of unequal length or form: *an oblique leaf.* **3.** *Anatomy.* Situated in a slanting position; not transverse or longitudinal: *oblique muscles or ligaments.* **4.a.** Indirect or evasive: *oblique political maneuvers.* **b.** Devious, misleading, or dishonest: *gave oblique answers to the questions.* **5.** Not direct in descent; collateral. **6.** *Grammar.* Designating any noun case except the nominative or the vocative. **—oblique** *n.* **1.** An oblique thing, such as a line, direction, or muscle. **2.** *Nautical.* The act of changing course by less than 90°. **—oblique** (ō-blīk', ə-blīk') *adv.* At an angle of 45°. [Middle English, from Old French, from Latin *oblīquus.*] **—o·blique'ly** *adv.* **—o·blique'ness** *n.*

Oblique is used in the above sentence as an adjective. Looking at the entries listed after *adj.* (adjective), you can skip over the definition under the heading *Mathematics,* as it wouldn't apply here. Definition 4a (indirect or evasive) best fits the way *oblique* is used in the sentence.

EXERCISE 3-15 Identifying the Correct Meaning of a Word

Directions: Each of the following sentences contains a boldfaced word that has several possible meanings. Write the answer that identifies the meaning that is appropriate for the way the word is used in the sentence on the line provided.

_____ 1. The engineer discovered an **obscure** flaw in the building's design.

    a. inconspicuous   c. humble

    b. dark   d. vague

_____ 2. Her father took a **dim** view of her decision to major in political science.

    a. indistinct   c. dull

    b. disapproving   d. faint

_____ 3. The recent surge in the stock market has many investors feeling **flush.**

    a. level   c. feverish

    b. embarrassed   d. affluent

_____ 4. The musicians agreed to play at the bluegrass festival for **scale.**

    a. a minimum wage fixed by contract   c. a system of ordered marks

    b. a progressive classification   d. a series of tones

_____ 5. A **knot** of onlookers had formed even before the police arrived.

    a. a fastening   c. a tight cluster

    b. a unifying bond   d. a complex problem

_____ 6. The shortstop caught the baseball and threw the runner out in one **fluid** motion.

    a. a continuous substance   c. readily reshaped; pliable

    b. smooth and flowing; graceful   d. tending to change

_____ 7. My son likes every kind of cookie, but he is **partial** to Oreos.

    a. incomplete   c. prejudiced

    b. affecting only a part   d. having a particular fondness
                                 for something

Using a Thesaurus

A thesaurus is a dictionary of synonyms. It groups words with similar meanings together. A thesaurus is particularly useful when you want to

➤ Locate the precise term to fit a particular situation

➤ Find an appropriate descriptive word

➤ Replace an overused or unclear word

➤ Convey a different or more specific shade of meaning

Suppose you are looking for a more precise word for the expression _look into_ in the following sentence:

The marketing manager will **look into** the decline of recent sales in the Midwest.

The thesaurus lists the following synonyms for "look into":

look into [*v.*] *check, research*
audit, check out, delve into, dig, examine, explore, follow up, go into, inquire, inspect, investigate, look over, make inquiry, probe, prospect, scrutinize, sift, study; SEE CONCEPT *103*

From *Roget's 21st Century Thesaurus*. Copyright © 1992, 1993, 1999, 2005 by The Philip Lief Group. Published by Dell Publishing. Reprinted by permission of The Philip Lief Group.

Read the above entry and underline words or phrases that you think would be more descriptive than *look into.* You might underline words and phrases such as *examine, scrutinize,* and *investigate.*

The most widely used thesaurus is *Roget's Thesaurus.* Inexpensive paperback editions are available in most bookstores. *Merriam-Webster's Collegiate Thesaurus* is available free online (http://www.merriam-webster.com/thesaurus.htm).

When you first consult a thesaurus, you will need to familiarize yourself with its format and learn how to use it. The following is a step-by-step approach:

1. **Begin by locating the word you are trying to replace.** Many thesauri are organized alphabetically, much like a dictionary. Following the word, you will find numerous entries that list the synonyms of that word. Select words that seem like possible substitutes. (The hardback edition of *Roget's* is organized by subject with an index in the back.)

2. **Test each of the words you selected in the sentence in which you will use it.** The word should fit the context of the sentence.

3. **Select the word that best expresses what you are trying to say.**

4. **Choose only words whose shades of meaning you know.** Check unfamiliar words in a dictionary before using them. Remember, misusing a word is often a more serious error than choosing an overused, vague, or general one.

Using a Thesaurus

Directions: Using a thesaurus, replace the boldfaced word or phrase in each sentence with a more precise or descriptive word. Write the word in the space provided. Rephrase the sentence, if necessary.

example   The union appointed Corinne Miller to act as the **go-between** in its negotiations with management. _____ liaison _____

1. The two interviewers **went back and forth** asking questions of the candidate.
   _____

2. On the night of the inauguration, the ballroom looked **very nice**. _____

3. More than anything, he **wanted** a new minivan. _____

4. The town had gone through an economic decline, but now it appeared to be on the verge of an **increase**. _____

5. The two brothers were opposites: Chester **liked to talk a lot**, whereas John was content to sit quietly and listen. _____

6. Freshwater lakes that are in the process of accelerated eutrophication are often **cloudy-looking**. _____

7. Daylilies range in color from **dark red** to yellow to almost white. _____

8. Today's trend toward casual clothing in the workplace has made the demand for high-quality custom suits **fall**. _____

9. The children were **so sad** over the loss of their old dog Chumley. _____

10. The first speaker was interesting, but the second one was so **dull** I almost fell asleep.
    _____

Using a Subject Dictionary

Specialized dictionaries that list most of the important words in a particular discipline are called *subject dictionaries*. They list technical and specialized meanings for words used in a particular field of study and suggest how and when to use them. For the fields of medicine and nursing, for example, there is *Taber's Cyclopedic Medical Dictionary*. Other subject dictionaries include *The New Grove Dictionary of Music and Musicians* and a *Dictionary of Economics*. Most subject dictionaries are available only in hardback; look for them in the reference section of your library. However, many are available online, either through a library that subscribes to them or as a free Web site. For a comprehensive directory of online subject dictionaries, visit the following Web site: http://www.yourdictionary.com/specialty.html. (Note that this is a commercial site, and it is unclear whether entries have been academically evaluated before they are included.)

Use a subject dictionary when you are unclear about the meaning of a term as used in your textbook and its glossary. You might also refer to a subject dictionary when you want to learn the distinction between several similar terms or when you want to learn more about the history and usage of a term.

EXERCISE 3-17 Using a Subject Dictionary

Directions: List the courses you are taking this semester. For three of your courses, find the name of a subject dictionary and evaluate its usefulness.

_____

_____

_____

_____

_____

_____

MASTERY test 1

Applying and Integrating Your Skills

Apply Your Skills in Biology

Directions: The following passage is taken from a biology textbook. The questions that follow illustrate situations in which you might apply the skills you have learned in this chapter. Answer each using a dictionary, thesaurus, or subject dictionary, if needed.

Body Defenses

Every second of every day, an army of **hostile** bacteria, viruses, and fungi swarms on our skin and invades our inner passageways—yet we stay amazingly healthy most of the time. The body seems to have developed a **single-minded** approach toward such foes—if you're not with us, then you're against us!

The body's defenders against these tiny but mighty enemies are two systems, simply called the *innate* and the *adaptive defense systems*. Together they make up the immune system. The innate defense system, also called the nonspecific defense system, responds immediately to protect the body from all foreign substances, whatever they are. You could say that we come fully equipped with our innate defenses, which are provided by intact skin and **mucous membranes,** by the **inflammatory response,** and by a number of proteins produced by body cells. This system reduces the workload of the second protective arm, the adaptive defense system, by preventing entry and spread of microorganisms throughout the body.

The adaptive, or specific defense, system mounts the attack against *particular* foreign substances. Although certain body organs (**lymphoid organs** and blood vessels) are **intimately** involved with the immune response, the immune system is a *functional system* rather than an organ system in an **anatomical** sense. Its "structures" are a variety of molecules and trillions of immune cells that inhabit lymphoid tissues and organs and circulate in body fluids. The most important of the immune cells are **lymphocytes** and **macrophages**.

When our immune system is operating effectively, it protects us from most bacteria, viruses, transplanted organs or grafts, and even our own cells that have turned against us. The immune system does this both directly, by cell attack, and indirectly, by releasing mobilizing chemicals and protective **antibody** molecules. The resulting highly specific resistance to disease is called immunity (*immun* = free).

1. Using a subject dictionary, find the meaning of the following words and phrases:

   a. mucous membranes _____

   _____

   b. inflammatory response _____

   c. lymphoid organs _____

   _____

   d. antibody _____

   _____

2. Identify three words that would be useful to add to your index file or vocabulary log.

   _____

3. Suppose you are writing a paraphrase—a word-for-word restatement of a passage—using your own words. Use a dictionary or a thesaurus to find an appropriate definition for each of the following words.

a. hostile _____

b. single-minded _____

c. intimately _____

d. anatomical _____

4. Use a dictionary to find the correct pronunciation of each of the following words. In the space provided, write each word the way it sounds.

a. mucous _____

b. lympocytes _____

c. macrophages _____

EXERCISE 3-19   Subject Dictionary Usage

Directions: For one of your courses, select three specialized words that appear in the glossary of your textbook and list them below.

Words: 1. _____ 2. _____ 3. _____

Using a subject dictionary, locate and read entries for the three words you selected above. Then answer the following questions:

1. In what ways did the subject dictionary definition differ from those in the glossary?

_____

_____

_____

_____

2. In what situations might you use a subject dictionary for this course?

_____

_____

_____

_____

This textbook excerpt was adapted from *Access to Health* by Rebecca J. Donatelle, published by Pearson/Benjamin Cummings in 2008. Read the passage to find out what stress is and to learn some stress management techniques. Then answer the questions that follow.

Stress Management

1   STRESS! You can't run from it, you can't hide from it, and it invades our waking and sleeping hours.

2   Often, stress is **insidious**, and we don't even notice the things that affect us. As we sleep, it **encroaches** on our **psyche** through noise or incessant worries over things that need to be done. While we work at the computer, stress may interfere in the form of noise from next door, strain on our eyes, and tension in our backs. Even when we are out socializing with friends, we feel guilty about not enough time and so much left to do. The exact toll stress **exacts** from us during a lifetime of stress overload is unknown, but it is much more than an annoyance. Rather, it is a significant health hazard that can rob the body of needed nutrients, damage the cardiovascular system, raise blood pressure, and **dampen** the immune system's defenses, leaving us **vulnerable** to infections and disease. In addition, it can drain our emotional reserves, contribute to depression, anxiety, and irritability, and **punctuate** social interactions with hostility and anger.

What Is Stress?

3   Often we think of stress as an externally imposed factor. But for most of us, stress results from an internal state of emotional tension that occurs in response to the various demands of living. Most current definitions state that stress is the mental and physical response of our bodies to the changes and challenges in our lives. Stress and strain are associated with most daily activities. Generally, positive stress, or stress that presents the opportunity for personal growth and satisfaction, is called eustress. Starting school, developing new friendships, and learning a new physical skill all give rise to eustress. Distress, or negative stress, is caused by events that result in debilitative stress and strain (such as financial problems, the death of a loved one, academic difficulties, and the breakup of a relationship).

Managing Your Stress

4   We cannot get rid of distress entirely: like eustress, it is a part of life. However, we can train ourselves to recognize the events that cause distress and to anticipate our reactions to them. One of the most effective ways to combat stressors is to build skills and coping strategies that will help **inoculate** you against them. Such

efforts are known collectively as stress management techniques. They range from doing something as simple as taking 20 minutes each day to be alone to developing an elaborate time management plan for eating, socializing, and exercising.

Social Support and Positive Thinking

5   As you plan a stress management program, don't underestimate the importance of social networks and social bonds. Friendships are an important aspect of inoculating yourself against harmful stressors. Studies have demonstrated the importance of social support in buffering individuals from the effects of stress. As you work to develop and cultivate friendships, look for individuals who are good listeners, tolerant, give and share freely, and do not rush to judgment. Avoid people who enjoy stirring things up and always seem to be in some crisis themselves. Such friends often **precipitate**, rather than reduce, stress responses.

6   As noted earlier, our reactions to situations are what makes these things stressful, not the situations themselves. To combat negative self-talk we must first become aware of it, then stop it, and finally replace the negative thoughts with positive ones. Several types of negative self-talk exist but among the most common are pessimism, or focusing on the negative; perfectionism, or expecting super-human standards; blaming, or condemning yourself or others for circumstances and events; and dichotomous thinking, in which everything is either black or white (good or bad) instead of in gradations. Once you realize that some of your thoughts may be irrational or overactive, interrupt this self-talk by saying "Stop" (under your breath or out loud) and make a conscious effort to adjust your thinking. Focus on more positive patterns. With any emotional response to a distressor, you are responsible for the emotion and the behaviors **elicited** by the emotion. Learning to tell the difference between normal emotions and those based on irrational beliefs can help you either stop the emotion or express it in a healthy and appropriate way.

Visualization and Meditation

7   Popular stress fighters include visualization and mediation. Visualization, or the creation of mental scenes, works by engaging one's imagination of the physical senses of sight, sound, smell, taste, and feel to replace stressful **stimuli** with peaceful or pleasurable thoughts. So the next time you feel stressed, close your eyes, imagine yourself at some **tranquil** location, and take a mini mental vacation.

8   There are many different forms of mediation. Most involve sitting quietly for 15 to 20 minutes, focusing on a particular word or symbol, controlling breathing, and getting in touch with the inner self. Practiced by Eastern religions for centuries, meditation is believed to be an important form of **introspection** and personal renewal. As a stress management tool, it can calm the body and quiet the mind, creating a sense of peace. As a meditative technique, mindfulness—the ability to be fully present in the moment—can aid relaxation, reduce emotional and physical pain, and help us connect more effectively with ourselves, with others, and with nature. The practice of mindfulness focuses on the cultivation of awareness, openness, and a nonjudgmental attitude that includes strategies and activities that contribute to overall health and wellness. In fact, mindfulness and wellness are interconnected and can be developed **concurrently**, reinforcing each other.

Directions: Use a dictionary to answer these questions that about the boldfaced words from the passage.

———   1. How is the word **insidious** (para. 2) correctly divided into syllables?

a. in si di ous

b. in sid i ous

c. in sidi ous

d. in sid ious

———   2. The word **encroaches** (para. 2) is a principal part of

a. encroach.

b. encroached.

c. encroaching.

d. encroacher.

———   3. What is the correct pronunciation of **psyche** (para. 2)?

a. psi KEE

b. si KEE

c. PSI chee

d. SI kee

———   4. Which of the following words is a derivative of **dampen** (para. 2)?

a. dampened

b. dampening

c. dampener

d. dampens

———   5. What part of speech is **punctuate** as it is used in paragraph 2?

a. adjective

b. intransitive verb

c. noun

d. transitive verb

———   6. What is the correct meaning of **elicited** as it is used in paragraph 6?

a. prevented

b. contradicted

c. provoked

d. complicated

———   7. What is the singular form of **stimuli** (para. 7)?

a. stimulate

b. stimulus

c. stimulate

d. stimula

———   8. Which of the following words is a synonym for **tranquil** (para. 7)?

a. entertaining

b. exotic

c. calm

d. familiar

———   9. Which syllable of **introspection** (para. 8) has a secondary accent?

a. in

b. tro

c. spec

d. tion

———   10. What is the origin of **concurrently** (para. 8)?

a. Old French

b. German

c. Middle English

d. Greek

Directions: Use the four sample dictionary entries shown below to complete the exercises that follow each entry. Write your answers in the spaces provided.

> **¹ex•act** (ig-'zakt) *vt.* [**ME**, to require as payment, fr. **L** *exactus*, pp. of *exigere* to drive out, demand, measure, fr. *ex-* + *agere* to drive — more at AGENT] (1564) **1** : to call for forcible or urgently and obtain (from them has been –ed the ultimate sacrifice —D.D. Eisenhower) **2** : to call for as necessary or desirable *syn* see DEMAND — **ex•act•able** (-'zak-tə-bəl) *adj*. — **ex•ac•tor** also **ex•act•er** (-'zak-tər) *n.*
> **²exact** *adj.* [**L** *exactus*] (1533) **1** : exhibiting or marked by strickt, particular, and complete accordance with fact or a standard **2** : marked by thorough consideration or minute measurement of small factual details *syn* see CORRECT — **ex•act•ness** (-'zak(t)-nəs) *n.*

1. Write the correct meaning of **exacts** as it is used in paragraph 2 of the "Stress Management" passage: _____

2. What is the orgin of the word **exact**: _____

> **vul•ner•a•ble** ('vəl-n(ə-)rə-bəl, 'vəl-nər-bəl) *adj.* [**LL** *vulnerabilis*, fr. **L** *vulnerare* to wound, fr. *vulner-*, *vulnus* wound; prob. akin to L *vellere* to pluck, Gk *oulē* wound] (1605) **1** : capable of being physically or emotionally wounded **2** : open to attack or damage : ASSAILABLE (–to criticism) **3** : liable to increased penalties but entitled to increased bonuses after winning a game in contract bridge — **vul•ner•a•bil•i•ty** (,vəl-n(ə-)rə-'bi-lə-tē) *n.* – **vul•ner•a•ble•ness** ('vəl-n)ə-)rə-bəl-nəs, 'vəl-nər-bəl-) *n.* — **vul•ner•a•bly** (-blē) *adv.*

3. Write the correct meaning of **vulnerable** as it is used in paragraph 2 of the "Stress Management" passage: _____

4. Write the subject label for a restrictive meaning of **vulnerable**: _____

> **in•oc•u•late** (i-'nä-kyə-lāt) *vt* **-lat•ed; -lat•ing** [**ME**, to insert a bud in a plant, fr. **L** *inoculatus*, pp. of *inoculare*, fr. *in-* + *oculus* eye, bud — more at EYE] (1721) **1 a** : to introduce a microorganism into (–mice with anthrax) (beans *inoculated* with nitrogen-fixing bacteria) **b** : to introduce (as a microorganism) into a suitable situation for growth **c** : to introduce immunologically active material (as an antibody or antigen) into esp. in order to treat or prevent a disease (–children against diphtheria) **2** : to introduce something into the mind of **3** : to protect as if by inoculation *syn* see INFUSE — **in•oc•u•la•tive** (-,lā-tiv) *adj.* — **in•oc•u•la•tor** (-,lā-tər) *n.*

5. Write the correct meaning of **inoculate** as it is used in paragraph 4 of the "Stress Management" passage: _____

6. Describe the etymology of **inoculate**: _____

¹pre·cip·i·tate (pri-'si-pə-,tāt) *vb.* **–tat·ed; –tat·ing** [L *praecipitatus*, pp. of praecipitare, fr. *praecipit-, praeceps*] *vt* (1528) **1a** : to throw violently ; HURL (the quandaries into which the release of nuclear energy has *precipitated* mankind — A.B. Arons) **b** : to throw down **2** : to bring about esp. abruptly (–a scandal that would end with his expulsion — John Cheever) **3a** : to cause to separate from solution or suspension **b** : to cause (vapor) to condense and fall or deposit –*vi* **1a** : to fall headlong **b** : to fall or come suddenly into some condition **2** : to move or act precipitately **3a** : to separate from solution or suspension **b** : to condense from a vapor and fall as rain or snow — **pre·cip·i·ta·tive** (-,tā-tiv) *adj.* — **pre·cip·i·ta·tor** (-,tā-tər) *n.*

²pre·cip·i·tate (pri-'si-pə-tət) *n.* [**NL** *praecipitatum* fr. **L**, neut. of *praecipitatus*] (1594) **1** : a substance separated from a solution or suspension by chemical or physical change usu. as an insoluble amorphous or crystalline solid **2** : a product, result, or outcome of some process or action

³pre·cip·i·tate (pri-'si-pə-tət) *adj.* (1615) **1a** : falling, flowing, or rushing with steep decent **b** : PRECIPITOUS, STEEP **2** : exhibiting violent or unwise speed — **pre·cip·i·tate·ly** *adv.* — **pre·cip·i·tate·ness** *n.* **syn** PRECIPITATE, HEADLONG, ABRUPT, IMPETUOUS, SUDDEN mean showing undue haste or unexpectedness, PRECIPITATE stresses lack of due deliberation and implies prematureness of action (the army's *precipitate* withdrawal). HEADLONG stresses rashness and lack of forethought (a *headlong* flight from arrest). ABRUPT stresses curtness and a lack of warning or ceremony (an *abrupt* refusal). IMPETUOUS stresses extreme impatience or impulsiveness (an *impetuous* lover proposing marriage). SUDDEN stresses unexpectedness and sharpness or violence of action (flew into a *sudden* rage).

7. Write the correct meaning of **precipitate** as it is used in paragraph 5 of the "Stress Management" passage: _____

8. What part of speech is the word **precipitate** used as in this selection? _____

9. Write two restrictive meanings for **precipitate**: _____
   _____

10. List two other words that are made up from the word **precipitate**: _____

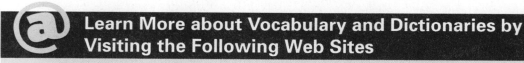

Learn More about Vocabulary and Dictionaries by Visiting the Following Web Sites

1. **Interpreting a Dictionary Entry**
   http://academic.cuesta.edu/acasupp/as/504.HTM

2. **Dictionaries: Frequently Asked Questions**
   http://www.askoxford.com/asktheexperts/faq/aboutdictionaries/?view=uk

3. **How to Use a Thesaurus**
   http://thesaurus.reference.com/features/howtousethesaurus.html

4. **How to Use Roget's II: The New Thesaurus**
   http://www.bartleby.com/62/11.html

4

Using Word Parts to Expand Your Vocabulary

Take your pick.

A. Study one word and learn one meaning. You could learn the meaning of *autopilot* or of *autonomy*, for example.

B. Study one prefix (word beginning) and learn the meaning of over 100 words. The prefix *auto-* is an example. It means "self." Knowing the meaning of *auto-* would help you figure out the meaning of *autopilot* and *autonomous,* as well as words such as *autoimmune, autocrat, autorotation, autotransfusion* and many others.

No doubt you picked choice B, which describes a method of building your vocabulary by learning word parts, the subject of this chapter.

Word Parts: The Bargain Table for Vocabulary Building

Word parts, beginnings, middles, and endings of words are the bargain table of vocabulary building. On a bargain table you buy merchandise for less than you would normally pay. On the word parts bargain table, you learn many more words that you would expect for the cost (your time).

If you study the meaning of the word *pseudonym*, you end up knowing one meaning (false name). If you study the prefix *pseudo-* (which means *false*) you might be able to figure out nearly 400 words that begin with that prefix (*pseudoscience, pseudonym, pseudobiological,* and so forth). The prefix *extra-* is used in approximately 225 words. The root *dict-* unlocks the meaning of over 175 words; the root *spec-* is the key to over 300 words.

By learning common beginnings, middles, and endings of words, called word parts, you unlock the meaning of many more words than you would by studying single meanings. Learning word parts is the bargain table of vocabulary building.

A letter or letters added to the beginning of a root is called a **prefix**.

Prefix + Root	Word
inter + change	interchange
mis + inform	misinform
trans + port	transport

A letter or letters added to the end of a root is called a suffix.

Root + Suffix	Word
sleep + y	sleepy
adopt + ion	adoption
normal + ly	normally

A **root** is a syllable, syllables, or an independent word that carries the basic meaning of the word.

	Roots	Words Formed from Roots
Single Syllable	path, graph, cred	sympathy, graphic, credible
Multiple Syllables	ortho, astro, photo	orthopedics, astronaut, photograph
Whole Words	light, advantage, heart	lightness, advantageous, heartless

Roots are the basic building blocks upon which other words, sometimes called variations or derivatives, are formed. Some roots are formed from Latin or Greek words. For example, the Latin root *-fid* (which means faith) is used to form words such as *fidelity* (faithfulness), *infidel* (a person who is not faithful), and *confidence* (having faith in yourself). Whole-word roots are found in the dictionary under their own entries. (Whole-word roots are sometimes called base words.) For example, the word *excite* is a root word. The word *excitable* is not. It is formed from the root word *excite*.

Here are a few things you need to know about prefixes, suffixes, and roots.

1. **Every word is built upon at least one root.**

2. **Words can have more than one prefix, root, or suffix.**
   ➤ Some words have two roots (*photo/graph*).
   ➤ Some words have two prefixes (*un/sub/stantial*).
   ➤ Some words have two suffixes (*beauti/ful/ly*)

3. **Not all words have a prefix and a suffix.**
   ➤ Some words have neither a prefix nor a suffix (*train*).
   ➤ Others have a suffix but no prefix (*train/able*).
   ➤ Others have a prefix but no suffix (*un/train*).

4. **The spelling of prefixes and roots may change when they are combined with other word parts.** For example, the prefix *com-* (meaning together) changes when combined with the root that follows it. The prefix *com-* along with the root word *relate* combines and changes spelling to form the word *correlate* (to show or establish a connection or relationship).

5. **Sometimes you may identify a group of letters as a prefix or root, but find that it does not carry the meaning of the prefix or root.** For example, the first three letters in the word *missile* are part of the root and are not the prefix *mis-*, which means wrong or bad.

EXERCISE 4-1 Root Words

Directions: Locate the whole word that functions as the root of each of the following boldfaced words. Write the root word and the meaning of the boldfaced word in the space provided.

example   The **generosity** of the city's restaurant owners was evident; the shelves of the food pantry were well-stocked.

generous; willingness to give

1. If you are color-blind, you cannot **differentiate** between shades of blue.

   difference → make change

2. Many Americans are guilty of conspicuous **consumption**.

   consum → take something

3. The title of the sculpture was accompanied by an **explanatory** note in the program.

   explan → provide information

4. The **likelihood** of my getting an A in the class seemed remote after the last exam.

   like → possibility

5. The judge pronounced sentence on the convicted killer **dispassionately**.

   passion → feel strongly

6. We thought her remarks at the rally were **inflammatory** and uncalled for.

   flamme → high degree of anger

7. The **righteousness** of their crusade was never in doubt.

   rights → correct way

8. The gentleman on my right at the dinner party was an **insufferable** bore!

   suffer → painful, intolerance

9. Several weightlifters were **disqualified** from the competition for having used steroids.

   qualifi → cannot do it. ineligible

10. Our **unsteadiness** on land was caused by a rough crossing on the ferry.

    steadi → instability

Word Parts and Academic Disciplines

WORD notes

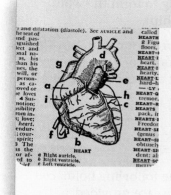

You are taking a human anatomy and physiology course, and you have hundreds of new terms to learn. You must learn names of muscles, joints, and nerves, not to mention the names of the 206 bones in the body. Learning all these words one by one would be a formidable task. One way to succeed in courses such as these is to learn prefixes, roots, and suffixes that will enable you to figure out many word meanings, rather than to memorize their individual meanings.

Each academic discipline, and especially the sciences, uses prefixes, roots, and suffixes as language building blocks. You can learn sets or groups of words with similar prefixes or roots. Here are a few common prefixes and roots used in medical, legal, and biological fields, along with a sampling of the words you can figure out based on them.

Common Prefixes and Roots Used in Medicine, Law, and Biology

Discipline	Prefixes and Roots	Words Using These Word Parts
Medicine	*derma-* (skin) *-itis* (inflammation of) *cardio-* (heart) *pod(o)-* (foot)	dermatologist, dermatitis bronchitis, appendicitis cardiac, cardiography, cardiogram podiatrist, podogram, pododynia
Biology	*-osis* (condition or process) *photo-* (light) *cyto-* (study of cells) *exo-* (outside)	symbiosis photosynthesis cytoplasm exoskeleton
Law	*feder-* (treaty, league) *judic-* (judgment) *jur(is)-* (law, right) *leg(is)-* (law, contract)	federal, federation judicial, adjudicant jury, justice legislation, legal

Some students find it helpful to create an index card file or computer file of important prefixes, roots, and suffixes. You can devise creative ways of organizing your files, depending on the discipline you are studying. For example, for an anatomy and physiology course, one student color-coded her index cards to correspond to various systems of the body.

Prefixes: Beginnings That Change Word Meanings

WORD notes

What do the words *reuse, reduce,* and *recycle* have in common? Each begins with the same prefix *re-*. If you did not know the meaning of these words, it would be helpful to know that *re-* means "again" or "back." *Reuse* means to use again, *recycle* means to process material so that it can be reused, and *reduce* means to lessen or go back in size or amount. Prefixes are powerful tools to building your vocabulary because they can unlock the meaning of thousands of words.

Not all prefixes create opposite meanings as those shown above. Prefixes can suggest negatives ("not"), or they can suggest quantities. They can also suggest direction, location, or placement. Some prefixes indicate particular fields of study as well.

Prefixes Meaning "Not" (Negative or Opposite)

Table 4-1 lists common prefixes that may give negative or opposite meanings to the roots to which they are attached. The prefix *ir-* added to the word *responsible* forms the word *irresponsible* (not responsible).

One factor that makes prefixes tricky to work with is knowing which prefix to add to which root word. For example, if you want to add a prefix meaning *not* to the base word *conclusive*, which of the prefixes meaning *not* should you add, *un-, in-,*

Table 4-1	Common Prefixes Meaning "Not" (Negative)	
Prefix	**Meaning**	**Sample Word**
a-	not	asymmetrical
anti-	against	antiwar
contra-	against, opposite	contradict
dis-	part, away, not	disagree
in/il/ir/im-	not	incorrect/illogical/irreversible/impossible
mal-	bad, wrong	malpractice
mis-	wrongly	misunderstand
non-	not	nonfiction
un-	not	unpopular
pseudo-	false	pseudoscientific

or *non-*? Unfortunately, there is no easy answer. The right answer is to add the prefix *in-*, forming the word *inconclusive*. *Nonconclusive* and *unconclusive* are not words. In these situations, there is usually no rule to follow. Instead, you should check your dictionary to be sure that you have combined a prefix and root or base word correctly to form a real word.

The prefixes *il-*, *im-*, and *ir-*, all of which mean *not*, are a special case. Which to use depends on the sound of the letter that follows the prefix. The prefix *il-* is added to words that begin with the letter *l* (*illegal*). The prefix *im-* is added to words that begin with the letters *b, m,* or *p* (*imbalance, immobile, impossible*). The prefix *ir-* is added to words that begin with the letter *r*.

EXERCISE 4-2   Prefixes I

Directions: For each boldfaced word in the following sentences, underline the prefix and write the meaning of the word in the space provided.

example   Be sure to use <u>non</u>sexist language. <u>not discriminating on the basis of gender</u>

1. Because my daughter's handwriting is nearly **illegible**, she got a D on her report card for handwriting.

    <u>il</u> → cannot read

2. When we found the kitten, it was suffering from **malnutrition**.

    <u>mal</u> → not good, wrong

3. Samuel Clemens wrote books under the **pseudonym** Mark Twain.

    _____

4. The diagnosis was difficult to make because the patient's symptoms were **atypical**.

    _____

5. It was **imprudent** of him to spend his last dollar on a lottery ticket.

    _____

6. The city councilman was accused of **misallocating** funds.

    _____

7. The earthquake **dislodged** several large boulders on the mountain.

    _____

8. His high blood pressure was a **contraindication** for surgery at this time.

    _____

9. The country maintained a policy of **nonaggression** toward its neighbors.

    _____

10. It was **demoralizing** to lose the game after having been ahead by ten runs.

    _____

EXERCISE 4-3   Prefixes II

Directions: For each of the following words, add a prefix to form a word opposite in meaning to the word given. Check a dictionary if you are unsure of which prefix to add.

example   trust _____distrust; mistrust_____

1. religious _____
2. conscious _____
3. perfect _____
4. familiar _____
5. social _____

6. belief _____
7. nutrition _____
8. moral _____
9. compliant _____
10. liberal _____

EXERCISE 4-4   Prefixes III

Directions: For each of the following sentences, write the letter of the choice that best explains the meaning of the boldfaced word. Use your knowledge of prefixes and a dictionary if necessary.

_____ 1. The counselor helped the teenager **redefine** her goals.

a. explain
b. restate
c. defend
d. manage

_____ 2. It was obvious that the mayor was **unacquainted** with the plight of immigrants in the city.

a. familiar
b. inexperienced
c. not knowledgeable about
d. not concerned about

_____ 3. Due to the group's radical position on animal rights, Janine **disaffiliated** herself from the Rights for Animals Association.

a. removed from involvement
b. remained partially involved
c. maintained several associations
d. carried a false association

_____ 4. We were **misinformed** about the store's hours.

a. distracted
b. given incorrect information
c. directed accurately
d. displeased

_____ 5. Our waiter laughingly tried to convince us that the triple chocolate cake was **noncaloric**.

a. fat free
b. not caffeinated
c. nutritious
d. having no calories

_____ 6. The federal official was charged with **misappropriation** of funds.

a. taking wrongly
b. receiving lawfully
c. losing
d. misplacing

——— 7. After being sprayed by a skunk, our **malodorous** dog hid under the porch.

    a. naughty   c. bad-smelling

    b. unhappy   d. ill

——— 8. The child's behavior was **unpredictable**.

    a. as expected   c. obviously aggressive

    b. outrageous   d. difficult to foretell

——— 9. The weather forecaster said that travel through the mountains was **inadvisable**.

    a. forbidden   c. impossible

    b. not wise   d. encouraged

——— 10. The talk show host was known for his **irreverent** sense of humor.

    a. bizarre   c. disrespectful

    b. dignified   d. unbiased

Prefixes Referring to Number or Amount

Some prefixes, when added to a root, suggest a number or an amount of something. The prefix *semi-* means *half*. A *semicircle*, then, is a half circle. Table 4-2 below lists common prefixes that refer to number or amount.

Table 4-2	Prefixes: Number or Amount	
Prefix	**Meaning**	**Sample Word**
mono/uni-	one	monocle/unicycle
bi/di/du-	two	bimonthly/divorce/duet
tri-	three	triangle
quad-	four	quadrant
quint/pent-	five	quintet/pentagon
deci-	ten	decimal
centi-	hundred	centigrade
milli-	thousand	milligram
micro-	small	microscope
multi/poly-	many	multipurpose/polygon
semi-	half	semicircle
equi-	equal	equidistant

EXERCISE 4-5   Prefixes: Numbers or Amounts I

Directions: Match the prefixes in column A with their meanings in column B. Write your answers in the spaces provided.

	Column A		Column B
1.	——— semi	a.	three
2.	——— micro	b.	ten
3.	——— centi	c.	two
4.	——— quad	d.	five
5.	——— tri	e.	half
6.	——— equi	f.	thousand
7.	——— bi/di/du	g.	many
8.	——— quint/pent	h.	one
9.	——— multi/poly	i.	hundred
10.	——— milli	j.	four
11.	——— deci	k.	equal
12.	——— mono/uni	l.	small

EXERCISE 4-6   Prefixes: Numbers or Amounts II

Directions: Supply a word that completes the meaning of each of the following sentences.

example   A **pentagon** has _____ sides.

1. A **multilingual** person can speak _____ languages.

2. A **bicentennial** celebration occurs every _____ years.

3. A **milliliter** is equal to _____ of a liter.

4. A **decapod** is a crustacean with _____ legs.

5. A **pentathlon** is an athletic contest in which each participant competes in _____ track and field events.

6. **Monosyllabic** words have _____ syllable(s).

7. The trillium is considered a **trifoliate** flower because it has _____ leaves.

8. An **equilateral** geometric figure has _____ sides.

9. A **duologue** is a conversation between _____ people.

10. A **semiannual** publication is issued _____ a year.

Table 4-3 Prefixes: Direction, Location, or Placement

Prefix	Meaning	Sample Word
ab-	away	absent
ad-	toward	adhesive
ante/pre-	before	antecedent/premarital
circum/peri-	around	circumference/perimeter
com/col/con-	with, together	compile/collide/convene
de-	away, from	depart
dia-	through	diameter
ex/extra-	from, out of, former	extramarital/ex-wife
hyper-	over, excessive	hyperactive
inter-	between	interpersonal
intro/intra-	within, into, in	introduction
peri-	around	perimeter
post-	after	posttest
re-	back, again	review
retro-	backward	retrospect
sub-	under, below	submarine
super-	above, extra	supercharge
tele-	far	telescope
trans-	across, over	transcontinental

Prefixes Suggesting Direction, Location, or Placement

Some prefixes suggest direction, location, or placement. For example, the prefix *post-* means *after*, and *postoperative care* refers to care given after (direction in time) an operation. Table 4-3 lists common prefixes that refer to direction, location, or placement.

EXERCISE 4-7 Prefixes: Direction, Location, or Placement I

Directions: Match the prefixes in column A with their meanings in column B. Write your answers in the spaces provided.

Column A	Column B
1. ——— con	a. back, again
2. ——— super	b. before
3. ——— retro	c. above, extra
4. ——— ad	d. away, from
5. ——— intro/intra	e. within, into, in
6. ——— de	f. toward
7. ——— re	g. across
8. ——— trans	h. backward
9. ——— ante/pre	i. around
10. ——— peri	j. with, together

EXERCISE 4-8   Prefixes: Direction, Location, or Placement II

Directions: Match the prefixes in column A with their meanings in column B. Write your answers in the spaces provided.

Column A	Column B
1. ——— inter	a. between
2. ——— hyper	b. far
3. ——— ex	c. under, below
4. ——— dia	d. from, out of, former
5. ——— circum	e. through
6. ——— com	f. with, together
7. ——— tele	g. after
8. ——— ab	h. over, excessive
9. ——— sub	i. away
10. ——— post	j. around

EXERCISE 4-9   Using Prefixes to Decode Words I

Directions: Write the letter that completes the meaning of each of the following sentences on the line provided.

——— 1. A **hyperactive** child has _____ energy.
   a. too little
   b. too much
   c. unsupervised
   d. over directed

_____ 2. A **periotic** device is one that is situated _____ the ear.

    a. around

    b. on

    c. in

    d. opposite

_____ 3. An **antebellum** mansion is one that was built _____ the Civil War.

    a. before

    b. during

    c. after

    d. as a result of

_____ 4. The **diameter** of a circle is the distance _____ the circle.

    a. around

    b. over

    c. under

    d. through

_____ 5. A **retrorocket** on a missile is used to _____ the motion of the missile.

    a. speed up

    b. reverse

    c. alter the direction

    d. accelerate

_____ 6. A **telephoto** lens on a camera allows you to photograph _____ objects.

    a. moving

    b. distant

    c. close-up

    d. stationary

_____ 7. **Extraterritorial** waters are those located _____ territorial boundaries.

    a. within

    b. below

    c. outside

    d. above

_____ 8. A musical **interlude** is a short piece inserted _____ the parts of a longer composition.

    a. before

    b. after

    c. between

    d. during

_____ 9. A thief who **absconds** with the money has _____.

    a. surrendered/given in

    b. returned

    c. been caught

    d. gone away

_____ 10. A **transdermal** patch works by supplying medication _____.

    a. across or through the skin

    b. only on the surface of the skin

    c. orally

    d. into veins

Prefixes Referring to Fields of Study

Other prefixes refer to particular fields of study or particular disciplines, as well as suggest other related meanings. The prefix _bio-_ means _life_, and _biology_ is the study of life. Related words also use the prefix. _Biopsy_ means a sample of tissue removed from a _living body_ for examination or study. A _biography_ is the story of a person's _life_. Table 4-4 lists common prefixes that refer to fields of study.

Table 4-4 Prefixes: Fields of Study

Prefix	Meaning	Sample Word
anthropo-	human being	anthropology, anthropomorphic
archaeo-	ancient	archaeology, archaic
bio-	life	biology, biotechnology
geo-	earth	geology, geography
gyneco-	woman	gynecology, gynecopathy
pysch-	mind	psychology, psychopath
theo-	God or gods	theology, theologian

EXERCISE 4-10 **Prefixes Referring to Fields of Study**

Directions: Underline the correct answer of the two given in parentheses.

1. A **biographer** is one who writes the story of (a fictional event, a person's life).

2. An **archaeopteryx** is (an ancient, a wild) bird.

3. **Theomorphism** is the depiction of human beings as having the form of (an animal, a god).

4. A **gynecocracy** is a society or government ruled by (men, women).

5. An **anthropocentric** person regards (human beings, plant life) as the central element of the universe.

6. A person suffering from **psychosis** has a severe (mental, physical) disorder.

7. A **bioastronaut** is concerned with the effects of space flight on (the solar system, living organisms).

8. **Geothermal** temperatures relate to the internal heat of the (earth, sun).

9. A **psychosurgeon** performs surgery to correct severe (mental, breathing) disorders.

10. If a law is considered **archaic**, it is (modern, out-of-date).

EXERCISE 4-11 **Using Prefixes to Decode Words II**

Directions: Write the choice that best states the meaning of each of the following boldfaced words on the line provided.

_____ 1. Many people are switching to **decaffeinated** coffee.

    a. strong   c. caffeine free

    b. weak   d. caffeine added

_____ 2. The will was **uncontested**.

    a. debated   c. not resolved

    b. not challenged   d. hostile

_____ 3. It was difficult to find an **impartial** judge for the talent contest.

    a. not biased   c. sympathetic

    b. unrelated   d. qualified

_____ 4. Their nightly routine included a **postprandial** walk around the neighborhood.

    a. before dinner   c. after dinner

    b. before dessert   d. before bed

_____ 5. The patient received **intramuscular** injections of cortisone to reduce the swelling.

    a. between muscles   c. away from the muscle

    b. into the muscle   d. under the muscle

_____ 6. The spaceship made a **circumlunar** voyage.

    a. away from the moon   c. to the moon

    b. beyond the moon   d. around the moon

_____ 7. She was **hypersensitive** about her cooking ability.

    a. overly sensitive   c. unconcerned

    b. unaffected   d. confident

_____ 8. Anders was much more **introverted** than his sisters.

    a. outgoing   c. shy

    b. entertaining   d. active

_____ 9. All members are expected to **adhere** to club rules.

    a. create   c. defend

    b. follow   d. ignore

_____ 10. Our ficus tree **defoliates** whenever we move it to another room.

    a. blooms   c. dries up

    b. shows new growth   d. loses leaves

EXERCISE 4-12   Using a Dictionary to Find the Meanings of Prefixes

Directions: There are many more prefixes than those listed in Tables 4-1, 4-2, 4-3, and 4-4. Use a desk dictionary to locate and write the meaning of each of the following prefixes. Then write two words using each prefix and use one in a sentence.

example   *ambi-* around, both; ambisexual, ambivalent _____

                My parents were ambivalent about their decision to sell their house. _____

1. *anti-* _____
    _____

2. *chrono-* _____
    _____

3. *co-* _____
    _____

4. *lacto-* _____
    _____

5. *hetero-* _____
    _____

6. *homo-* _____
    _____

7. *hydro-* _____
    _____

8. *idio-* _____
    _____

9. *patho-* _____
    _____

10. *ultra-* _____
    _____

EXERCISE 4-13   Using Prefixes to Decode Words III

Directions: Read the following paragraphs and use your knowledge of prefixes to identify the meaning of each of the words in boldfaced type. Use a dictionary if necessary.

A. How can we **reconcile** such **contradictory** conclusions about heroin addiction? Certainly William Burroughs' description of his own addiction to heroin (and similar reports by others) is accurate. He did not make it up. At the same time, Johnson and his associates are also accurate. They did not make up their findings either. And other researchers have noted that some people use heroin on an **irregular** basis, such as at weekend parties, without becoming addicted. Where does this leave us? From the mixed reports, it seems reasonable to conclude that heroin is addicting to some people, but not to others. Some people do become addicts and match the **stereotypical** profile. Others use heroin on a recreational basis. Both, then, may be right. With the evidence we have at this point, it would be **inappropriate** to side with either extreme.

—Adapted from Henslin, *Social Problems,*
Sixth Edition, p. 118.

1. reconcile _____

2. contradictory _____

3. irregular _____

4. stereotypical _____

5. inappropriate _____

B. Why are there such **unaccounted** for differences in promiscuity and commitment between male and female **homosexuals**? Some would argue that the chief reason can be traced to differences in their socialization. Girls are more likely to associate sex with emotional relationships, and, like their **heterosexual** counterparts, lesbians tend to conform to this basic expectation. Similarly, boys tend to learn to separate sex from affection, to validate their **self-images** by how much sex they have, and to see fidelity as a restriction on their **independence**.

—Adapted from Henslin, *Social
Problems,* Sixth Edition, p. 72.

6. unaccounted _____

7. homosexuals _____

8. heterosexual _____

9. self-images _____

10. independence _____

C. An especially **unstable** class of molecules are oxygen free radicals, sometimes just called free radicals. Some free radicals are accidentally produced in small amounts during the normal process of energy transfer within living cells. Exposure to chemicals, radiation, **ultraviolet** light, cigarette smoke, and air pollution may also create free radicals. We now know that certain enzymes and nutrients called **antioxidants** are the body's natural defense against oxygen free radicals. Antioxidants may prevent oxidation by **inactivating** them quickly before they can damage other molecules. Many health experts believe that antioxidant vitamins reduce the chance of certain cancers and the risk of **cardiovascular** death.

—Adapted from Michael D. Johnson,
Human Biology, Second Edition, p. 27.

11. unstable _____

12. ultraviolet _____

13. antioxidants _____

14. inactivating _____

15. cardiovascular _____

Roots: The Building Blocks of Language

WORD notes

Did you know that . . .

➤ The word *automatic*, as in *automatic transmission*, comes from the ancient Greek word *automatos,* which means self-acting? (Wouldn't the ancient Greeks who traveled on foot be pleased to know they helped name a part of modern automobiles?)

➤ The word *hamburger* may have originated in Hamburg, Germany, where pounded beef steak was served.

➤ The word *dandelion* is borrowed from an Old French word meaning "tooth of the lion," referring to the sharp leaves of the plant.

Roots are the building blocks of our language. Every word has at least one. Some roots, such as *dict-* and *spec-,* are used in hundreds of English words. By learning the meaning of common root words, you will have the key to thousands of previously unknown words. There are hundreds of roots that are not whole words. They form the basis for thousands of words. It is important to know that the spelling of roots can change as they are combined with other roots. Often the spelling of the root changes to make pronunciation of the newly formed word easier.

The following list shows ten of the most useful roots and how different words are derived from them.

1. *cap-* **(take, hold):** Someone who is **captured** is taken away or held. **Capacity** is the amount something can hold.

   captivate (verb): To hold one's attention.
   The six-year-old was **captivated by** *Sesame Street.*

   captor (noun): One who holds.
   The **captor** treated his prisoners well.

   capacious (adjective): Capable of holding a large amount, roomy.
   The hotel room was surprisingly **capacious**.

2. *-cede* **(go):** To **precede** is to go before. To **secede** is to withdraw or go away from.

   exceed (verb): To go beyond.
   The Broadway show **exceeded** our expectations.

   intercede (verb): To go between.
   The attorney **interceded** in the argument between the divorced couple.

   proceed (verb): To go forward.
   The couple decided to **proceed** with their plans for divorce.

   recede (verb): To go back.
   The flood waters finally **receded**.

3. *cred-* (**trust or believe**): Someone who is **credible** is believable. **Credentials** are records that cause others to believe in someone.

credit (noun): Trust, as in financial trust.
   It is wise to check your **credit** rating.

credulous (adjective): Gullible, believing too readily.
   She was **credulous** enough to believe she would win the sweepstakes.

incredible (adjective): Beyond belief, implausible, not easy to believe.
   Teachers hear some **incredible** explanations from their students about missing or incomplete homework.

4. *dict-* (**tell, say**): A **dictionary** tells what words mean. In a **dictatorship**, the ruler has final say. In English words, the spelling may change to *dic-* or *dit-*.

contradict (verb): To say the opposite.
   The child **contradicted** her parents.

dictate (verb): To express orally to another person, to command.
   The manager **dictated** the new accounting procedures to the staff.

dictatorial (adjective): Exercising excessive power or authority.
   The nursery school teacher seemed **dictatorial** when she told students how to play the game.

diction (noun): Wording, use of words in speech and writing.
   Ellen was given a C for the poor **diction** in her essay.

5. *mis-/mit-* (**send**): A **message** is something that is sent to someone. To **omit** something is to leave it out (send it away).

intermittent (adjective): coming and going at intervals (to send at intervals).
   The rain was **intermittent**.

missile (noun): A weapon fired (sent) toward a target.
   The **missile** struck the village.

promise (verb): To send forth, to indicate what might be expected.
   He **promised** us that the check was in the mail.

transmit (verb): To send across a distance.
   The message was **transmitted** overseas.

6. *port-* (**carry**): Something that is **portable** can be carried. To **transport** something is to carry it across a distance.

portend (verb): To carry a warning.
   Those dark clouds in the east **portend** a storm.

porter (noun): One who carries something.
   The **porter** delivered the bags to our hotel room.

portfolio (noun): A case for carrying a document.
   Kerry brought his **portfolio** of drawings to the interview.

portly (adjective): To carry weight, stocky.
   The **portly** man had trouble getting into his seat on the airplane.

7. *sen-* (**feel**): Someone who is **sensitive** to criticism feels or is affected by it. **Sensory** organs allow us to feel and experience our environment.

senseless (adjective): Unconscious, lacking feeling.
   The destruction of our neighbor's mailbox was a **senseless** crime.

sensibility (noun): Mental receptivity, capacity for refined feelings.

A musician's **sensibility** to pitch and tone is essential when composing music.

sensor (noun): Device that responds to (senses) a physical event.
Our skin serves as a **sensor** for heat, cold, pressure, touch, and pain.

sentimental (adjective): Having tender feelings or emotions.
The wedding photos made my grandmother **sentimental**.

8. *spec-/spect-* **(look, see): Spectacles** are eyeglasses that enable one to see. A **spectacle** is a public performance or display, often of bad behavior.

inspect (verb): To look closely, to examine critically.
The customs agent **inspected** our passports.

spectator (noun): One who views, onlooker, witness.
One thousand **spectators** attended the stadium's opening ceremony.

retrospect (noun): The act of looking backwards or thinking about the past.
In **retrospect**, I realize I made the wrong decision.

perspective (noun): Point of view, the relative position of an object or of events.
From my **perspective**, the crowd appeared unruly and threatening.

9. *sym-/syn-* **(same, together):** A **symphony** orchestra plays together. **Synonyms** have similar meanings.

symbiosis (noun): The living together of different species of organisms.
A kind of **symbiosis** exists between a parasite and its host.

symmetry (noun): Regularity (sameness) in form.
Pansies are characterized by the **symmetry** of their petals.

syndrome (noun): A set of symptoms that suggest a disease.
She suffered from chronic fatigue **syndrome**.

synthesis (noun): Combination of elements into a whole.
The project was a **synthesis** of several architects' work.

10. *voc-/vok-* **(call):** Think of a **vocation** as a calling. To **revoke** is to call back. (His driver's license was revoked.) Something that is **irrevocable** cannot be called back.

advocate (verb): A person who pleads on another's behalf.
The governor appointed a former social worker as the chief child **advocate** for the state.

avocation (noun): A calling away, a hobby or special interest.
Horseback riding has become my **avocation**.

evoke (verb): To call out, to draw out.
The campfire **evoked** pleasant childhood memories.

provoke (verb): To call forth, to bring about, to cause anger.
Witnesses report that the football player **provoked** the crowd to jeer.

EXERCISE 4-14   Roots

Directions: Match the roots in column A with their meanings in column B. Write your answers in the spaces provided.

Column A	Column B
1. ——— sym/syn	a. take, hold
2. ——— dict	b. trust, believe

3. _____ cede   c. feel

4. _____ mis/mit   d. look, see

5. _____ sen   e. carry

6. _____ voc/vok   f. call

7. _____ cap   g. tell, say

8. _____ spec/spect   h. same, together

9. _____ port   i. send

10. _____ cred   j. go

EXERCISE 4-15   Roots and Context

Directions: From the list of words below, choose a word that fits the context of each of the following sentences and write the word in the space provided.

synchronized	perspective	invoked	omitted	preceded	portable
sensitized	credulity	capacity	dictum	retrospect	

example   In ___retrospect___, I realized that I should have offered my sister a loan.

1. From our _____ on the top of the mountain, islands in the sea looked tiny and unoccupied.

2. The concert hall was filled to _____.

3. The plot of the action movie strained the audience's _____.

4. Before the race, we _____ our watches.

5. The company's CEO issued a _____ that all purchases must be approved in advance.

6. She deliberately _____ her maiden name from the application.

7. We couldn't believe they brought a _____ TV to the beach!

8. The witness _____ the Fifth Amendment.

9. His experience in Honduras _____ him to the plight of poor people everywhere.

10. The minister typically _____ each sermon with a moment of silence.

Twenty-Five Common Roots

Table 4-5 on page 91 lists many of the most common roots—those that will be most useful to you in figuring out unknown words. See Table 4-6 on p. 93 for additional roots.

Table 4-5 Twenty-five Common Roots

Root	Meaning	Sample Word
aud/audit	hear	audible, audition
aster/astro	star	asteroid, astronaut
bene	good, well	benefit
bio	life	biology
chron(o)	time	chronology
corp	body	corpse
duc/duct	lead	introduce
fact/fac	make, do	factory
fid	trust	confident
graph	write	telegraph
geo	earth	geophysics
log/logo/logy	study, thought	psychology
loqu	speak	colloquial
mort/mor	die, death	immortal
path	feeling	sympathy
phono	sound, voice	telephone
photo	light	photosensitive
scrib/script	write	inscription
sen/sent	feel	insensitive
tend/tent/tens	stretch or strain	tension
terr/terre	land, earth	territory
theo	god	theology
ven/vent	come	convention
vert/vers	turn	invert
vis/vid	see	invisible/video

Roots and Context

Directions: From the list of words below, choose a word that fits the context of each of the following sentences and write the word in the space provided.

chronology	beneficence	mortality	aster	facilitates	corporal
loquacious	intense	advent	inscribed	captive	

example   The _____captive_____ panther paced around her cage.

1. The _____ rate among infants is shockingly high among the rural poor.

2. The flower called _____ is so named because it is shaped like a star.

3. His parents do not believe in spanking or _____ punishment of any kind.

4. The actor—who typically played the strong, silent type—was _____ in the interview.

5. An English professor _____ our book club discussions.

6. Trying to study while your neighbors give a party requires _____ concentration.

7. Mother Teresa was known around the world for her _____.

8. The book was even more valuable because it had been _____ by the author.

9. With the _____ of the Internet, our ways of viewing the world are changed forever.

10. The detective tried to determine the _____ of events that led up to the crime.

EXERCISE 4-17   Roots and Prefixes

Directions: Using your knowledge of prefixes and roots, write the choice that best states the meaning of each boldfaced word or phrase on the line provided.

_____ 1. Scientists are searching for **extraterrestrial life**.

   a. life beyond the earth   c. microscopic life

   b. life beneath the earth's surface   d. underwater life

_____ 2. The defendant's reply to the prosecutor was **inaudible**.

   a. nonsense   c. impossible to hear

   b. unmistakable   d. difficult to see

_____ 3. His **infidelity** was a major factor in the divorce.

   a. unhappiness   c. bad temper

   b. dishonesty   d. unfaithfulness

_____ 4. The exterior of the building was **nondescript**, but the interior was filled with treasures.

   a. lacking distinctive qualities   c. unmarked

   b. unusual   d. covered with writing

_____ 5. His unethical behavior put his assistant in an **untenable** position.

   a. easier   c. secretive

   b. impossible   d. excusable

_____ 6. The **biodiversity** in the Amazon rain forest is astounding.

    a. animals   c. plant life

    b. climate   d. variety of life

_____ 7. The manuscript was **revised** several times prior to publication.

    a. written   c. corrected/improved

    b. turned down   d. printed

_____ 8. The developer had a reputation for trying to **circumvent** zoning restrictions.

    a. strictly follow   c. understand and apply

    b. go around   d. debate

_____ 9. The surface of the moon appears to be **abiotic**.

    a. lifeless   c. unknown

    b. life-sustaining   d. unseen

_____ 10. The children performed especially **euphonious** selections for the nursing home residents.

    a. complicated   c. unrestrained

    b. harsh-looking   d. pleasant-sounding

Roots for Additional Study

Table 4-6 below presents an additional 20 roots that will help you expand your knowledge of word parts.

Table 4-6 Roots for Additional Study					
Root	**Meaning**	**Sample Word**	**Root**	**Meaning**	**Sample Word**
am	love	amorous	*man*	hand	manual
ann	year	annual	*nat*	born	native
cord	heart	cordial	*ped*	foot	podiatrist
cur	run	excursion	*pel*	drive	propel
dent	tooth	dentist	*pop*	people	populace
form	shape	transform	*rupt*	break	interrupt
ject	throw	reject	*sect*	cut	intersection
lab	work	laborer	*tract*	pull	attraction
liber	free	liberty	*vac*	empty	vacant
lust	shine	luster	*ver*	turn	inversion

Roots and Context

Directions: Supply the missing word in each of the following sentences. Choose words from the list supplied below.

lusterless	bisected	manufactured	vacuous	laboriously	vacant
pedometer	recurring	cordate	projectiles	annuity	

example   Although the apartment was _____vacant_____, the landlord claimed he had no time to repaint it.

1. Many household products are _____ in foreign countries.

2. We used a _____ to measure how far we went this morning.

3. Every April, Carlos receives a $500 _____ from his uncle.

4. The small town was _____ by the railroad tracks.

5. The _____ expression on her face revealed that she was not paying attention.

6. We carried stones _____ from the riverbed to the house.

7. The actor appeared in a _____ role on the soap opera.

8. The lovely, _____ leaves of the wild ginger make it an appealing ground cover.

9. The unpopular player had to duck several _____ as he ran onto the field.

10. The violinist blamed her _____ performance on jet lag.

EXERCISE 4-19   **Using Roots**

Directions: Underline the correct answer of the two given in parentheses, based on the root of the boldfaced word.

1. Someone with a **morbid** sense of humor (never laughs, laughs at gloomy things).

2. A **chronoscope** measures (sound, time) intervals.

3. A person who wears **dentures** has false (teeth, hair).

4. **Astrophysicists** are primarily concerned with the physics of (stars, space).

5. Many modern **monotheistic** religions are based on the belief in one (god, prophet).

6. Your friend who likes to (laugh, talk) a lot is loquacious.

7. If you can identify with another person's (feelings, situation), you are said to be **empathic**.

8. When musicians are **inducted** into the Rock and Roll Hall of Fame, they are (brought in, invited) as members.

9. Dams **divert** water by forcing it to (stay back, go in a new direction).

10. After the (birth, death) of her son, she experienced **postnatal** depression.

EXERCISE 4-20   Using Roots to Determine Meaning

Directions: For each boldfaced word in the following sentences, underline the root and write the meaning of the word in the space provided.

1. The view of the Olympic Mountains from Hurricane Ridge was **spectacular**.

   _____

2. New arrivals to this country must follow certain procedures to avoid being **deported** to their homelands.

   _____

3. The new regulations **supersede** those put in place a decade ago.

   _____

4. The school board members were **incredulous** when they heard of the allegations against a well-respected teacher.

   _____

5. Not even the most astute political observer could have **predicted** the unexpected election results.

   _____

6. When the city officials heard about the coming blizzard, they called for an early **dismissal** for all government employees.

   _____

7. Since the new manager had once been a union worker, she **sympathized** with the plight of the workers under her supervision.

   _____

8. Now that Carmen had decided to study biology, he had to learn the **vocabulary** of the field.

   _____

9. Many screenwriters study the lives of famous people looking for interesting stories to develop into **biopics**.

   _____

10. Some of the smaller candy companies still make their chocolates by hand in their **factories**.

   _____

EXERCISE 4-21   The Meaning of Roots

Directions: There are many more roots than those listed in this chapter. For each of the following roots, several words are given that use that root. Look the words up in a desk dictionary to discover the meaning of the root. Write that meaning in the space provided.

example	-spire	inspire, perspire, transpire	**Root Meaning:**	breathe

1. *-clude/-cluse*   include, recluse, preclude   **Root Meaning:** _____

2. *-plic*   explicit, implicate   **Root Meaning:** _____

3. *-cite*   excite, incite   **Root Meaning:** _____

4. *-pos*   deposit, disposable, impose   **Root Meaning:** _____

5. *-creas*   increase, decrease   **Root Meaning:** _____

6. *-volve*   revolve, involve, evolve   **Root Meaning:** _____

7. *-mature*   premature, immature   **Root Meaning:** _____

8. *-cept*   accept, except, susceptible   **Root Meaning:** _____

9. *-press*   compress, expression, depressed   **Root Meaning:** _____

10. *-fer*   infer, defer, prefer   **Root Meaning:** _____

EXERCISE 4-22   **Using Roots to Determine Meaning**

Directions: Read each of the following paragraphs and use your knowledge of roots to determine the meaning of each of the words in boldface. If you have difficulty, consult a dictionary.

A. Is it possible that humankind is now, at last, at the end of its ability to increase food supplies? The answer to this question is a cautious "probably not." If demographers are correct in their **projections** of Earth's future **population**, the population can be fed. **Humankind** has scarcely begun to maximize **productivity** with the best contemporary technology, and that leading technology has been applied to only a small portion of Earth. Spreading **urbanization** is replacing agriculture in many places, but more lands can still be farmed.

—Bergman and Renwick, *Introduction to Geography*, Second Edition, p. 323.

1. projections _____

2. population _____

3. humankind _____

4. productivity _____

5. urbanization _____

B. Many of the problems found in Mexico's **agricultural** economy can also be found in Africa. Landholding is often **communal**, so successful farmers cannot expand their productivity. Many African governments themselves hold ownership of agricultural land and lease it to farmers. In Zimbabwe, for example, the government **nationalized** numerous large white-owned private farms that were **exporting** food. The government **relocated** black settlers onto the properties but retained ownership, so the farmers cannot borrow to invest in increasing productivity.

—Bergmann and Renwick, *Introduction to Geography*, Second Edition, p. 332.

6. agricultural _____

7. communal _____

8. nationalized _____

9. exporting _____

10. relocated _____

C. No country is completely self-sufficient in food. Most countries both import and export food despite the fact that portions of their own populations are **undernourished**. This may be due to **injustice** or civil strife. Political **instability** contributes to hunger. Several African countries, for example, are environmentally richly endowed, yet a great many of their people go hungry. Peter Rosset, director of the Institute for Food and Development Policy, wrote, "There is no relationship between the **prevalence** of hunger in a given country and its population. The world today produces more food per **inhabitant** than ever before."

—Bergman and Renwick, *Introduction to Geography*, Second Edition, p. 329.

11. **undernourished** _____

12. **injustice** _____

13. **instability** _____

14. **prevalence** _____

15. **inhabitant** _____

Suffixes: Endings That Change a Word's Part of Speech

WORD notes

Adapt is a verb meaning to change in order to fit a specific situation.

What word describes a person who can change easily?* _____

What word describes the ability to change easily?* _____

What word describes a change that has been made?* _____

*Answers are on the bottom of page 98.

Suffixes are word endings that change the part of speech of a word. For example, adding the suffix *-y* to the noun *cream* forms the adjective *creamy*. A change of meaning also occurs when the part of speech is changed. For example, *teach* (to instruct) is a verb; by adding the suffix *-able* the adjective *teachable* (able to be taught, capable of learning) is formed and carries a different meaning.

Often several different words can be formed from a single root word by adding different suffixes.

Root	Suffix	New Word
right	*-ly*	rightly
right	*-ful*	rightful
right	*-ist*	rightist
right	*-eous*	righteous

If you know the meaning of the root word and the ways in which different suffixes affect the meaning of the root word, you will be able to figure out a word's meaning when a suffix is added. A list of common suffixes and their meanings appears in Table 4-7.

You can expand your vocabulary by learning the variations in meaning that occur when suffixes are added to words you already know. When you find a word that you do not know, look for the root. Then, using the sentence the word is in (its context), figure out what the word means with the suffix added. Occasionally you may find that the spelling of the root word has been changed. For instance, a final *e* may be dropped, a final consonant may be doubled, or a final *y* may be

Table 4-7 Common Suffixes

Suffix	Sample Word	Suffix	Sample Word
Suffixes that refer to a state, condition, or quality		Suffixes that mean "one who"	
		-an	Italian
-able	touchable	*-ant*	participant
-ance	assistance	*-ee*	referee
-ation	confrontation	*-eer*	engineer
-ence	reference	*-ent*	resident
-ible	tangible	*-er*	teacher
-ion	discussion	*-ist*	activist
-ity	superiority	*-or*	advisor
-ive	permissive	Suffixes that mean "pertaining to or referring to"	
-ment	amazement		
-ness	kindness	*-al*	autumnal
-ous	jealous	*-ship*	friendship
-ty	loyalty	*-hood*	brotherhood
-y	creamy	*-ward*	homeward

*Answers: adaptable, adaptability, adaptation. *Adaptable* is an adjective; *adaptability* and *adaptation* are nouns.

98 PART ONE General and Academic Vocabulary

changed to *i*. Consider the possibility of such changes when trying to identify the root word. Here are some examples.

The article was a **compilation** of facts.
root + suffix
compil(e) + -ation = something that has been compiled, or put together into an orderly form

We were concerned with the **legality** of our decision to change addresses.
root + suffix
legal + -ity = pertaining to legal matters

Our college is one of the most **prestigious** in the state.
root + suffix
prestig(e) + -ious = having prestige or distinction

EXERCISE 4-23   Suffixes I

Directions: For each suffix shown in Table 4-7, write another example of a word you know that has that suffix.

EXERCISE 4-24   Suffixes II

Directions: For each of the words listed below, add a suffix so that the word will complete the sentence. Write the new word in the space provided. Check a dictionary if you are unsure of the spelling.

example   **sex:** _____Sexist_____ language should be avoided in both speech and writing.

1. **eat:** We did not realize that the plant was _____ until we tasted its delicious fruit.

2. **compete:** The gymnastics _____ was our favorite part of the Olympics.

3. **decide:** It was difficult to be _____ in such a stressful situation.

4. **Portugal:** Our favorite restaurant specializes in _____ food.

5. **active:** She gained fame as a civil rights _____ in the 1960s.

6. **parent:** _____ is one of the most rewarding experiences in life.

7. **vaccine:** You must receive several different _____ before your trip to Africa.

8. **member:** We inadvertently allowed our _____ to the botanical garden to lapse.

9. **drive:** The abandoned car did not appear _____ so a tow truck was summoned.

10. **celebrate:** The girls waited at the airport for hours to catch a glimpse of their favorite _____ .

How Suffixes Change Parts of Speech

You need to know how to change a word's part of speech, especially when you are writing or speaking. For example, you may want to use a verb that means to divide something into groups or classes. The noun *class* can be converted to a verb by adding the suffix *-ify*, forming the word *classify*. Or you may want to find a noun that describes the condition of being an individual. You could add the suffix *-ism*, forming the word *individualism*. A list of suffixes divided according to the part of speech they form appears in Table 4-8.

Table 4-8   Adding Suffixes to Form New Parts of Speech

Suffix	Sample Word	Suffix	Sample Word
Suffixes Used to Form Verbs		*-some*	wholesome
-ate	motivate	*-y*	cloudy
-ify	quantify	Suffixes Used to Form Nouns	
-ize	customize		
Suffix Used to Form Adverbs		*-ac*	insomniac
-ly	lively	*-ance, -ancy*	pregnancy
Suffixes Used to Form Adjectives		*-ary*	adversary
-able, -ible	touchable	*-dom*	kingdom
-ac, -ic	psychic	*-ence*	independenec
-al	minimal	*-er*	teacher
-ant	belligerent	*-hood*	parenthood
-ary	contrary	*-ion, -tion*	transaction
-dom	freedom	*-ism*	tourism
-en	brazen	*-ist*	activist
-ful	faithful	*-ment*	employment
-ive	attentive	*-ness*	kindness
-like	birdlike	*-ship*	friendship
-ous, -ious	anxious	*-ure*	tenure

EXERCISE 4-25   Suffixes and Context

Directions: For each of the following sentences choose the word from the list below that best fits the context.

qualifications	preferential	occupational	preferable	predictions	predicament
variations	predictable	qualifier	occupant	variable	

example   Before our marriage, we never anticipated the financial ___predicament___ we would face.

1. I decided that electing to take a pass/fail grade was _____ to withdrawing from sociology.

2. The study focused on _____ in color among parakeets.

3. After the food critic was recognized, he was given _____ treatment by the restaurant staff.

4. Out of ten athletes from his country, Ian was the only _____ for the finals.

5. The _____ hazards for coal miners are many.

6. Her _____ for the job were outstanding.

7. The reviewer said the movie was weighed down by poor acting and a _____ plot.

8. The only _____ we couldn't control was the weather.

9. Most of the mail was addressed simply to _____ .

10. Stock analysts were unable to make any _____ about the company's future success.

EXERCISE 4-26   Suffixes and Parts of Speech

Directions: For each word below, underline the suffix and indicate what part of speech the word is, using both Tables 4-7 and 4-8 as applicable.

example   **hardship** ___ noun, "pertaining to" ___

1. **actor** _____

2. **peaceful** _____

3. **employee** _____

4. **admission** _____

5. **starry** _____

6. **neighborhood** _____

7. **qualify** _____

8. **happily** _____

9. **toxic** _____

10. **vegan** _____

Creating New Words with Suffixes

Directions: Match the suffix in column B to the word in column A it can combine with to create the requested type of word. Write the new word in the blank. The first one has been done for you.

Column A

Forms a verb:

  F   1. donor _____donate_____

Forms a noun:

_____ 2. harmony _____

_____ 3. happy _____

_____ 4. fascist _____

_____ 5. designate _____

Forms an adjective:

_____ 6. fervor _____

_____ 7. harm _____

_____ 8. consider _____

_____ 9. vary _____

Forms an adverb:

_____ 10. quick _____

Column B

A. -ent/-ant

B. -ly

C. -ism

D. -ion, -tion

E. -ful

F. -ate

G. -able

H. -ize

I. -ous, ious

J. -ness

EXERCISE 4-28 Creating New Words with Suffixes

Directions: For each word, create at least two new words by adding or changing suffixes. Indicate the part of speech for each new word.

example   **fish:** fishy (adj.), fishlike (adj.), fisher (noun) _____

1. **might:** _____

2. **participation:** _____

3. **clear:** _____

4. **equal:** _____

5. **depend:** _____

6. **tech:** _____

7. **prevent:** _____

8. **system:** _____

9. **function:** _____

10. **relation:** _____

EXERCISE 4-29 **Using Prefixes, Roots and Suffixes to Determine Meaning**

Directions: Read the following paragraphs and use your knowledge of prefixes, roots, and suffixes to determine the meaning of the words in boldface listed below.

A. **Professional** criminals make their **livelihood** from crime. They include not only the highly **romanticized** jewel thieves, **safecrackers,** and **counterfeiters**, but also professional shoplifters, pickpockets, and fences—those who buy stolen goods for resale. Their activities, although illegal, are a form of work, and they pride themselves on their skills and successes.

—Henslin, *Social Problems*, Sixth Edition, p. 187.

1. professional _____

2. livelihood _____

3. romanticized _____

4. safecrackers _____

5. counterfeiters _____

B. Certain types of crime are easier to get away with than others. Running less risk are **political** criminals who attempt to maintain the status quo and white-collar criminals who commit crimes in the name of a **corporation**, and those who comprise the top levels of organized crime. **Respectability**, wealth, power, and underlings insulate them. Those in the second group are insulated by the corporation's desire to avoid negative **publicity**. Those who run the highest risk of arrest are "soldiers" at the lowest levels of organized crime, who are considered **expendable**.

—Adapted from Henslin, *Social Problems*, Sixth Edition, p. 192.

6. political _____

7. corporation _____

8. respectability _____

9. publicity _____

10. expendable _____

C. The proponents of capital punishment argue that it is an appropriate **retribution** for **heinous** crimes, that it deters, and, of course, that it is an effective **incapacitator**. Its critics argue that killing is never justified. Opponents also argue that the death penalty is **capricious**: Jurors deliberate in secrecy and indulge their prejudices in recommending death, and judges are **irrational**—merciful to some but not to others.

—Adapted from Henslin, *Social Problems*, Sixth Edition, p. 205.

11. retribution _____

12. heinous _____

13. incapacitator _____

14. capricious _____

15. irrational _____

EXPLORING language

Abbreviations and Acronyms—Shortcuts for Words and Phrases

Sarah wants to finish her MBA asap so she can apply for a job with an ISP; she plans to work her way up to becoming CEO.

Each of the underlined words is an **abbreviation**; it is formed from the initial letters of a name of a series of words. *MBA* stands for master's of business administration, *asap* means as soon as possible, an *ISP* is an Internet service provider, and a *CEO* is a chief executive officer. Unlike an abbreviation, an **acronym** uses the first letters and/or parts of words to form a new word. For example, the word *sonar* was formed from the words sound navigation ranging.

Use a dictionary or an Internet search to discover what each of the following acronyms or abbreviations stands for.

1. scuba _____

2. laser _____

3. radar _____

4. NASA _____

5. Wi-Fi _____

Compound Words

A **compound word** is created when two regular words are put together. Both word parts are individual words that stand on their own. When they are joined, they form a new word, with a new meaning. For example, *newspaper* is created when the words *news* and *paper* are put together. The meanings of the two words helps you to understand the meaning of the compound word: a paper with news in it. Following are a few more examples of compound words:

thumbprint	thumb + print
eyebrow	eye + brow
bedroom	bed + room
drawback	draw + back
outspoken	out + spoken

Some words commonly appear in compound words. The word *under*, for example, as in:

> *under*water
>
> *under*ground
>
> *under*standing
>
> *under*educated
>
> *under*hand

EXERCISE 4-30   **Compound Words**

Directions: For each boldfaced compound word in the following sentences, draw a line to separate the two words it is composed of and write the meaning of the word in the space provided.

example   The driver struggled to stay on the road when the **sand/storm** hit.
high winds carrying sand and dust

1. The cottage was built on the **sea side**. _____

2. A **loop hole** in the tax code allowed the corporation to keep a lot of income tax-free.

_____

3. The computer program was **fool proof**.

_____

4. She received a notice on **letter head** from the lawyer's office about her inheritance.

_____

5. The college offered a **guide book** listing all its resources.

_____

MASTERY test 1

Applying and Integrating Your Skills

> **EXERCISE 4-31**   Apply Your Skills in Psychology

Directions: Read the following passage and use your knowledge of word parts and context to figure out the meaning of each boldfaced word. Write a synonym or definition in the space provided. Consult a dictionary if necessary.

Erik Erikson proposed that each individual must successfully **navigate** a series of psychosocial stages, each of which presented a particular conflict or crisis. Erikson identified eight stages in the life cycle. Each stage requires a new level of social interaction; success or failure in achieving it can change the course of **subsequent** development in a positive or negative direction.

In Erikson's first stage, an infant needs to develop a basic sense of trust in the environment through interaction with caregivers. Trust is a natural **accompaniment** to a strong attachment relationship with a parent who provides food, warmth, and the comfort of physical closeness. But a child whose basic needs are not met, who experiences **inconsistent** handling, lack of physical closeness and warmth, and the frequent absence of a caring adult, may develop a **pervasive** sense of mistrust, insecurity, and anxiety. This child will not be prepared for the second stage, which requires the individual to be adventurous.

With the development of walking and the beginnings of language, there is an **expansion** of a child's exploration and **manipulation** of objects (and sometimes people). With these activities should come a comfortable sense of **autonomy** and of being a capable and worthy person. Excessive restriction or criticism at this second stage may lead instead to self-doubts, while demands beyond the child's ability can discourage the child's efforts to **persevere** in mastering new tasks. The 2-year-old who insists that a particular ritual be followed or demands the right to do something without help is acting out of a need to **affirm** his or her autonomy and adequacy.

—Adapted from Zimbardo and Gerrig, *Psychology and Life*, Fifteenth Edition, pp. 404–405.

1. navigate: _____

2. subsequent: _____

3. accompaniment: _____

4. inconsistent: _____

5. pervasive: _____

6. expansion: _____

7. manipulation: _____

8. autonomy: _____

9. persevere: _____

10. affirm: _____

Directions: Read the following passage and use your knowledge of word parts and context to figure out the meaning of each boldfaced word. Write a synonym or definition in the space provided. Consult a dictionary if necessary.

The most obvious yet elusive component of small group communication is the spoken word. Words lie at the very heart of who and what people are. Their ability to represent the world **symbolically** gives humans the **capacity** to foresee events, to reflect on past experiences, to plan, to make decisions, and to consciously control their own behavior. Words are the tools with which people make sense of the world and share that sense with others.

While words can **empower** people and can influence attitudes and behaviors, they can also **impede** a process. While speech communication gives individuals access to the ideas and inner worlds of other group members, it can also set up barriers to effective communication. Some more subtle but pervasive word barriers are (1) bypassing, (2) allness, and (3) fact-inference confusion.

Bypassing takes place when two people assign different meanings to the same word. In groups, the problem of bypassing is **compounded** by the number of people involved; the possibility for multiple misunderstandings is always present. To overcome word barriers, people must understand that words are subjective. They need to check that what they understand from others is really what those others intend.

Allness statements are simple but untrue **generalizations**. The danger of allness statements is that you may begin to believe them and to **prejudge** other people unfairly based on them. Therefore, be careful not to overgeneralize; remember that each individual is unique.

Fact-inference confusion occurs when people respond to something as if they have actually observed it when, in reality, they have merely drawn a conclusion. While statements of fact can be made only after direct observation, **inferences** can be made before, during, or after an occurrence. No observation is necessary. The key distinction is that in statements of inference people can **speculate** about and interpret what they *think* occurred. Like bypassing and allness statements, fact-inference confusion can lead to **inaccuracy** and misunderstanding.

—Adapted from Beebe and Masterson, *Communication in Small Groups*, Sixth Edition, pp. 120–122.

1. symbolically: _____

2. capacity: _____

3. empower: _____

4. impede: _____

5. compounded: _____

6. generalizations: _____

7. prejudge: _____

8. inferences: _____

9. speculate: _____

10. inaccuracy: _____

Directions: Read the following passage and use your knowledge of word parts and context to figure out the meaning of each boldfaced word or phrase. Write a synonym or definition in the space provided. Consult a dictionary if necessary.

Internal Structures: The Eyeball

The eye itself, commonly called the eyeball, is a hollow sphere. The outermost layer, called the fibrous layer, consists of the protective sclera (skle'rah) and the **transparent** cornea (kor'ne-ah). The sclera, thick, glistening white **connective** tissue, is seen **anteriorly** as the "white of the eye." The central anterior portion of the fibrous layer is crystal clear. This "window" is the cornea through which light enters the eye. The cornea is well supplied with nerve endings. Most are pain fibers, and when the cornea is touched, blinking and increased tearing occur. Even so, the cornea is the most exposed part of the eye, and it is very **vulnerable** to damage. Luckily, its ability to repair itself is **extraordinary**. Furthermore, the cornea is the only tissue in the body that can be transplanted from one person to another without the worry of **rejection**. Because it has no blood vessels, it is beyond the reach of the immune system.

The middle layer of the eyeball, the vascular layer, has three distinguishable regions. Most **posterior** is the choroid (ko'roid), a blood-rich nutritive tunic that contains a dark pigment. The pigment prevents light from scattering inside the eye. Moving anteriorly, the choroid is modified to form two smooth muscle structures, the ciliary (sil'e-er-e) body, to which the lens is attached by a **suspensory ligament** called the ciliary zonule, and then the iris. The pigmented iris has a rounded opening, the pupil, through which light passes. Circularly and radially arranged smooth muscle fibers form the iris, which acts like the diaphragm of a camera. That is, it regulates the amount of light entering the eye so that one can see as clearly as possible in the available light. In close vision and bright light, the circular muscles **contract**, and the pupil **constricts**. In distant vision and dim light, the radial fibers contract to enlarge (dilate) the pupil, which allows more light to enter the eye.

—Marleb, *Essentials of Human Anatomy & Physiology,* Ninth Edition, pp. 408–409.

1. transparent _____

2. connective _____

3. anteriorly _____

4. vulnerable _____

5. extraordinary _____

6. rejection _____

7. posterior _____

8. suspensory ligament _____

9. contract _____

10. constricts _____

MASTERY test 2

Applying and Integrating Your Skills in Geography

This textbook excerpt is adapted from *Introduction to Geography* by Edward F. Bergman and William Renwick. Read the selection to learn about the possible consequences of global warming. Then answer the questions that follow.

Global Warming

1   Forecasting weather beyond five days is very difficult, so **prediction** of future climate is an immense challenge. At the present state of the art, we cannot plan for the next 10 or 20 years with confidence. Keep this in mind when trying to understand the dilemma that scientists and government officials face when considering actions to limit global warming.

2   During the twentieth century, Earth's temperature increased slightly less than 1°C (1.8°F). Throughout the 1990s the body of scientific evidence linking this temperature rise to **emissions** of CO_2 accumulated rapidly, so that today few scientists doubt that increased CO_2 is the principal cause of global warming. The future of global warming is always **uncertain**, but the **consensus** is that unless **output** of CO_2 slows dramatically, world average temperature could rise by a few degrees celsius in the next century.

3   Despite this scientific consensus, there are many uncertainties. One is that we do not know how rapidly **atmospheric** CO_2 content will increase. That will depend on whether we continue to expand our use of fossil fuels as we have in the past. Another uncertainty is that we are not sure how water in the atmosphere, which plays a major role in regulating climate, will be affected by the increased levels of greenhouse gases.

4   Thus, we can only guess how global warming will affect specific regions. Will storm tracks shift? How will a place's current levels of rainfall, snowfall, and temperature change? Will the seasons change? How will plants and animals be affected? How large an effect will this have on sea level, worldwide energy use, and food supply?

The Consequences of Global Warming

5   One serious effect of global warming that is widely believed to be possible is a worldwide rise in sea level of perhaps 1 to 5 meters (3 to 16 feet). People living near coasts would face danger from rising seas. The danger would not be from constant inundation, because sea level would rise very gradually over years, allowing people time to **relocate**, raise structures, or build dikes. The danger would be from occasional severe storms that would cause sudden flooding farther **inland**. The Dutch have shown that well-built dikes can hold back the sea, but poorer countries cannot afford such protection.

6   Another possibility is that climate change could reduce water supply in some regions. Consider a mid-latitude environment such as eastern Nebraska that averages 60 centimeters (24 inches) precipitation and 55 centimeters (22 inches) evapotranspiration. The 5 centimeters (2 inches) of precipitation that is not transpired by plants flow into streams and rivers. A small increase in evapotranspiration, due to a

warmer climate, could sharply reduce water flow to the region's streams and rivers. **Semiarid** regions and **densely** populated subhumid areas depend on river flow for irrigation, drinking water, and waste removal. These areas might suffer severe water shortages if warming increases evapotranspiration and decreases river flow. However, if this warming brings greater precipitation, agriculture may be helped rather than harmed. Agricultural production might be especially helped in areas currently receiving little precipitation. Warming could also lengthen the growing season in high-latitude areas and make agriculture possible in areas of Canada and Siberia where today it is not. There is some evidence to suggest that the warming in the western Pacific that is tied to droughts in the southeastern U.S. and elsewhere (as well as the November 2002 storms discussed at the beginning of the chapter) may be related to global warming, but as yet we are not certain of these effects.

7   A third possibility is that warming will increase **storminess**. More heat in the atmosphere can mean more humidity, and atmospheric humidity is the energy source driving hurricanes and other intense storms. While we do not know whether global warming is a factor in the increased frequency of weather-related disasters, there is **statistical** evidence to suggest as much, and certainly the possibility of more frequent weather disasters is alarming.

Should We Attempt to Halt Global Warming?

8   Although global warming is in progress and humans are significant **contributors** to the problem, we have not reached global consensus on how we should try to stop it or if we should stop it at all. Those who argue for immediate action **emphasize** the potentially severe consequences of warming in some areas. But it is hard to convince people to spend money to prevent an event that does not have **dramatic**, obvious effects on our lives and one that occurs over long periods of time rather than in the short term.

9   Reducing carbon dioxide **concentrations** will be difficult because we depend on fossil fuels in our daily lives, and energy producers employ many people and earn billions of dollars each year. Significantly reducing fossil-fuel use is possible only if we consume less energy or shift to alternative energy sources. An alternative to reducing fossil-fuel use is to try to trap and store ("sequester," in the scientific jargon) CO_2. Several alternatives are being discussed, from storing CO_2 in the deep ocean or underground to increasing **photosynthesis** by fertilizing plants in the ocean. Any of these alternatives would be expensive. Would people prefer to cut back on their use of coal-generated electricity or spend money on new ways to produce electricity? Either alternative is expensive and inconvenient.

10   Another reason for not acting to curb global warming is the belief that it is easier to adapt to climatic change than to prevent it. People already adjust to changing weather, commodity prices, and technology from year to year, so why shouldn't we be able to adjust to climate change, too? The United States has refused to join the Kyoto Protocol, an international treaty that would limit CO_2 emissions (see Chapter 13) on the grounds that a strategy of adapting to global warming would be less costly and more effective than attempting to reduce it.

11   We must remember, though, that humans are not the only life on the planet. We are only one form of life and one part of many interacting **ecosystems**. Some animals and plants could not adapt to a climate change, and thus *our* human-environment **interaction** might be responsible for the extinction of other species. Is the possibility that we can adapt to climate change a **credible** reason not to halt our contribution to global warming?

EXERCISE 4-34   Word Parts I

Directions: **(Part A)**   For each boldfaced word in the following sentences, underline the prefix and write the meaning of the word in the space provided.

1. A new job caused the family to **relocate** (para. 5) to a different city.
    _____

2. The plane took off by the ocean and flew **inland** (para. 5), toward the mountains.
    _____

3. When the baking soda was added to the water, it caused a bubbling **interaction** (para. 11).
    _____

Directions: **(Part B)**   For each boldfaced word in the following sentences, underline the root and write the meaning of the word in the space provided.

4. Many cars are now carefully engineered to control **emissions** (para. 2) of carbon dioxide.
    _____

5. The water crashed over the waterfall with a **dramatic** (para. 8) splash.
    _____

6. The botanist wrote a paper about **photosynthesis** (para. 9) in orchid plants.
    _____

7. The lawyer offered **credible** (para. 11) evidence to the jury that the man did not commit the crime. _____

Directions: **(Part C)**   For each boldfaced word in the following sentences, underline the suffix and write the meaning of the word in the space provided. Consult a dictionary if necessary.

8. The meteorologist tracked the **atmospheric** (para. 3) storms on Mars.
    _____

9. The **densely** (para. 6) crowded streets made it difficult to walk.
    _____

10. The Bermuda Triangle is a portion of the ocean known for its **storminess** (para. 7) and bad weather. _____

EXERCISE 4-35   Word Parts II

Directions: Use your knowledge of prefixes, roots, and suffixes to answer the following questions about words used in the passage. Write the letters of the correct answers on the lines provided.

_____ 1. A **prediction** (para. 1) is
           a. a newly created word   c. something said in the past
           b. an answer given too early   d. a statement about the future

_____ 2. **Uncertain** (para. 2) means
           a. not definite   c. not helpful
           b. not affordable   d. not understandable

_____ 3. **Consensus** (para. 2) refers to

    a. answers

    b. agreement

    c. opposite opinions

    d. different experiences

_____ 4. **Output** (para. 2), as used in this selection, means

    a. amount produced

    b. items given as gifts

    c. carefully measured work

    d. slowdown of production

_____ 5. A **semiarid** (para. 6) climate is one that is identified as being

    a. cold in the winter

    b. solidly frozen

    c. prone to hurricanes

    d. somewhat dry

_____ 6. **Statistical** (para. 7) means

    a. having to do with data

    b. involving ideas

    c. related to the future

    d. facts that cannot be proven

_____ 7. **Contributors** (para. 8) are those who

    a. solve something

    b. add or supply

    c. ignore a problem

    d. discover a new method

_____ 8. **Emphasize** (para. 8) means to

    a. take immediate action

    b. be able to understand someone's feelings

    c. cause a reaction

    d. stress as important

_____ 9. The word **concentrations** (para. 9), as used in this selection, refers to

    a. remaining amounts of fossil fuels

    b. the amounts of one substance in another substance

    c. the weight of a gas

    d. amounts of conservation

_____ 10. The word **ecosystems** (para. 11) refers to

    a. biological dangers that are caused by human misuse of the environment

    b. chemical reactions that occur over time

    c. gases that protect the earth from radiation

    d. animals, plants, and environments that work together

Learn More about Word Parts by Visiting the Following Web Sites

1. **Practice Quizzes with Greek and Latin Roots**
   http://english.glendale.cc.ca.us/roots.html

2. **Word Part Exercise**
   http://www.southampton.liunet.edu/academic/pau/course/webex1.htm

3. **Prefix and Suffix Word Search**
   http://learn.midsouthcc.edu/LearningObjects/softchalk/Prefix_Suffix/Prefix_Suffix.html

5

Vocabulary On the Move!

Everything Changes, Even Words!

The most common meaning of the word **green** refers to color. Recently, however, the word **green** has been widely used to mean something that is environmentally friendly or beneficial. What is the difference between a fight and a tiff? Both suggest a disagreement of sorts, but one is much more serious than the other. In the sentence, "It is a tie," what does *tie* mean? Does it mean a neck garment worn by men or does it mean a draw in a sporting event?

As you can see, words have different meanings in different situations. This chapter will illustrate how new words enter our language, change meaning, and get used in new and different ways.

Language is fluid and constantly changing and you can move ahead with it by learning to use words creatively and in the new, interesting ways suggested in this chapter. Your choice of words reveals a great deal about you. You can use them to hide or reveal your feelings, to cover up information, to suggest but not directly state ideas, to provoke feelings in others, or to state clearly and precisely what you want to say.

Idioms: Words with Uncommon Meanings

WORD notes

Does a *flea market* sell fleas?

Does the *graveyard shift* mean you work in a graveyard?

Does *"Close, but no cigar"* involve tobacco?

Each of these italicized expressions is an idiom. **Idioms** are phrases that have a different meaning than the common meaning of the word in them, than what the common meaning of the words in the phrase mean. For example, the phrase *to turn over a new leaf* does not refer to leaves on a tree. Instead it means *to start fresh* or *begin over again in a new way*. There are thousands of idioms in use in the English language, and they are often particularly puzzling to nonnative speakers. To find the meaning of an idiom, look in a dictionary under one of the key words. For instance, look under *crow* to find the meaning of the idiom *as the crow flies*. In a dictionary, idioms are often labeled "idiom" and followed by the complete phrase and its meaning.

EXERCISE 5-1 Idioms

Directions: Write the letter of the answer that best explains the meaning of each of the following idioms.

_____ 1. to keep tabs on

    a. to encourage or promote   c. to keep secret

    b. to observe carefully   d. to compliment

_____ 2. to steal someone's thunder

    a. to ask someone for help

    b. to make someone look foolish

    c. to form an opinion about someone's behavior

    d. to use someone else's idea without his or her consent

_____ 3. to make no bones about

    a. to be forthright and candid   c. to pretend to understand a situation

    b. to withhold important information   d. to live humbly or modestly

_____ 4. in the dark

    a. uninhabited   c. uninformed

    b. alone or friendless   d. fearful

5. to bite the bullet

    a. to defend one's actions   c. to undergo a transformation

    b. to face a painful situation bravely   d. to control one's temper

---

EXERCISE 5-2   Defining Idioms

Directions: Write a definition of each of the following idioms.

1. the blind leading the blind _____

_____

2. to learn the ropes _____

_____

3. like a chicken with its head cut off _____

_____

4. peeping tom _____

_____

5. pin money _____

_____

6. rule of thumb _____

_____

7. straight from the horse's mouth _____

_____

8. three dog night _____

_____

9. under the weather _____

_____

10. let the cat out of the bag _____

_____

 Learn More about Idioms by Visiting the Following Web Site

http://humanities.byu.edu/elc/student/idioms/idiomsmain.html

Words on Loan: Foreign Words and Phrases

WORD notes

Pretzel, umbrella, Iowa, tornado, banjo, and *stove*—all of these are words that English speakers know and use. But did you know that *umbrella* was originally an Italian word (*ombrella*)? The word *Iowa* is an American Indian word that originally meant "drowsy ones." *Tornado* is a Spanish word; *pretzel* is a German word; *banjo* is an African word; and *stove* is a Dutch word. Each of these words has become an ordinary English word, but each was originally borrowed from another language.

Over hundreds of years, thousands of words have been borrowed from other languages in this manner, gradually becoming part of our standard English vocabulary. Often a change in spelling or pronunciation occurred as each word was adopted.

There are a few words and phrases, however, that are taken directly from a foreign language and retain their original pronunciation and spelling. Often, there is not a word or phrase in English that carries exactly the same meaning or expresses it in such a concise manner. An example is the French phrase *faux pas*. Its direct translation is "false step." It has come to mean a social blunder—an embarrassing, unintentional social error. If, for example, in a conversation with a sightless person, you said, "Don't you see?" meaning don't you understand, you might feel as if you made a *faux pas*. Your question was not quite the right thing to ask and you felt embarrassed. There is no single word or phrase that expresses exactly this situation in English, so the French phrase is used. This section presents a list of common foreign words and phrases that are frequently used by English speakers and writers.

Since the largest number of words and phrases have been borrowed from Latin and French, lists of common Latin and French words and phrases follow.

Useful Latin Words and Phrases

ad nauseam (ăd nô′zē-əm) Adverb. To a disgusting or ridiculous degree, causing disgust or boredom, to the point of nausea. The speaker repeated his sales pitch *ad nauseam.*

bona fide (bō′nə fīd′) Adjective. In good faith, sincere, authentic, genuine. The real estate agent thought the purchase offer was *bona fide.*

caveat emptor (kä′vē-ät ĕmp′tôr′) Noun. Let the buyer beware. The buyer is responsible for making sound buying decisions. The consumer advocate urged his radio listeners to repeat the phrase *caveat emptor* whenever they shopped for a used car.

de facto (dā făk′tō) Adjective. Actual. What is done, whether lawful or not. *De facto* racial segregation still exists in some parts of the country.

et cetera (ĕt sĕt′ər-ə) Noun. Abbreviated *etc.* And so forth, and so on. A number of unspecified similar items. On our trip to the Southwest we visited historical sites, national parks, *etc.*

modus operandi (mō′dəs ŏp′ə-răn′dē) Noun. A method, style, or manner of working or functioning. Beginning each class with a review of the prior lecture followed by a brief anecdote was Professor Yu's *modus operandi.*

non sequitur (nŏn sĕk′wĭ-tər) Noun. A statement or conclusion that does not follow from the evidence that preceded it. My neighbor made a *non sequitur* when he said, "It's raining because I washed my car this morning."

per annum (pər ăn′əm) Adverb. Annually or by the year. The library's subscription to the periodical is renewed *per annum.*

per capita (pər kăp′ĭ-tə) Adverb. Per person or by a fixed unit or group of population. Among nonwhite households, the average cost of transportation is $1,212 *per capita.*

per diem (pər dē′əm) Adverb. By the day, per day. The laborers were paid $50 *per diem.*

persona non grata (pər-sō′nə nŏn grä′tə) Adjective. A person who is unacceptable or unwelcome. Often used as reference to a foreign government policy or decision. The former congressman was *persona non grata* in Argentina.

postmortem (pōst-môr′təm) Adjective. After death or following a difficult or unpleasant event. A *postmortem* examination revealed the victim died of head wounds. At a *postmortem* conference, the sales staff analyzed their failure to win the multimillion-dollar contract.

status quo (stā′təs kwō) Noun. The way things are, an existing state of affairs. The presidential candidate promised to maintain the *status quo* of the social security system.

vice versa (vī′sə vûr′sə) Adverb. The other way around, with the order reversed. James suspected Martha and *vice versa.*

EXERCISE 5-3 **Latin Words and Phrases I**

Directions: Match the Latin words or phrases in column A with their meanings in column B. Write your answers in the spaces provided.

Column A	Column B
1. _____ non sequitur	a. By the day, per day
2. _____ et cetera	b. A person who is unacceptable or unwelcome
3. _____ per diem	c. The way things are, an existing state of affairs
4. _____ modus operandi	d. Per person or by a fixed unit or group of population
5. _____ per annum	e. Annually or by the year
6. _____ caveat emptor	f. Let the buyer beware, the buyer is responsible for making sound buying decisions

7. ——— status quo   g. A statement or conclusion that does not follow from the evidence that preceded it

8. ——— per capita   h. A method, style, or manner of working or functioning

9. ——— de facto   i. And so forth, and so on

10. ——— persona non grata   j. What is done, whether lawful or not

---

EXERCISE 5-4   Latin Words and Phrases II

Directions: Using the list of Latin words and phrases above, supply a word or phrase that fits the meaning of each of the following sentences.

example   The catalog contained dolls, trucks, electronic games, _____ etc _____.

1. He has been _____ at the restaurant ever since he insulted the chef.

2. The couple went on and on _____ about their trip to the Everglades.

3. All of my expenses at the convention were paid, in addition to a $100 _____.

4. The sign over the flea market entrance warned shoppers with the words: _____!

5. The pickpocket's _____ was to create a distraction by dropping a large package in a crowd.

6. We shook hands and parted, satisfied that we had made a _____ agreement.

7. The board of directors wanted to shake up the _____ by hiring a female president.

8. After every loss, the coach conducted a _____ in which he discussed what went wrong during the game.

9. Li thought her sister was being difficult, and _____.

10. "The doorbell rang because I had just gotten in the bathtub" is a _____.

Useful French Words and Phrases

avant-garde (ä'vänt-gärd') Noun. People active in the invention of new ideas or techniques in a particular field. The Computer Task Group was considered *avant-garde*. Adjective. Describing an innovative or creative person or group. Jackson Pollack was considered an *avant-garde* artist.

carte blanche (kärt blänsh') Noun. Freedom to use one's own judgment or authority, unconditional authority to act. In negotiating the new contract, the sales director was given *carte blanche*.

cause célèbre (kōz' sā-lěb'rə) Noun. A situation or issue involving widespread interest, public concern, or debate. The young illegal immigrant became a *cause célèbre* last year.

coup (koō) Noun. A sudden clever move or action. Persuading several Republicans to vote against the bill was quite a *coup* for the governor.

double entrendre (dŭb'əl ä-tän'drə). Noun. A word or expression with two meanings; one of the meanings is often improper or indelicate. The comedy act contained so many *double entendres* that we understood why children were not admitted.

esprit de corps (ĕ-sprē' də kôr') Noun. Group spirit, comradeship. The sales team needs *esprit de corps* to work well together.

fait accompli (fā'tä-kôn-plē') Noun. An accomplished fact, an irreversible or unchangeable act or decision. The family move to Arizona is a *fait accompli*.

faux pas (fō' pä') Noun. An embarrassing social blunder. The attorney's *faux pas* made the jury laugh aloud.

joie de vivre (zhwä' də vē'vrə) Noun. Joy of living, enjoyment of life. Martin's *joie de vivre* is evident through his carefree lifestyle.

laissez-faire (lĕs'ā fâr'). Noun. The principle that business should operate without government interference and regulation; the principle of allowing others to do as they please. Nick had a *laissez-faire* attitude about the tenants in his building.

nouveau riche (nōō'vō rēsh'). Noun. A person who has recently become rich, especially in a showy manner. Computer gurus who have started dot-com companies are among the *nouveau riche*.

savoir faire (săv'wär-fâr') Noun. Knowledge of the right thing to do or say, social grace or tact. Cary Grant was an actor who always projected a certain *savoir faire*, both on screen and off.

tête-à-tête (tāt 'ə tāt') Adverb or adjective. Two together in private. Noun. A private conversation between two people. The two friends were engaged in a *tête-à-tête*.

vis-à-vis (vē'z-ə-vē'). Preposition. Face to face with, compared with. The earnings report was a disappointment *vis-à-vis* the optimism earlier in the year.

EXERCISE 5-5   **French Words or Phrases I**

Directions: Match the French words or phrases in column A with their meanings in column B. Write the letters of your answers in the spaces provided.

Column A	Column B
1. ——— avant-garde	a. Freedom to use one's own judgment or authority, unconditional authority to act
2. ——— esprit de corps	b. A situation or issue involving widespread interest, public concern, or debate
3. ——— tête-à-tête	c. A sudden clever move or action
4. ——— carte blanche	d. An accomplished fact, an irreversible or unchangeable act or decision
5. ——— joie de vivre	e. The principle that business should operate without government interference and regulation; the principle of allowing others to do as they please

6. ——— savoir faire

    f. A word or expression with two meanings; one of the meanings is often improper or indelicate

7. ——— double entendre

    g. Group spirit, comradeship

8. ——— cause célèbre

    h. Face to face with, compared with

9. ——— fait accompli

    i. Two together in private; a private conversation between two people

10. ——— coup

    j. Knowledge of the right thing to do or say; social grace or tact

11. ——— vis-à-vis

    k. People active in the invention of new ideas or techniques in a particular field

12. ——— laissez-faire

    l. Joy of living, enjoyment of life

EXERCISE 5-6 French Words and Phrases II

Directions: Using the list of French words and phrases above, supply a word or phrase that fits the meaning of each of the following sentences.

1. She considered it a _____ to host the national convention in her hometown.

2. A certain _____ developed among the people who had been stranded at the airport.

3. We were given _____ with regard to ordering supplies for the festival.

4. The many _____ in the film made me wish I had taken my mother to another movie.

5. During our brief and hectic visit, we were able to find time for a quiet _____.

6. The dishonest employee accepted his reprimand and dismissal as a _____.

7. Wyclef Jean is too _____ a musician to appeal to the masses.

8. The south side of town was mainly "old money," but the west side was strictly for the _____.

9. We realized our _____ when he introduced the young lady as his wife, not his daughter.

10. The new chairperson's hands-on approach to running the business was a departure from her predecessor's _____ style.

Learn More about Foreign Phrases by Visiting the Following Web Site

http://en.wikipedia.org/wiki/Lists_of_English_words_of_international_origin

Words Have Feelings, Too: Denotative versus Connotative Meanings

WORD notes

Would you rather be part of a *crowd* or *mob*?

If you were wearing a leather-looking jacket that was made out of manmade fibers, would you prefer that it be called *fake* or *synthetic*?

Would you rather be called a *college student* or a *college kid*?

Each of the above pairs of words has basically the same meaning. A *crowd* and a *mob* are both groups of people. Both *college student* and *college kid* refer to someone who attends college. If the words have similar meanings, why did you choose *crowd* rather than *mob* and *college student* rather than *college kid*? Although the pairs of words have similar primary meanings, they carry different shades of meaning; each creates a different image or association in your mind. This section will explore these shades of meaning, called connotative meanings.

All words have one or more standard meanings. These meanings are called **denotative meanings**. Think of them as those meanings listed in the dictionary. They tell us what the word names. Many words also have connotative meanings. **Connotative meanings** include the feelings and associations that may accompany a word. For example, the denotative meaning of *mother* is female parent. However, the word carries many connotations. For many, *mother* suggests a warm, loving, caring person. Let's take another example, the word *home*. Its denotative meaning is "a place where one lives," but to many its connotative meaning suggests comfort, privacy, and coziness. Figure 5-1 on the next page shows some connotative meanings of the word *mother*.

Writers and speakers use connotative meanings to stir emotions or to bring to mind positive or negative associations. Suppose a writer is describing how someone walks. The writer could choose words such as *strut, stroll, swagger,* or *amble*. Do you see how each creates a different image of the person? Connotative meanings, then, are powerful tools of language. When you read, be alert for meanings suggested by the author's word choice. When writing or speaking, be sure to choose words with appropriate connotations.

Connotations can vary from individual to individual. The denotative meaning for the word *flag* is a piece of cloth used as a national emblem. To many, the American flag is a symbol of patriotism and love of one's country. To some people, though, it may mean an interesting decoration to place on their clothing. The word *cat* to cat lovers suggests a fluffy, furry, cuddly animal. To those who are allergic to cats, however, the word *cat* connotes discomfort and avoidance—itchy eyes, a runny nose, etc.

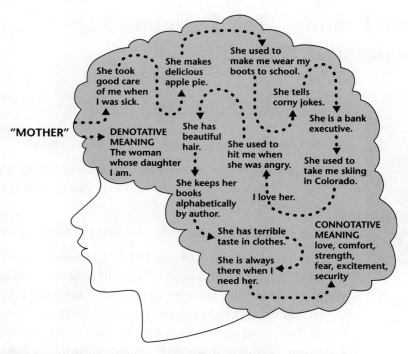

Figure 5-1   One person's connotations for the word "mother."

The cloud contains:
- "MOTHER" → **DENOTATIVE MEANING** The woman whose daughter I am.
- She took good care of me when I was sick.
- She makes delicious apple pie.
- She used to make me wear my boots to school.
- She tells corny jokes.
- She is a bank executive.
- She has beautiful hair.
- She used to hit me when she was angry.
- She used to take me skiing in Colorado.
- She keeps her books alphabetically by author.
- I love her.
- She has terrible taste in clothes.
- She is always there when I need her.
- **CONNOTATIVE MEANING** love, comfort, strength, fear, excitement, security

---

EXERCISE 5-7   Connotative Meanings

Directions: Discuss the differences in connotative meaning of each of the following pairs or sets of words. Consult a dictionary, if necessary.

example   To improve: **mend—reform**
Mend implies repairing something that is broken; reform means changing something, often a

document or law, to improve it or eliminate its faults.

1. To find fault: **admonish—reprimand**

_____

_____

2. A competitor: **rival—opponent**

_____

_____

3. Working together: **accomplice—colleague**

_____

_____

4. Stated briefly: **pithy—concise**

_____

_____

5. Long lasting: **perpetual—interminable—eternal**

_____

_____

_____

6. Inactive: **idle—lethargic—languid**

_____

_____

_____

7. Ability: **proficiency—aptitude—dexterity**

_____

_____

8. Old: **antique—old-fashioned—obsolete—dated**

_____

_____

_____

9. Cautious: **wary—vigilant—careful**

_____

_____

_____

10. Trip: **excursion—pilgrimage—vacation—tour**

_____

_____

_____

EXERCISE 5-8   Using Connotation to Make a Point

Directions: For each of the following sentences, underline the word in parentheses that best completes the sentence. Consult a dictionary, if necessary.

1. The price of the dinner was (exorbitant, extravagant).

2. The discipline policy at the boarding school was (stiff, rigid).

3. Using coupons at the grocery store is one way of being (frugal, stingy).

4. Jay had several friends with tattoos, but he never felt (influenced, pressured) to get one himself.

5. The neighbors were embroiled in a (dispute, debate) over property lines.

6. The restaurant manager (warned, threatened) us that it could be well over an hour before we were seated.

7. The couple (hesitated, wavered) several times before finally deciding to put their house on the market.

8. The millionaire made his fortune through several (bold, brash) investments.

9. He had a (forcible, forceful) personality that was difficult to ignore.

10. The physician is (dedicated, pledged) to the well-being of her patients.

 Learn More about Connotative Meaning by Visiting the Following Web Site

Connotations
http://leo.stcloudstate.edu/grammar/connotations.html

Not Saying What You Mean: Euphemisms

WORD **notes**

Where is the ladies' room?

My aunt passed away.

I work for the sanitation department.

What do each of these sentences have in common? Each uses an expression called a euphemism—a word or phrase that is used in place of a word that is unpleasant, embarrassing, or otherwise objectionable. The expression *passed away* replaces the word *died, ladies' room* is a substitute for *toilet*, and *sanitation* is a more pleasing term than *garbage*.

The word *euphemism* comes from the Greek roots *eu-*, meaning "sounding good," and *-pheme*, meaning "speech." Euphemisms have a long history going back to ancient languages and cultures. Ancient people thought of names as extensions of the things themselves. To know and say the name of a person or object gave the speaker power over that person or object. Thus, calling something by its name was avoided, even forbidden. God, Satan, deceased relatives, and hunted animals would often be referred to indirectly. For example, in one culture God was called the Kindly One; the bear was called the Grandfather. Today, many euphemisms are widely used in both spoken and written language. Here are a few more examples:

The objective of the air strike was to neutralize the enemy. (kill the enemy)

Some collateral damage occurred as a result of the air strike. (death to civilians)

When it is hot, people perspire. (sweat)

Euphemisms tend to minimize or downplay the importance or seriousness of something. They are often used in politics and advertising. They can be used to camouflage actions or events that may be unacceptable to readers or listeners if bluntly explained. For example, the word *casualties of war* may be used instead of the phrase *dead soldiers* to lessen the impact of the attack. To say that a politician's statement was *at variance with the truth* is less forceful than to say that the politician *lied*.

When you speak or write, be sure to avoid euphemisms that obscure or interfere with your intended meaning. Euphemisms can lead your listeners or readers to believe that you have something to hide or that you are not being completely truthful with them.

EXERCISE 5-9   Euphemisms

Directions: For each of the boldfaced euphemisms, write a substitution that does not minimize or avoid the basic meaning of the term.

example   The theater had only one **ladies room**. <u>toilet for women</u>

1. The search continued for the **remains** of the victims of the air crash. _____

2. The advertising campaign was an **incomplete success**. _____

3. The presidential aide was accused of spreading **disinformation**.

   _____

   _____

4. We took our broken refrigerator to the **sanitary landfill**. _____

5. The company announced that it would be **downsizing** several hundred employees over the next few months. _____

   _____

6. The business recorded a **negative cash flow** last month. _____

7. We noticed that she **was carrying a little extra weight**. _____

8. The car dealership sold both new and **previously owned** automobiles. _____

9. Witnesses reported that the two men **exchanged words** before the gun was fired.

   _____

   _____

10. The veterinarian recommended that the elderly cat be **put to sleep**. _____

 Learn More about Euphemisms by Visiting the Following Web Site

http://en.wikipedia.org/wiki/Lists_of_English_words_of_international_origin

Untangling a Tangle of Words: Doublespeak

WORD **notes**

The letter from the Air Force colonel in charge of safety said that rocket boosters weighing more than 300,000 pounds "have an explosive force upon surface impact that is sufficient to exceed the accepted overpressure threshold of physiological damage for the exposed personnel."[1]

What does the colonel's statement mean in simple words? *Answer*: If a 300,000-pound rocket falls on a person, it will kill him or her.

The language the colonel used is an example of doublespeak. Here are a few more examples. Can you translate each of the following phrases into simple language? (Answers are on the bottom of the next page.)

1. pink slip_____

2. ground-mounted confirmatory route markers _____

3. vertically deployed antipersonnel devices_____

Doublespeak is deliberately unclear or evasive language. Often, it exaggerates or overstates information that could be expressed simply. William Lutz, an expert on doublespeak, defines it as "language that pretends to communicate but does not."[2]

Doublespeak uses euphemisms (see p. 124), but it tangles language in other ways, as well, that are intended to confuse or overwhelm the listener or reader. Doublespeak may also use (1) technical language that is likely to be unfamiliar to the audience, (2) inflated language, or words that tend to make something seem more important or complex than it really is, and (3) long, polysyllabic words. It may scramble the order of words in a sentence to create confusion or avoid giving complete information. For example, the passive voice may be used to avoid saying who performed an action. In the sentence "The bombs were released, injuring many civilians," we do not know who released the bombs.

In your own writing, avoid doublespeak at all costs; it is the opposite of clear, concise expression. When reading doublespeak, be suspicious of the writer's motives. Ask yourself: Why is the writer being purposefully evasive or unclear? What is he or she trying to hide?

EXERCISE 5-10   Doublespeak

Directions: Untangle each of the following examples of doublespeak and write a translation in simple English.

example   Most hospitals are reluctant to publicize negative patient care outcomes.
Hospitals are reluctant to publicize patient deaths.

1. Human rights violations in Country X included the "unlawful or arbitrary deprivation of human life." (U.S. State Department)

   _____

2. Corporations involved in staff reduction activities often offer excessed employees reemployment engineering.

   _____

3. Preliminary reports showed a negative gain in test scores in the state's public schools.

   _____

4. Please allow the more vertically challenged individuals to come to the front of the group so they may have a clearer line of sight.

   _____

5. The merchandise order you have placed cannot be accommodated due to current shortages in inventory.

   _____

6. Your request for assistance will be processed in a timely manner by customer service representatives in the order in which it was received.

   _____

7. A corporate climate specialist will join us today to facilitate the positive exchange of ideas.

   _____

8. After the less-than-positive earnings of last quarter, it has become necessary to eliminate redundancies in various areas of the company.

   _____

9. The couple entered interrelational therapy in an effort to work out some of their compatibility issues.

   _____

10. A low pressure system will be moving into the area later this evening, bringing with it the possibility of an accumulation of precipitation.

   _____

Learn More about Doublespeak by Visiting the Following Web Sites

http://www.Issu.edu/banished/current/default.html

http://www.cord.edu/faculty/sprunger/e315/dbltk.html

Where Do New Words Come From?

WORD notes

Here are a few newly coined (created) words. Do you know their meanings?

- ➤ anime
- ➤ slamming
- ➤ senior moment
- ➤ sky surfing

Answers: *Anime* refers to a type of animation that originated in Japan. *Slamming* is the change of long-distance telephone service without the customer's permission. A *senior moment* is a brief lapse of memory or confusion. *Sky surfing* is aerial skateboarding.

New words enter our language each year. These new words are called *neologisms* (neo–new plus logo–word).

English is a language that is constantly changing; new words are added and words that have become outdated are classified as obsolete. One way new words enter our language is through social and cultural change. Many of our great grandparents never heard of words like *taco, quiche, croissant, piña colada, tofu*, and *pita bread*— nor ventured to taste the foods they described. Now these words and food items have become standard fare.

Computer technology has brought hundreds of new words into our language. Our grandparents never heard of *e-mail, CD-ROMs, modems*, and so forth. Here are a few other ways new words enter our language:

- ➤ **People make up new words.** Writers and speakers create new words. It is estimated that one-tenth of the words Shakespeare used were never used before. Developers of new products make up words to describe their products. The word *sneaker* entered our language this way.

- ➤ **Words are created by error.** According to the *Oxford English Dictionary*, at least 350 English words came into existence because of typographical errors or misreadings. Others came into existence by mishearings (people thought they heard a word pronounced a certain way and pronounced it that way themselves). Because of such errors, for example, *shamefast* became *shamefaced*.

➤ **Meanings of existing words change.** Often a word itself does not change. Rather its meaning does. For example, *tell* used to mean *count*. (Think of a *bank teller*.)

➤ **Words are shortened:**
Examination has become *exam*.
Gymnasium has become *gym*.
Laboratory has become *lab*.

➤ **Words are combined to make new words.** (Some are compound words; others may be two separate words; others are hyphenated.)
Seaplane
High school
Half-moon

EXPLORING language

Ghost Words—Mistakes That Became Words

A ghost word is a word that has come into the language by mistake. The mistake might be a misreading of a manuscript, a typographical error, or a misunderstanding. Approximately 350 words were introduced into the English language in one of these ways.

Here are a few examples:

➤ *Asparagus* was originally called *sparrow-grass*.

➤ *Buttonhole* was once *buttonhold*.

➤ *Sweetheart* was originally *sweetard*, as in a dullard or dotard (someone who is senile).

EXERCISE 5-11   Neologisms I

Directions: Each of the following words recently entered the English language and appeared in one of the more recently revised dictionaries. Write the meaning of each, consulting a recent hard-copy dictionary or using an online dictionary.

example   cross trainer: A type of athletic shoe designed for use with a variety of sports.

1. carjacking: _____

    _____

2. antiglare: _____

    _____

3. energy bar: _____

    _____

4. megaplex: _____

_____

5. e-tailing: _____

_____

6. Gen Y'ers: _____

_____

7. date rape: _____

_____

8. fashionista: _____

_____

9. spamming: _____

_____

10. televangelist: _____

_____

EXERCISE 5-12 Neologisms II

Directions: Each of the following is a newly created word or phrase listed on a Web site that features neologisms. Try to figure out the meaning of each. *Note*: Most of them are not yet accepted as authentic English words; if they do not appear in the dictionary, they should not be used in academic writing.

example   body Nazis: <u>workout fanatics who look down on anyone who does not work out</u>

1. baggravation (*Hint*: think about airlines and baggage problems):

_____

_____

2. mouse potato (*Hint*: think computers and couch potato):

_____

3. blamestorming (*Hint*: modify brainstorming):

_____

4. forklift upgrade: _____

_____

5. Gutenberg: _____

_____

_____

6. netizen: _____

7. mallrats: _____

8. flaming: _____

9. netiquette: _____

_____

10. losingest: _____

_____

@ Learn More about Neologisms by Visiting the Following Web Site

http://www.owlnet.rice.edu/~ling215/NewWords

Let Your Creativity Show: Using Figurative Language

WORD notes

Golconde (1953), **Magritte**

The cake tasted like sawdust.

Her answer was as unexpected as a white tiger appearing in my yard.

Today, my boss, Martha Yarfield, is as nervous as an expectant father.

You know that a cake cannot really be made of sawdust, that answers are not white tigers, and that the boss is not an expectant father. Instead, you know that the writer means that the cake was dry and tasteless, that the answer was totally unexpected, and that the boss is full of anxious anticipation.

Each of these statements is an example of *figurative language*—a way of describing something that makes sense on an imaginative or creative level like the Magritte painting of raining business people but not on a factual or literal level. None of the above statements is literally true, but each is meaningful. In many figurative expressions, one thing is compared with another for some quality they have in common. Two unlike objects, the cake and sawdust, share the characteristic of dryness.

The purpose of figurative language is to paint a word picture that will help the reader or listener visualize how something looks, feels, or smells. Figurative language allows the writer or speaker the opportunity to be creative and to express attitudes and opinions without directly stating them. Figurative language is used widely in literature, as well as many forms of expressive writing. Here are a few examples:

➤ I will speak daggers to her, but use none. (Shakespeare, *Hamlet*)

➤ An aged man is but a paltry thing, / a tattered coat upon a stick ... (W. B. Yeats, *Sailing to Byzantium*)

➤ Time is but the stream I go a-fishing in. (Henry David Thoreau, *Walden*)

➤ Announced by all the trumpets of the sky, / arrives the snow ... (Ralph Waldo Emerson, *The Snowstorm*)

The two most common types of figuricic language are metaphors and similes. A *simile* uses the word *like* or *as* to make a comparison. A *metaphor* states or implies that one thing *is* another thing. If you say, "Mary's dress looks <u>like</u> a whirlwind of color," you have created a simile. If you say, "Mary's dress <u>is</u> a whirlwind of color," you have created a metaphor. Notice that each compares two unlike things, the dress and the whirlwind.

EXERCISE 5-13   Figurative Expressions

Directions: For the figurative expression indicated in each sentence, write the choice that best explains its meaning on the line provided.

———   1. It was **an uphill battle** to get the insurance claim approved.

    a. dangerous   c. physically tiring

    b. extremely difficult   d. complicated

———   2. His face **clouded over** as soon as she said no.

    a. looked unhappy   c. cooled off

    b. cleared up   d. was shaded

———   3. She asked for the favor in a voice **dripping with honey.**

    a. sentimental   c. unpleasant

    b. overly sweet   d. sticky

———   4. At sunset, the surface of the lake was **like a piece of glass.**

    a. sharp   c. wavy

    b. smooth   d. hard

———   5. After dining at the all-you-can-eat buffet, he was **as full as a tick.**

    a. still hungry   c. rude

    b. like a parasite   d. stuffed with food

———   6. She politely asked her visitors to leave, but **icicles were hanging on every word.**

    a. it was winter   c. she spoke in a cold, unwelcoming manner

    b. she had a sparkling voice   d. she used fancy words

7. As he dozed in the hammock, the sun slowly moved across the yard and dropped **a soft, golden blanket** on him.

   a. warmth

   b. yellow leaves

   c. rain

   d. pollen

8. The sound of the chainsaw outside her window was **like a dentist drilling on her nerves.**

   a. a pleasant humming

   b. a sound she could ignore

   c. an extremely unpleasant sound

   d. an important and necessary sound

9. His birthday money was **burning a hole in his pocket**!

   a. on fire

   b. too heavy for his pocket to hold

   c. causing people to look at him

   d. making him anxious to spend it

10. Our computer is **a dinosaur.**

    a. huge

    b. awkward

    c. heavy

    d. outdated

 Learn More about Figurative Language by Visiting the Following Web Site

http://www.cod.edu/people/faculty/fiten/readlit/figspch.htm

Stretching Your Thinking with Words: Analogies

WORD notes

Can you fill in the blank?

evil is to good as right is to _____.

If you answered "left," you are correct. You have just completed an analogy. You can think of an analogy as a comparison made between sets of words. Understanding and working with analogies is an excellent means of sharpening your vocabulary as well. Analogies force you to use language, stretch your thinking, and strengthen your logical reasoning skills. Analogies also crop up on all sorts of standardized tests, so it is useful to be familiar with how they work. For example, various graduate school admission tests, licensing exams, civil service exams, and employment tests contain analogies.

An analogy is an abbreviated statement expressing the same relationship between two pairs of items. Analogies are usually written in the following format:

black : white :: dark : light

This can be read in either of two ways:

1. *Black is to white as dark is to light.* (The words in each pair are opposites.)

2. *White has the same relationship to black as light does to dark.* (White is the opposite of black, and light is the opposite of dark.)

In analogies, the relationship between the words or phrases is critically important.

Analogies become problem-solving and critical-thinking exercises when one of the four items, usually the fourth, is left blank and you are instructed to supply or choose a correct answer.

Here are a few simple analogies that demonstrate how analogies work; supply a correct answer for each blank.

1. celery : vegetable :: orange : _____

2. shotgun : bullet :: bow : _____

3. video : watch :: audio : _____

4. hot : cold :: heavy : _____

5. hamburgers : Burger King :: chicken : _____

In the first analogy, the correct answer is fruit because celery is a type of vegetable and an orange is a type of fruit. Other answers should be (2) arrow, (3) listen, (4) light, and (5) KFC (or another fast-food restaurant featuring chicken).

Tips for Solving Analogies

The key to solving analogies is to analyze the relationship that exists between the first pair of words or between the first and third items. The relationship you uncover between the first pair must be expressed in the second pair.

Analogies typically explore several common relationships. These include:

1. **Opposites**—*Example*: yes : no :: stop : start
   (The words in each pair are opposites.)

2. **Whole/part**—*Example*: year : month :: week : day
   (A month is part of a year; a day is part of a week.)

3. **Synonyms**—*Example*: moist : damp :: happy : glad
   (The words in each pair are interchangeable.)

4. **Categories**—*Example*: dessert : cake :: meat : beef
   (Cake is a type of dessert; beef is a type of meat.)

5. **Similarities**—*Example*: lemon : orange :: celery : cabbage
   (The words in each pair are similar because they belong to the same category of things.)

6. **Association or action**—*Example*: train : conductor :: airplane : pilot
   (A conductor operates a train; a pilot operates a plane.)

In addition to the ability to analyze relationships, analogies often require background knowledge or information. For example, the following analogy requires that you know that red light waves are the longest whereas violet ones are the shortest.

red : longest :: violet : (shortest)

EXERCISE 5-14   Analogies

Directions: Complete each of the following sets of analogies by writing the appropriate word or phrase on the line provided. Each set is increasingly more difficult. Check a dictionary for the meaning of unfamiliar terms.

Set I

1. sculptor : statue :: musician : _____
   a. art
   b. songwriters
   c. music
   d. notes

2. brush : painter :: pen : _____
   a. pencil
   b. book
   c. paper
   d. writer

3. coffee : cup :: hamburger : _____
   a. beef
   b. milkshake
   c. bun
   d. eat

4. halibut : fish :: lamb : _____
   a. animal
   b. chicken
   c. mutton
   d. wool

5. dress : wear :: apple : _____
   a. peel
   b. eat
   c. fruit
   d. food

6. tennis : ball :: hockey : _____
   a. stick
   b. game
   c. puck
   d. ice

7. like : dislike :: respect : _____
   a. inspect
   b. expect
   c. admire
   d. disrespect

8. snake : reptile :: whale : _____
   a. fish
   b. mammal
   c. ocean
   d. aquatic

9. word : sentence :: sentence : _____
   a. line
   b. write
   c. paragraph
   d. report

10. New Orleans : Louisiana :: Chicago : _____

    a. Illinois   c. Midwest

    b. Lake Michigan   d. Indiana

Set II

1. aviary : birds :: greenhouse : _____

    a. bugs   c. gardener

    b. plants   d. outdoors

2. Alps : Europe :: Rockies : _____

    a. North America   c. Switzerland

    b. mountains   d. Colorado

3. podiatrist : feet :: ophthalmologist : _____

    a. doctor   c. organs

    b. head   d. eyes

4. United States : president :: England : _____

    a. Great Britain   c. prime minister

    b. United Kingdom   d. monarchy

5. horn : honk :: whistle : _____

    a. shrill   c. lips

    b. blow   d. tune

6. Iowa : state :: Jupiter : _____

    a. planet   c. Mars

    b. space   d. moon

7. fresh : rancid :: unique : _____

    a. appearance   c. rare

    b. characteristic   d. common

8. Picasso : painter :: Shakespeare : _____

    a. plays   c. literature

    b. writer   d. words

9. hasten : speed up :: outdated : _____

    a. old-fashioned   c. slow

    b. current   d. timely

10. solar : sun :: lunar : _____

    a. planets   c. moon

    b. earth   d. stars

Set III

1. expunge : delete :: repel : _____
   a. resist
   b. erase
   c. remove
   d. attract

2. perceive : understand :: ostentatious : _____
   a. plain
   b. showy
   c. understated
   d. exterior

3. quart : pint :: 1 : _____
   a. 1
   b. 2
   c. 3
   d. 8

4. Allah : Islam :: God : _____
   a. America
   b. Jesus
   c. Christianity
   d. Creator

5. United States : dollar :: Japan : _____
   a. money
   b. dollar
   c. peso
   d. yen

6. odometer : mileage :: barometer : _____
   a. atmospheric pressure
   b. temperature
   c. weather
   d. precipitation

7. present : past :: sit : _____
   a. sat
   b. walk
   c. sitting
   d. stand

8. old age : geriatrics :: infancy : _____
   a. babies
   b. families
   c. childhood
   d. pediatrics

9. Adam Smith : capitalism :: Karl Marx : _____
   a. German
   b. communism
   c. society
   d. atheism

10. export : import :: malignant : _____
    a. cancerous
    b. tumor
    c. benign
    d. health

 Learn More about Analogies by Visiting the Following Web Site

http://www.quia.com/pop/121261.html
Try the analogies test.

Is It *Lie* or *Lay*? Commonly Confused Words

WORD **notes**

Which sentence in each of the following pairs is correct?

➤ The *stationary* bike is broken.
The *stationary* is on my desk.

➤ *Lay* the package on the table.
Lie the package on the table.

➤ The couple will divide the settlement *between* them.
The couple will divide the settlement *among* them.

Answers: The first sentence in each pair is correct.

There are many word pairs or groups, such as those above, that are commonly confused and misused. Use the following list to be sure you use words correctly in your speech and writing.

Commonly Confused Words

Accept	(to receive) She will **accept** the gift.
Except	(other than) Everyone was invited **except** me.
Adapt	(to adjust or accommodate to) The children **adapted** easily to life in Panama.
Adopt	(to accept and put into effect) The council members agreed to **adopt** the new budget beginning in May.
Advice	(guidance or information) My teacher offered **advice** on how to study.
Advise	(to offer guidance) My teacher **advised** me to drop the course.
Affect	(to influence) Smoking **affects** one's health.
Effect	(result) The **effects** of smoking are obvious.
Allusion	(indirect reference or hint) Her **allusions** about his weight were embarrassing.
Illusion	(false idea or appearance) Cosmetic surgery creates the **illusion** of youth.

Between	(refers to two things or people) My wife and I will divide the household chores **between** us.
Among	(refers to three or more people or things) The vote was evenly divided **among** the four candidates.
Beside	(next to, along the side of) He wants to sit **beside** you.
Besides	(in addition to) **Besides** the regular players, the team has three reserve players.
Bring	(describes movement of an object toward you) **Bring** me the newspaper.
Take	(describes movement away from you) **Take** these letters to the mailbox.
Censor	(to edit or ban from the public) The school board will **censor** the controversial novel from the library.
Censure	(to criticize or condemn publicly) The mayor was **censured** for misusing public funds.
Cite	(to summon to appear in court; to quote) I couldn't believe I was **cited** for jaywalking. She **cited** Toni Morrison in her acceptance speech.
Sight	(something seen) The best **sight** in the world is your own child's smile.
Site	(location) The **site** for the new civic center has not yet been determined.
Complement	(to add to or go with) Their personalities **complement** one another.
Compliment	(to praise or flatter) I must **compliment** you on your quick wit.
Conscience	(awareness of the moral right and wrong of your own actions) Her **conscience** has been bothering her ever since she told that lie.
Conscious	(aware or alert) He remained **conscious** during the surgery.
Continual	(repeated regularly) We have enjoyed everything about our house except for the **continual** need to pay the mortgage.
Continuous	(happens without stopping) They sailed **continuously** for two months before they reached land.
Coarse	(rough) Stone-ground grits have a pleasantly **coarse** texture.
Course	(class or path) Many students considered the film **course** their favorite. The **course** was quite hilly but we enjoyed the exercise.
Elicit	(to draw out or extract) It is sometimes difficult to **elicit** information from a teenager.
Illicit	(unlawful, illegal) The mobsters were charged with several **illicit** activities, including gambling and extortion.

Eminent	(something evident or outstanding) The **eminent** Dr. Sullivan will be the keynote speaker at the conference.
Imminent	(something about to happen) Everyone felt sure that an announcement was **imminent**.
Explicit	(clearly expressed) I gave her **explicit** instructions about taking care of the cats while we were out of town.
Implicit	(implied or complete) We had an **implicit** agreement not to mention her first marriage. I trust him **implicitly**.
Farther	(at or to a greater distance) We hiked much **farther** than we had intended.
Further	(to a greater extent, more; or help forward) After grounding him, we sent him to his room to **further** contemplate his bad behavior. Her support went a long way toward **furthering** our cause.
Fewer	(a smaller number of persons or things) Every year, there seem to be **fewer** television programs that I really enjoy.
Less	(a smaller amount or to a smaller extent) However, there does seem to be **less** violence during prime time.
Good	(satisfactory, adequate (adjective)) Milo felt **good** about his performance on the final exam.
Well	(satisfactorily, fortunately (adverb)) Most of the class did very **well** on the bonus question.
Imply	(to suggest or state indirectly) I didn't mean to **imply** that you were a thief.
Infer	(to guess or conclude) There were no signs of forced entry, so the detective **inferred** that the intruder had a key to the house.
Its	(of or relating to it or itself (adjective)) The old barn is in terrible shape—**its** roof is about to fall in.
It's	(contraction of *it is*) I'm taking the car to be serviced tomorrow because **it's** making an odd noise.
Lay	(to set down) Please **lay** those drawings on the table.
Lie	(to be in a horizontal position) I would like to **lie** down for a minute.
Loose	(not rigidly fastened) Part of the problem with your car is the **loose** fan belt.
Lose	(to misplace or miss) Orinthia put the key in her pocket so she wouldn't **lose** it.
Principal	(most important; a sum of money) The **principal** reason I've called you here today is to discuss your finances; the **principal** you invested with us six months ago has doubled!
Principle	(a rule or code of conduct) He refused to compromise his **principles** so he was fired.
Proceed	(to move forward) After obtaining a loan, we were able to **proceed** with our remodeling plans.
Precede	(to go before) The couple who **preceded** us in line bought the last pair of tickets.

Raise	(collect; lift up) The booster club was able to **raise** $4,000 for the school's athletic teams. It was impossible to **raise** the windows because they had been painted shut.
Rise	(to get up or to move upward) We watched the hot-air balloons **rise** into the sky.
Set	(to place) Please **set** that vase down very carefully.
Sit	(to occupy a seat) Please **sit** wherever you'd like.
Stationary	(fixed or unchanging) We bought a **stationary** bicycle so we could exercise during the winter.
Stationery	(writing paper) She ordered new **stationery** with her initials embossed on it.
Than	(in comparison with) I like classical music better **than** rap.
Then	(at that time, next) First we went out to eat, and **then** we decided to see a movie.
Their	(of or relating to them or themselves) It's not **their** fault that they ran out of gas; **their** gas gauge was broken.
There	(used to introduce a sentence (pronoun), or that place (noun)) **There** is no time for dawdling; we'll have to hurry if we want to get **there** on time!
They're	(contraction of *they are*) They promised to be on time, but **they're** always late.
Threw	(past tense of to throw) The pitcher **threw** the ball as hard as he could.
Through	(from one side to the other; finished) We decided to go **through** the forest instead of around it. After he injured his knee, he knew he was **through** with soccer.
To	(toward (preposition); also used for marking a verb that follows as an infinitive (as in *to see*)) They went **to** New England in October **to** see the fall colors.
Too	(also; very) We would have gone **too**, but the trip was **too** long.
Two	(a whole number meaning one more than one) The **two** men agreed to meet for coffee at **two** o'clock.
Weather	(atmospheric conditions) The **weather** was stormy the whole time we were at the beach.
Whether	(if; in case; if it happens that) I plan to go, **whether** you join me or not.
Who's	(contraction of *who is*) **Who's** going on the canoe trip?
Whose	(of or relating to whom, especially as possessor) I wonder **whose** truck is parked in front of her house.

EXERCISE 5-15   Commonly Confused Words

Directions: Underline the correct words in parentheses to complete each of the following sentences.

1. Please (sit, set) my laptop on my desk (beside, besides) those papers.

2. It is my pleasure to (accept, except) your offer.

3. They had hoped to meet us for dinner before the play, but (their, they're, there) babysitter was late, so (their, they're, there) going to meet us (their, they're, there).

4. Baked apples make a delicious (complement, compliment) to roast pork.

5. My husband is (to, too, two) years younger (than, then) his brother.

6. We allowed the funeral procession to (precede, proceed) us, then we (preceded, proceeded) on our way.

7. The severe (weather, whether) had such an (affect, effect) on her that she gave (explicit, implicit) instructions not to be disturbed for the rest of the day.

8. A debate appeared to be (eminent, imminent), but I still had not decided (who's, whose) side I was on.

9. She made several (allusions, illusions) to his mysterious past, but we were unable to (imply, infer) what she was trying to (imply, infer).

10. Even though (its, it's) getting late, I'd like to drive you by the building (cite, sight, site).

Learn More Commonly Confused Words by Visiting the Following Web Site

http://homepage.smc.edu/reading_lab/words_commonly_confused.htm

END NOTES

1. *Source*: http://www.geocities.com/CollegePark/6174/jokes/doublespeak.htm
2. From William Lutz, *Beyond Nineteen Eighty-Four*

MASTERY test 1

Applying and Integrating Your Skills

Applying Your Skills in Literature

Directions: Read the passage and answer the following items in the space provided.

An Excerpt from *A Beautiful Mind*

John Forbes Nash, Jr.—mathematical genius, inventor of a theory of rational behavior, visionary of the thinking machine—had been sitting with his visitor, also a mathematician, for nearly half an hour. It was late on a weekday afternoon in the spring of 1959, and, though it was only May, uncomfortably warm. Nash was slumped in an armchair in one corner of the hospital lounge, carelessly dressed in a nylon shirt that hung limply over his unbelted trousers. His powerful frame was slack as a rag doll's, his finely molded features expressionless. He had been staring dully at a spot immediately in front of the left foot of Harvard professor George Mackey, hardly moving except to brush his long dark hair away from his forehead in a fitful, repetitive motion. His visitor sat upright, oppressed by the silence, acutely conscious that the doors to the room were locked. Mackey finally could contain himself no longer. His voice was slightly querulous, but he strained to be gentle. "How could you," began Mackey, "how could you, a mathematician, a man devoted to reason and logical proof . . . how could you believe that extraterrestrials are sending you messages? How could you believe that you are being recruited by aliens from other space to save the world? How could you . . . ?"

Nash looked up at last and fixed Mackey with an unblinking stare as cool and dispassionate as that of any bird or snake. "Because," Nash said slowly in his soft, reasonable southern drawl, as if talking to himself, "the ideas I had about supernatural beings came to me the same way that my mathematical ideas did. So I took them seriously."[1]

—Sylvia Nasar, p. 11

1. Write a sentence describing the overall impression the author creates of John Forbes Nash.

   _____

2. Identify 5 words or phrases whose connotative meaning contribute to the overall impression of Nash. _____

   _____

3. Identify at least one figurative expression used in the passage.

   _____

   _____

Applying Your Skills in Technology

Directions: Read the passage on the next page. It contains numerous neologisms, words that have recently entered our language. For each of the following neologisms, write a brief definition. Do an online search for meanings, if needed.

Bluetooth Technology

Zoom Technologies, Inc. (NASDAQ: ZOOM) today published on their web site a detailed description of how to easily move pictures, music, and Outlook contact names between a mobile phone and a computer using Bluetooth wireless capability. The phone must have built-in Bluetooth, and the computer must have Bluetooth either built into the computer or added by way of a low-cost Bluetooth USB adapter.

With the proper Bluetooth and hardware moving pictures, music, and contacts is a simple "drag and drop" operation. You can easily take a picture using a Bluetooth phone and move it to your computer, or move pictures from your computer onto your phone. You can also move music from a computer to your phone's MP3 player. Similarly, it's easy to select contacts from your computer's Outlook and to move them and their phone numbers into your phone's contact list, or to move contacts from your phone's contact list into Outlook. A detailed "How To" and useful Bluetooth information are provided in the new paper, "How to use Bluetooth® to move pictures, music, and contact names between your mobile phone and your computer," available at www.zoom.com/graphics/datasheets/bluetooth/BlueTooth_HowTo.pdf.

—from Marketwire News Releases, 2/4/08.

1. Bluetooth _____

_____

2. Outlook _____

3. "drag and drop" _____

_____

4. MP3 player _____

EXERCISE 5-18   Applying Your Skills in Literature

Directions: Read the passage. Then, explain the meaning of each of the following uses of figurative language.

An Excerpt from *That Old Ace In the Hole*

A sudden burst of wind threw hailstones against the post office window. Lightening flickered as he ran for his car. On the way back to the bunkhouse the wind shoved and hustled the Saturn. Hail and rain mixed, the hail increasing in size, smacking the car, the road, and rebounding with dull purple flashes. The lightening shot around him in blinding streamers. He pulled off near Saddle Blanket bridge and parked under a black willow for some shelter. The wind was terrific and frightening. The sky flickered, its sickening strobe light revealing corn clouds, leaves flashing white. Rain and hail and twigs and plastic bags scraped over the windshield. He could just make out hailstones the size of walnuts lashing the stream into froth. It was less frightening to watch the brown ripped water than to look at the jittery horizon. A brown wave swept down the Saddle Blanket, no longer pencil-size, but a snarling river. He watched in horrified amazement as the water swelled out of its banks and began spreading over the road behind him, then, with thin, watery fingers, crept over the bridge roadway. He saw he could be cut off and swept away in the flood.

—Annie Proulx, p.359

1. "the sky flickered its sickening strobe light" _____

_____

2. "a snarling river" _____

3. the water ... "with thin, watery fingers crept over the bridge roadway" _____

_____

MASTERY test 2

Applying and Integrating Your Skills in Communication

This textbook excerpt is adapted from *The Media of Mass Communication* by John Vivian. Read the passage to learn about how the music business is changing. Then answer the questions that follow.

Changes in the Music Business

1   Technology has put sophisticated low-cost recording and mixing equipment within the means of a lot of garage bands. As little as $15,000 can buy digital recorders and 24-channel mixing boards, plus remodeling, to do what only a major studio could do a few years ago. Back then, only big-name artists could afford their own studios. Now almost everyone can. Home recording studios in the United States now number more than 100,000. Since 1980 commercial studios have **dwindled** from 10,000 to 1,000. Dan Daley, an editor at the trade journal *Mix*, calls this the democratization of the recording industry, which has returned an **avant-garde** attitude among artists that record companies have been forced to recognize.

2   The widespread availability of mini-studios is contributing to a demassification in recorded music that, in some respects, should please elitists. **Bona fide** music that flows from the soul and heart of the musicians, reflecting the life experiences of the artists without strong commercial imperatives, is being recorded. And some of this music moves the culture in new directions. Early rap and **hip-hop** for example, had authenticity. So did early Seattle grunge. Elitists note, though, that breakthroughs are always devitalized by **derivative artists** who try to pick up on a new sound that's become popular. The result, at worst, is a cultural setback and, at best, the **cultural stagnation that comes from homogenization.**

Streaming Crisis

3   Besides losing much of the creative control over its products, the record industry faced even more serious challenges from technology at the start of the 21st century. In 2000, Shawn Fanning's Napster technology ushered in a frenzy of free music-swapping. Suddenly, record stores found themselves unable to move inventory. Major music retailer Best Buy shut down hundreds of its Sam Goody's Musicland, Suncoast, Media Play, On Cue and other brand-name record outlets that had seemed sure money-makers only a few months earlier. The situation worsened. After two years of **slippage,** CD sales slid another 8.2 percent in 2002. Record-makers braced for worse to come. For the first time the record industry was not in control of new technology—unlike the earlier adjustments when the companies exploited developments to **goose** sales, like the introduction of electrical recording and format adjustments like the switches to long-playing records, then stereo and high-fidelity, eight-tracks, cassettes and CDs.

4   Its survival threatened, the record industry **flailed** for answers. In one twist, Germany-based media giant Bertelsmann, whose brands included RCA Records, invested in its **nemesis** Napster, in hopes of somehow finding retailing possibilities in Shawn Fanning's technology. Slightly longer-lived was a Universal-Sony joint venture, PressPlay, a subscription service that allowed guilt-free **downloading**. Bertelsmann, EMI and Time Warner rolled out a similar guilt-free subscription service, MusicNet. The fact, however, was that few illicit downloaders felt guilt. At its peak, PressPlay drew only 225,000 subscribers.

5   Meanwhile, the Recording Industry Association of America was in court against Napster. A federal judge bought the record-makers' argument that Napster was participating in copyright infringements by facilitating illicit copying of protected intellectual property. RIAA prevailed. Napster was **toast**. But other illicit file-swapping mechanisms soon were serving music fans who had been hooked on free downloading by their Napster experience. These services were harder to **tackle**. Kazaa, for example kept moving its operations from one offshore site to another where legal actions were impossible. The Napster successors had no central site for downloads, so when RIAA went after these in court, a judge found that these services could not be sued because they didn't have any mechanism to control illegal downloading.

6   In a surreal initiative in 2003, the RIAA began legal action against individuals who downloaded music without paying. The industry recognized that it couldn't sue the millions of people who were engaged in illegal downloading, but it hoped that some showcase suits would discourage the free downloading. Also, record-makers put pressure on colleges to monitor their servers and **crack down** on their own students. This record industry heavy-handedness engendered hard feelings in the very consumers that the big record companies were trying to **entice** with PressPlay and MusicNet. It made little sense.

Steve Jobs and the iPod

7   **Doomsayers** said the record industry as we knew it was about to disappear—and much of the music too. Without the financial engine that had driven the business, and creativity, the incentive to produce music would be blunted. It was a dire scenario.

8   Then came the **iPod**. Late in 2002 Steve Jobs, the innovator behind the Apple computer, introduced a handheld music download and playback device. He called it the iPod. Then Jobs followed with the iTunes Music Store. With iTunes, people could sample a song with a single click and then download with another click for 99 cents. iTunes had no ongoing subscription charge. With MusicNet and PressPlay not only was there a download charge, but the music would disappear if a subscriber missed a monthly payment, which ranged from $4 to $18. Also, unlike MusicNet and PressPlay, iTunes music could be transferred to other devices at no charge. It was like owning the music, not renting. In iTunes' first week, more than 1 million songs were downloaded, **juicing** a 27 percent spike in Apple stock.

9   Also, the sound quality was exceptional. The iPod used a new format, AAC, which not only was superior to MP3 but, by compressing more efficiently than MP3, could be downloaded faster and consumed less disc space. Even then, why pay? Jobs noted that Kazaa, Morpheus, Grokster and other free swap systems had been infected with annoying **viruses**. Also, Jobs figured that the guilt trip that RIAA was trying to lay on illegal downloaders wouldn't hurt.

10   Perhaps most significant was that Jobs recognized a new reality: the value of singles. For years the record industry had been thinking of music in terms of albums that typically included 12 to 20 songs. Too, many artists regarded their work not as songs but coherent bodies of music packaged in albums. People bought the packages for songs they wanted because there was no choice. Clunkers were part of the deal. With Napster, people began thinking in terms of personal playlists and mixes that they could configure to suit their individual tastes. The big record companies were still trying to peddle albums, but not Jobs. About Jobs' iPod and iTunes, rap producer Dr. Dre said: "Somebody finally got it right."

11   Almost immediately, the major record companies, realizing all their own failures, signed on with iTunes to sell their music. Predictably, imitators sprouted within months using the iTunes model, but they were **Johnny-come-latelies.**

EXERCISE 5-19   Context Clues and Word Parts

Directions: Choose the word or phrase from the list that best fits into each of the following sentences. If you are unsure of the meaning of a word, use your knowledge of context clues and word parts to figure out its meaning as it is used in the sample passage. Consult a dictionary if necessary.

dwindled (para. 1)	**tackle** (para. 5)	**doomsayers** (para. 7)
bona fide (para. 2)	**crack down** (para. 6)	**juicing** (para. 8)
slippage (para. 3)	**entice** (para. 6)	**viruses** (para. 9)
downloading (para. 4)		

1. _____ predicted that nuclear weapons would end the human race.

2. The jeweler examined the stone and agreed it was a _____ diamond, not a fake.

3. There are a variety of computer programs available to detect _____ that can damage files.

4. The investor sold the stock at a loss after six months of _____ in value.

5. The essay portion of the exam was going to be difficult to _____, but practice and lots of study made it easier than expected.

6. The supply of paint _____ until there was almost none left.

7. The constant text messaging ended up _____ the cell phone bill up $200 more than usual.

8. The confusing voicemail system made it difficult to _____ the person who could help me fix the problem with my account.

9. Samples of food were distributed to passing pedestrians in the hope that it would _____ them to try the new restaurant.

10. She opened the e-mail and clicked on the attachment to begin _____ the photos.

Directions: The following questions test your knowledge of the meaning of words or phrases used in the selection. Write the letters of the correct answers on the lines provided.

———   1. The word **avant-garde** (para. 1) means

    a. unskilled

    b. innovative

    c. orchestral

    d. inexpensive

———   2. **Hip-hop** (para. 2), as used in this selection, is a newly coined word that describes

    a. a style of dance

    b. a type of music

    c. a style of dress

    d. a type of language

———   3. The phrase **derivative artists** (para. 2) is a euphemism for

    a. pirated recordings

    b. digital music

    c. karaoke sessions

    d. musicians who sound like other artists

———   4. The phrase **cultural stagnation that comes from homogenization** (para. 2) is doublespeak for

    a. the lack of anything new in music

    b. the prevalence of black artists in some types of music

    c. too much remixing of music

    d. decreases in popularity of CDs

———   5. A **goose** (para. 3) may be a bird with a long neck, but in this selection the author uses this word as a verb meaning to

    a. chase unsuccessfully

    b. frighten easily

    c. increase in a sudden way

    d. cook slowly or roast

———   6. The word **flailed** (para. 4) has the connotation of

    a. anger

    b. panic

    c. excitement

    d. anticipation

———   7. The word **nemesis** (para. 4) is used instead of a word like "enemy" to connote

    a. admiration

    b. deep hatred

    c. unexpected sympathy

    d. jealousy

———   8. The word **toast** (para. 5) is used figuratively to mean

    a. totally brown

    b. entirely used up

    c. completely ruined

    d. mostly unimportant

———   9. An **iPod** (para. 8) is a word that refers to

    a. a portable player for downloaded music

    b. a subscription charge

    c. offshore music servers

    d. an online music service

———   10. The author uses the idiom **Johnny-come-latelies** (para. 11) to refer to

    a. artists who model their music on that of other artists

    b. people who illegally download music

    c. artists who are still releasing albums

    d. companies that weren't fast enough to come up with an iTunes-like success

PART two Discipline-Specific Vocabulary

Most academic disciplines have their own language—a set of specialized words and phrases that have very specific meanings within the field. The following chapters, arranged by academic discipline, will familiarize you with some of the key terminology used in college courses. You will also find these words helpful in everyday life and in the workplace. Here is a list of the disciplines included in this part, along with page references.

6

Computers and
Information Systems

Learning Core Terms

The following list is representative of the terminology you will be expected to learn in the computer and information systems fields.

1. **cookie** An entry or a file placed on the user's hard drive that stores user profiles. It is often used to personalize a Web site for a frequent visitor.

2. **cyberspace** The Internet and other networks, and the virtual communities they form.

3. **download** To receive and transfer a file electronically from a remote computer.

4. **emoticons (smileys)** Small graphic images produced using keyboard characters that writers substitute for facial expressions. For example, a "smile" is indicated by a colon and a right parenthesis.

5. **GUI (graphical user interface)** An interface that represents programs, files, and options as graphical images instead of text.

6. **hacker** A highly skilled computer user who accesses computer files and systems illegally or without authorization.

7. **homepage** A Web page that functions as an introduction or front door entrance to a Web site.

8. **links (hyperlinks)** A text or image that connects the user to other pages or to other Web sites.

9. **listserv** An ongoing discussion group on a particular topic or issue in which participants subscribe through a central service. Listservs may have a moderator who manages information flow and content.

10. **MIME (Multipurpose Internet Mail Extensions) attachment** A file that is attached to an e-mail message.

11. **multimedia** Software that combines words, graphics, sound, and video.

12. **netiquette** The appropriate behavior expected on the Internet; a combination of the words *Net* (from Internet) and *etiquette*.

13. **network** A computer system that uses communication equipment to connect two or more computers.

14. **RAM (random access memory)** and **ROM (read-only memory)** RAM is the computer's electronic memory; it contains data that can be entered into a computer file. ROM is the computer's preprogrammed memory; it can be read but not altered.

15. **search engine** A research tool that allows users to enter keywords to search the Internet for information.

16. **upload** To send a file or application from a local computer to another computer over the Internet.

17. **URL (Uniform Resource Locator)** A string of characters that serves as an address for a file or site on the World Wide Web.

18. **virtual reality (VR)** A system that uses three-dimensional graphics to create an imaginary place that seems very realistic.

19. **virus** An unauthorized program that attaches itself to other computer programs and, after reproducing itself, causes damage or destroys data in those programs.

20. **World Wide Web (WWW)** Part of the Internet containing documents and images connected by hyperlinks.

Note: If you are unfamiliar with computers, be sure to learn the following terms as well: *cursor, data, CD-ROM, mouse, modem, terminal, monitor, hardware, software, CPU, Internet, e-mail.*

Learn More about Computer–Related Terminology by Visiting the Following Web Site

http://foldoc.org/

Defining Computer and Information Systems
Vocabulary I

Directions: Choose the definitions in column B that best match each word or phrase in column A.
Write your answers in the spaces provided.

Column A	Column B
1. _d_ listserv	a. The Internet and other networks, and the virtual communities they form
2. _f_ homepage	b. A computer system that uses communication equipment to connect two or more computers
3. _e_ download	c. A computer's electronic preprogrammed memory
4. _h_ MIME attachment	d. An ongoing discussion group on a particular topic or issue
5. _b_ network	e. To receive information from another computer
6. _c_ ROM	f. A Web page that introduces a Web site
7. _j_ virus	g. A research tool that uses keywords to search for information
8. _g_ search engine	h. A file attached to an e-mail message
9. _i_ links	i. Text or an image that leads to other pages or sites
10. _a_ cyberspace	j. A program that damages or destroys data

EXERCISE 6-2   Using Computer and Information Systems Vocabulary

Directions: Supply the words from the list at the beginning of the chapter that complete the
meanings of each sentence.

1. Because data was missing from her computer, Kyoka wondered if a ___virus___ had
   invaded her system.

2. The instructor warned her students to use appropriate _____ when online during
   class time.

3. The company is trying to find the ___hacker___ who illegally accessed credit card numbers
   from its computer files.

4. Abbey realized her computer did not have enough ___Rom___ when she tried to install
   her new software program.

5. Because his business was expanding, Jeff decided to use a ___network___ to connect all the
   computers in the office.

6. Eva found a ___mime___ attached to one of her e-mail messages.

7. The professor told her students they could ___download___ files from the library Web site.

8. Jeff went to the university's _____ to find the academic department's listing.

9. The museum's Web site has many ____links____ connecting to all its art galleries and to other museum sites.

10. Because her keywords were not getting enough results, Judith decided to try another ____search engine____

Defining Computer and Information Systems Vocabulary II

Directions: Choose the definition in column B that best matches each word or phrase in column A. Write your answer in the space provided.

Column A	Column B
1. _____ virtual reality	a. A text or image that connects to other pages or Web sites
2. _____ multimedia	b. To send information from one's own computer to another
3. _____ World Wide Web	c. A part of the Internet containing documents and images connected with links
4. _j_ netiquette	d. A system that uses three-dimensional images to create an imaginary place
5. _a_ links	e. Graphic images that substitute for facial expressions
6. _____ cookie	f. A file that stores data about a computer user's visits to Web sites
7. _h_ hacker	g. Software that combines words, graphics, sound, and video
8. _____ URL	h. A computer user who accesses files without authorization
9. _e_ emoticons	i. An address for a file or site on the Web
10. _____ upload	j. Appropriate behavior expected on the Internet

Applying Your Skills in Computers and Information Systems

This passage is taken from *Tomorrow's Technology and You* by George Beekman and Michael J. Quinn. Read the selection to learn about how Google came about. Then practice the skills you have learned in Part I of this text by answering the questions that follow.

The Google Guys Search for Success

1   Google is one of the most successful companies to **spring** from the World Wide Web. The Google search engine, which helps people find relevant Web pages, handles hundreds of millions of **queries** a day, making it the most popular search engine in the English-speaking world. To many Web users, the term "google" is **synonymous** with "search" (as in, "Have you **googled** yourself lately?"). People routinely use Google to find facts, track down quotes, locate other people, and even do background checks on blind dates.

2   This amazing venture was launched by two **entrepreneurs** from opposite sides of the globe. Sergey Brin was born in Moscow in the former Soviet Union. Larry Page is the son of a computer science professor at Michigan State University. The two met while they were computer science Ph.D. students at Stanford University.

3   Soon after enrolling at Stanford, Page talked with his **advisor**, Professor Terry Winograd, about ways to improve Web search engines. Early Web search engines determined the extent to which a Web page related to a key word or phrase by counting how many times that word or phrase appeared in the page. **Low-quality** sites could fool these search engines by repeating a particular phrase hundreds of times. Winograd and Page had the idea of determining a Web page's **relevance** by counting the number of times *other* related Web pages linked to it.

4   Page teamed up with Brin and began writing the software to **implement** a new kind of search engine. They called it BackRub, since the reputation of one site depends on links to it from other sites. BackRub essentially **tallied** "votes" from all over the Web to determine a site's worthiness.

5   Page borrowed money and built a Web server hosting BackRub in his dorm room; Brin's dorm room became the business office. In 1998 twenty-six-year-old Page and twenty-five-year-old Brin raised $1 million and officially launched their company, **renamed** Google. (The name Google is a play on the huge number *googol*—a 1 followed by 100 zeroes.) At first, the **start-up** operated out of a garage, but in just a few months, it outgrew its **humble** quarters. Today, Google has thousands of employees around the globe.

6   In 2004 Google offered shares to the public, making Brin and Page instant billionaires. Google's management defied **convention** by establishing procedures to ensure the company could stay focused on long-term **strategic** investments rather

than short-term profits. In their letter to potential investors, Brin and Page wrote, "Google is not a conventional company. We do not intend to become one."

7   Today Google is one of the fastest-growing Web companies. In addition to basic information search tools, Google offers image searches, book content searches, comparison shopping, mapping, e-mail, and more. In every **venture**, Google tries to honor its do-no-evil mission statement.

8   But Google's phenomenal growth has occasionally challenged that mission. For example, in 2005 Google, like many other companies, agreed to allow the Chinese government to **censor** certain searches made by Chinese citizens. Company officials decided that it was better to have a restricted presence in the most **populous** country in the world than to not be there at all.

9   In spite of occasional **growing pains**, the company continues to soar. By combining **database** technology with a seemingly **endless** supply of creative ideas. Google has become one of the most important shapers of the Web.

EXERCISE 6-4   Context Clues and Word Parts

Directions: Listed below are ten words boldfaced in the selection. Use your knowledge of context clues and word parts to work out their meanings as they are used in the passage and write them below. Then, for each word, write a sentence that contains the word and uses it to mean the same as it means in the passage. Consult a dictionary if necessary.

example   Endless (para. 9) without limit; The amount of work the students had to do before the end of the semester felt endless

1. queries (para. 1) _____

_____

2. entrepreneurs (para. 2) _____

_____

3. advisor (para. 3) _____

_____

4. low-quality (para. 3) _____

_____

5. implement (para. 4) _____

_____

6. renamed (para. 5) _____

_____

7. humble (para. 5) _____

_____

8. convention (para. 6) _____

_____

9. strategic (para. 6) _____

_____

10. venture (para. 7) _____

_____

EXERCISE 6-5   **Using Your Vocabulary Skills**

Directions: The following questions are about the words or phrases boldfaced in the passage. Write the letter of the correct answer in the space provided.

_____d_____ 1. The author uses the word **spring** (para. 1) instead of a word such as *develop* to connote a sense of

    a. relevancy and accuracy   c. carefulness and planning

    b. riskiness and danger   d. energy and freshness

_____ 2. If a synonym can be used in place of another word without a change in meaning, then **synonymous** (para. 1) means

    a. similar to   c. hard to understand

    b. descriptive   d. routinely

_____c_____ 3. The newly coined word **googled** (para. 1) means

    a. counted something   c. did a search for

    b. looked for   d. sorted

_____d_____ 4. If the word *relevant* means being connected to the subject at hand, then the word **relevance** (para. 3) means

    a. likelihood of finding   c. number of times an item is repeated

    b. similarity to something else   d. importance in relation to other sites

_____b_____ 5. Complete this analogy:
tallied (para. 4): votes :: _____ : money

    a. spent   c. elected

    b. counted   d. sorted

_____d_____ 6. Google is referred to as a **start-up** (para. 5). This means that it is

    a. an Internet business   c. an unsuccessful venture

    b. a get-rich-quick scheme   d. a recently formed company

_____c_____ 7. To **censor** (para. 8) an online search is to

    a. read it carefully   c. not permit it to be done

    b. expand on it   d. move it to a different search engine

_____a_____ 8. The root *pop* refers to people, so the most **populous** country (para. 8) is the one

    a. that has the greatest number of citizens

    b. the most people would prefer to live in

    c. that exercises the greatest control over its residents

    d. that is most often considered Communist

_____ a_ 9. The figurative phrase **growing pains** (para. 9) is used to indicate

    a. the difficulties experienced when a young company expands quickly

    b. the high costs of starting a new company from the ground up

    c. immediate commercial success

    d. technological advances

_____ b_ 10. The compound word **database** (para. 9) means

    a. an endless amount of facts   c. numerical statistics

    b. a collection of information   d. Web site components

7

Law and Criminal Justice

Learning Core Terms

The following list is representative of the terminology you will be expected to learn in the fields of law and criminal justice.

1. **affidavit** A voluntary written statement sworn to before an authorized official.

2. **arraignment** An appearance in court prior to a criminal trial. Often the identity of the defendant is established, the defendant is informed of the charges and of his or her rights, and the defendant is required to enter a plea.

3. **defendant** A person accused of a crime against whom legal action is brought.

4. **deposition** A statement made under oath outside of court that is intended to be used as evidence in court.

5. **entrapment** Improper or illegal encouragement by law enforcement agents for a person to commit a crime.

6. **fraud** Intentional deception in order to secure unfair or unlawful gain.

7. **hearsay** Something not based on the personal observations of a witness; it is not usually allowed to be entered as evidence.

8. **indictment** A formal written accusation, submitted to the court by a grand jury, alleging that a certain person has committed a serious crime.

9. **infringement** A violation of a right, law, or contract; wrongful use of a copyright or trade name.

10. **injunction** A court order prohibiting a person from doing a specific act.

11. **jurisdiction** The territory, subject matter, or people over which a court has authority.

12. **lien** The right to take, hold, or sell the property of a debtor as security or payment for a debt.

13. **litigation** Legal proceedings.

14. **misdemeanor** A criminal offense lesser than a felony usually punishable by a fine or by imprisonment other than in a penitentiary.

15. **plaintiff** A person who initiates or begins a legal action.

16. **plea bargain** To plead guilty to a lesser charge than that of which one is accused; often used in exchange for information or cooperation as a witness by the accused.

17. **proxy** A document in which one person is legally appointed to represent another.

18. **statute** A law enacted by a legislative body.

19. **tort** Damage, injury, or wrongful act done willingly against a person or property for which a civil suit can be brought.

20. **venue** The place where a crime is committed. Also, the geographical area in which a court may hear or try a case.

Learn More about Legal Terminology by Visiting the Following Web Site

http://jurist.law.pitt.edu/dictionary.htm

EXERCISE 7-1   Using Law and Criminal Justice Terminology I

Directions: Supply the words from the list at the beginning of the chapter that complete the meanings of each sentence.

1. When a police officer improperly encourages a citizen to commit a crime, the officer is guilty of ___entrapment___ .

2. The abused wife sought an ___injunction___ to prevent her ex-husband from entering her home.

3. In a trial, the ___plaintiff___ is the person who initiates the legal action.

4. A statement made under oath outside of court that is intended to be used as evidence in court is called a ___deposition___ .

5. Mr. Hargrave signed an _____affidavit_____ before a notary stating that he had no knowledge of his son's criminal activities.

6. If you copy several pages of a book and do not give the author credit for the work, you are guilty of copyright _____infringement_____.

7. When Harrison took out a car loan, the finance company placed a _____lien_____ against the car's title.

8. At his _____plea bargain_____, Jay, who was accused of car theft, pleaded not guilty.

9. A _____ is less serious than a felony and is punishable by fine or imprisonment.

10. The president of the corporation was shocked when she received the news of her _____proxy_____ for theft of corporate funds.

EXERCISE 7-2 Defining Law and Criminal Justice Vocabulary

Directions: Choose the definitions in column B that best match the words or phrases in column A. Write your answers in the spaces provided.

Column A	Column B
1. __F__ fraud	a. Something not based on personal observation
2. __e__ statute	b. Legal proceedings
3. __j__ plea bargain	c. A voluntary written statement sworn before an authorized official
4. __h__ defendant	d. A relatively minor criminal offense
5. __i__ venue	e. A law enacted by a legislative body
6. __d__ misdemeanor	f. Intentional deception
7. __c__ affidavit	g. Statement made under oath
8. __a__ hearsay	h. Person accused of a crime
9. __b__ litigation	i. Place where a crime is committed
10. __g__ deposition	j. To plead guilty to a lesser charge

EXERCISE 7-3 Using Law and Criminal Justice Vocabulary II

Directions: Use words from the list at the beginning of this chapter to complete each sentence.

1. In a court case, a person accused of a crime is called the _____defendant_____.

2. In a courtroom, when a witness reports something he or she has not directly experienced, the testimony is known as _____hearsay_____.

3. _____ for consumer fraud cases is expected to take two years.

4. A health care ____proxy____ allows a person to make medical decisions for another person who is unable to do so.

5. A _____ refers to a damage or injury for which a civil suit can be brought.

6. A person who deliberately does not report income on his or her federal tax statement is guilty of ____fraud____.

7. The man accused of first degree murder agreed to accept a __plea bargain__ that reduced the charge to accidental homicide.

8. The defense attorney requested a change of ____venue____; he hoped to move the trial to a district with stronger ethnic representation.

9. The state legislature passed a _____ making smoking illegal in public buildings.

10. The judge refused to hear the case because it was out of her _____.

This passage is taken from *Criminal Justice Today* by Frank Schmalleger. Read the selection to learn about factors that influence people's choices about eating. Then practice the skills you have learned in Part I of this text by answering the questions that follow.

As Shocks Replace Bullets, Questions Arise

1   The police in Seattle have had their share of high-profile violent or deadly run-ins with protesters, mentally ill suspects, and other lawbreakers. But in 2003, for the first time in 15 years, no one here was shot and killed by the police.

2   Miami, a city with a long history of police shootings and ensuing civil **unrest**, had no police shootings last year, fatal or otherwise, for the first time in 14 years. In Phoenix, where such shootings reached a level over the last several years that far **outpaced** the rate of much larger cities, deadly police shootings fell sharply in 2003, to their lowest rate in 14 years.

3   In these cities and in a fast-growing number of the nation's police departments, officers are carrying a **slick** new weapon, the Taser gun, which looks a lot like a pistol but does not shoot to kill.

4   Though officials say the Taser gun, which fires a stunning jolt of electricity, is not solely responsible for a decline in police killings, many departments say it has made a huge difference. Its supporters say the Taser is saving lives, protecting officers and suspects in standoffs that might otherwise have left someone dead or seriously injured.

5   "This is 100 percent more **humane**" said Officer Tom Burns, who has carried a Taser gun for the past two and a half years on bicycle patrol in Seattle.

6   But as the Taser spreads rapidly, it is raising questions about whether the weapon, which can also be applied directly to the skin as a stun gun, could be abused by the police. The Taser **zaps** suspects with 50,000 volts of electricity, disabling them for five seconds at a time. Critics say the weapon is **ripe** for abuse because the shock leaves no obvious mark, other than what looks like a small bee sting. Human rights groups in the United States and abroad have called Tasers potential instruments of torture.

7   They are now being used by more than 4,000 police departments. Roughly 170 new departments are buying the high-tech electro-shock guns every month, and the Army has begun using them in Iraq, according to Taser International, the Arizona company that makes them. More than one-third of Seattle's 600 patrol officers carry Tasers. In Miami, Phoenix and a growing number of cities, every officer has one.

8   Tasers have often been introduced in the wake of public outcry over deadly police shootings. That was the case in Seattle, Denver, Austin, Tex., and Portland, Ore., as part of an effort to reduce killings through the use of training programs and "less lethal" weapons.

9   "You have to think about the alternatives," said Officer Burns, who also carries pepper spray and a .40-caliber Glock pistol. He said he had used the Taser five times on suspects who seemed eager to attack or were difficult to control. "And without this technology you might have to break it down to very brutal methods."

10   Officer Burns was on the scene in 1999 when Seattle police shot and killed a mentally ill man, a widely **publicized** incident that led to soul-searching in the department and a plan that among other things involved the purchase of Tasers.

11   The newest Tasers are an advanced version of technology that was developed in the 1970's but was not considered by the police to be effective until recently. The electrical pulses travel from the gun through two 21-foot-long wires that look like a stretched-out Slinky tipped with barbed probes. If the probes pierce skin or a layer of clothing two inches thick or less, the jolt contracts the muscles and throws the suspect off balance. It makes the suspect unable to move and gives the police a full five seconds with every **tasing** to handcuff the suspect. The police say that 50,000 volts is a safe amount of electricity to absorb and that suspects shot with a Taser recover immediately.

A promotional photo showing the effects of Taser International's Advanced Taser®. This less lethal weapon, intended for use in law enforcement and private security, incapacitates potential attackers by delivering an electrical shock to the person's nervous system. The technology is intended to reduce injury rates to both suspects and officers.

12   But critics and watchdog groups say the Taser could be used to torture suspects and prison inmates to **extract** confessions or taunt them, and Amnesty International has called for a ban on their use pending studies on their long-term effects. Human rights and civil liberties groups are also questioning whether the electro-shocks that Tasers deliver are potentially deadly.

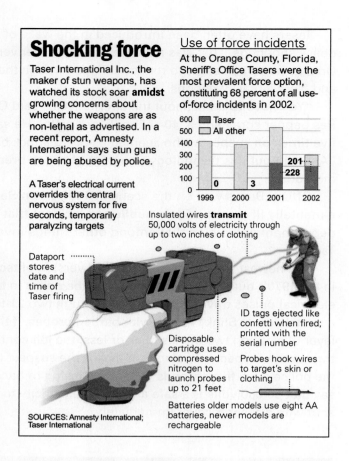

Shocking force

Taser International Inc., the maker of stun weapons, has watched its stock soar **amidst** growing concerns about whether the weapons are as non-lethal as advertised. In a recent report, Amnesty International says stun guns are being abused by police.

A Taser's electrical current overrides the central nervous system for five seconds, temporarily paralyzing targets

Use of force incidents

At the Orange County, Florida, Sheriff's Office Tasers were the most prevalent force option, constituting 68 percent of all use-of-force incidents in 2002.

Insulated wires **transmit** 50,000 volts of electricity through up to two inches of clothing

Dataport stores date and time of Taser firing

ID tags ejected like confetti when fired; printed with the serial number

Disposable cartridge uses compressed nitrogen to launch probes up to 21 feet

Probes hook wires to target's skin or clothing

Batteries older models use eight AA batteries, newer models are rechargeable

SOURCES: Amnesty International; Taser International

13   "Surely it's better than being killed," said Dan Handelman, a founder of Portland Copwatch, a group that has been critical of that city's growing use of Tasers over the last year. "But it's not necessarily an acceptable replacement because it's not being used—at least in Portland—in place of lethal force; it's being used for **compliance**."

14   Across the country in recent months, several suspects who were shot with Tasers, sometimes repeatedly, have died. But officials said other health problems, like heart conditions and drug overdoses, were the cause.

15   The American Civil Liberties Union of Colorado urged the Denver Police Department two weeks ago to limit its use of Tasers. The group cited a rising number of deaths nationally, saying 16 suspects in custody had died after being subdued with Tasers or stun guns in 2003, up from 10 in 2002 and 3 in 2001. But none of the deaths were officially **attributed** to the effect of the weapons.

16   In Las Vegas, William Lomax, 26, died last month after being arrested and, according to witnesses and the police, shot with a Taser four or five times, which critics of the Police Department said was an excessive use of force. Investigators said that Mr. Lomax had been under the influence of drugs, but that the cause of death was still under investigation.

17   Marsha Bell, 22, said she saw Mr. Lomax, her cousin, arrested on February 21 at her apartment complex, where he often visited his family. After he had a run-in with security guards, the police were called.

18   "He was on the ground," Ms. Bell said in a telephone interview: "He had two pairs of handcuffs on him, and I didn't know the Taser was being used until I heard him screaming. He kept screaming and screaming, saying, 'Oh God, Jesus, please no.' He was screaming in pain; he was hurt and he didn't resist."

19   Lt. Tom Monahan of the Las Vegas Metropolitan Police Department, which bought several hundred Tasers last year, said that Mr. Lomax had struggled with officers, security guards and paramedics, and that the Taser was used while officers were trying to handcuff him.

20   Officer Thomas Miller, who conducts Taser training for the Las Vegas department, said that there were clear guidelines on when Tasers should be used.

21   "In the past, an officer would have to fight," Officer Miller said. "Now we have an option to stop that before it gets to that point, greatly reducing the risk to the officer and the suspect."

22   The police do say that a Taser would never replace lethal weapons if an officer felt his life was in **imminent** danger, like when a suspect is wielding a knife or a gun at close **proximity** or when no other officer is available to provide "**lethal cover**" for an officer using the Taser. Most departments allow officers on the scene to make that judgment call.

23   In the New York City Police Department, supervisors and members of the large Emergency Service Unit, which helps patrol officers in violent situations, carry Tasers, but patrol officers do not, the police said.

24   The newest models cost $799 each, according to Taser International, the leading producer of the weapons. But company officials, who have seen their stock **skyrocket** over the last year, say the savings to police departments that might otherwise be sued over violent confrontations or shootings are potentially huge.

25   The police and other supporters of the new technology also say there are built-in **safeguards** to prevent abuse of the guns. Each Taser, which is powered by batteries, has a data port that records each shock and is used by police departments when they prepare incident reports, allowing supervisors to count how many times a Taser was fired.

26   Steve Tuttle, a spokesman for Taser International, which is based in Scottsdale, Ariz., said the company continually reviewed data and had found few instances among about 70,000 episodes so far of abuse or inappropriate use.

27   "If there's a **bad apple** out there, the technology we made will catch that bad apple," Mr. Tuttle said. "We've won the lottery in terms of great success, stock market-wise, but with that comes much more scrutiny."

28   Officer Burns of the Seattle department said the police could not deny that a misguided officer could abuse any weapon. But he said that there had been numerous instances in Seattle where officers had used the Taser instead of fists, nightsticks, guns or pepper spray, which can have much longer effects than Taser shocks, and that suspects had recovered immediately.

29   "Shooting someone is not a **badge of honor**," Officer Burns said. "It's something no one wants to do. No police officer in the world is paid to die; no police officer in the world is paid to get hurt."

EXERCISE 7-4   Context Clues and Word Parts

Directions: Use your knowledge of context clues to figure out the meaning of each of the following words as they are used in the passage. Then create a context clue of your own for each word, which conveys the same meaning the word has in the selection. If you cannot work out the meaning of the word from the reading, consult a dictionary.

1. The government's decision to go to war led to **unrest** (para. 2), as seen when people

   _____ .

2. The programmer used a **slick** (para. 3) new program to create the Web site—one that was

   _____ .

3. Because electrocution was painful, some states began executing prisoners in more **humane** (para. 5) or _____ ways.

4. Mount Vesuvius is a volcano that has erupted **amidst** (box) the cities that surround it, in contrast to other volcanoes, particularly undersea ones, which erupt _____

   _____ .

5. Marconi used the telegraph to **transmit** a message across the ocean, becoming the first person to _____ a transoceanic telegram.

6. The anthropologist began to **extract** (para. 12) the pottery shard from the sandstone, carefully

   _____ .

7. As the clouds darkened and the wind picked up, it was clear that the tornado was **imminent** (para. 22) and likely to happen _____ .

8. The soldier ran out into the open to rescue the woman while his partner provided **lethal cover** (para. 22) by _____ .

9. The recession caused retail prices to **skyrocket** (para. 24), meaning they _____

   _____ .

10. The _____ are all examples of the **safeguards** (para. 25) in place in the chemistry lab.

EXERCISE 7-5   Using Your Vocabulary Skills

Directions: The following questions are about the words or phrases boldfaced in the passage. Write the letters of the correct answers on the lines provided.

_____ 1. The compound word **outpaced** (para. 2) means
   a. grew more quickly than   c. lagged behind
   b. was impossible to track   d. became much more dangerous

_____ 2. Instead of using a word such as *shoots*, the author uses **zaps** (para. 6) to connote
   a. the close angle of the shot   c. the decreased danger of the gun
   b. how similar the gun is to a   d. the sense of an electric shock
      computer game

3. The definition of the word **ripe** (para. 6), as it is used in the passage, is
   a. fully grown
   b. having mature knowledge of
   c. smelly or stinking
   d. open to

4. If the word *public* means "open to all people," then **publicized** (para. 10) means
   a. shown on television
   b. widely shared with many
   c. carefully controlled
   d. known to everyone

5. The author uses the word **tasing** (para. 11) to mean
   a. teasing incessantly
   b. immobilizing completely
   c. shooting with a Taser
   d. shocking news

6. If the word *comply* means "to obey," then **compliance**, as used in paragraph 13, refers to
   a. enforced obedience
   b. nonlethal acts
   c. illegal use of a weapon
   d. obedient distribution

7. **Attributed** (para. 15) means
   a. formally numbered
   b. predicted to be caused by
   c. considered to be caused by
   d. made symbolic of

8. A synonym for the word **proximity** (para. 22) is
   a. wielding
   b. imminent
   c. gun
   d. close

9. The phrase **bad apple** (para. 27) is used in this passage to refer to someone who
   a. is afraid of guns
   b. uses a weapon inappropriately
   c. steals police weapons
   d. acts wrongly

10. A **badge of honor** (para. 29) is figurative language for
    a. something to be proud of
    b. an official reprimand
    c. an award of money
    d. an honest mistake

8

Allied Health and Medicine

Learning Core Terms

The following list is representative of the terminology you will be expected to learn in the fields of allied health and medicine.

1. **acute** Sudden and requiring immediate treatment, as in *acute appendicitis*.

2. **asymptomatic** Without symptoms.

3. **benign** Nonthreatening, noncancerous, as in a *benign tumor*.

4. **biopsy** The removal of tissue for the purpose of determining the presence of cancerous cells.

5. **contraindications** Conditions suggesting that a drug should not be used.

6. **health care proxy** A legal document that designates another person who can make medical decisions for a person who is unable to direct his or her own care.

7. **holistic** Viewing the body as a whole organism.

8. **HMO (health maintenance organization)** An organization established to provide health care to its members at a fixed price.

9. **idiosyncratic** Unusual or abnormal, as in an *idiosyncratic response* to a drug or food by an individual.

10. **inoculation** The injection or transfer of a substance into the body.

11. **intravenous** Inserting a medication or fluid into the vein using a needle or tube.

12. **living will** A document that specifies the type of care a person does and does not want to receive when his or her death is likely.

13. **malignant** Cancerous.

14. **malpractice** Professional negligence.

15. **noninvasive procedures** Tests or treatments in which the skin and body are not entered.

16. **nurse practitioner (NP)** A registered nurse who has received additional training in an area of specialty, such as obstetrics.

17. **outpatient** Medical treatment that does not require overnight hospital care.

18. **predisposition** The tendency or susceptibility to develop a certain disease or condition.

19. **prognosis** Prediction of the course and outcome of a disease or illness.

20. **rehabilitation** The process of assisting patients to regain a state of health.

Learn More about Health-Related Terminology by Visiting the Following Web Site

http://www.mlanet.org/resources/medspeak/index.html

EXERCISE 8-1 Using Allied Health and Medicine Vocabulary I

Directions: Use the words from the list at the beginning of the chapter that complete the meanings of each sentence.

1. The physician advises all of her elderly patients to prepare a _____ that specifies their wishes for medical care.

2. Arturo had _____ appendicitis; he was rushed into surgery.

3. The _____ of the tumor on Martha's knee indicated it was not malignant.

4. Because my doctor was unavailable for an immediate appointment, I was given an appointment with the _____ .

5. A _____ allows you to name the person who will make medical decisions for you if you are unable to do so.

6. _____ medicine considers the body as a whole, complete organism.

7. The doctor who operated on his patient's wrong knee was charged with _____ .

8. The antibiotic was administered using an _____ needle.

9. The doctor told the patient that his low white blood cell count was _____; there were no visible symptoms.

10. Due to the history of heart attacks in his family, Jonathan has a _____ toward heart disease.

EXERCISE 8-2   Defining Health/Medicine Vocabulary

Directions: Write the letter of the correct answer in the space provided.

_____ 1. **Acute** refers to

        a. pain in the joints   c. muscle spasms

        b. a sudden injury or illness   d. a type of cancer

_____ 2. A **living will** specifies

        a. when a person is declared legally deceased

        b. who can be named in a person's will

        c. the type of care a person wants when his or her death is likely

        d. the wishes of a diseased person

_____ 3. **Prognosis** refers to

        a. prediction of the course or outcome of a disease or illness

        b. the type of treatment needed

        c. a medical chart used in hospitals for tracking medications

        d. any procedure using a needle

_____ 4. **Asymptomatic** refers to a patient

        a. with symptoms that come and go   c. in a lot of pain

        b. with only minor pain   d. with no symptoms

_____ 5. **Malignant** means

        a. cankerous   c. noncancerous

        b. cancerous   d. dyspeptic

_____ 6. A person who receives **outpatient** treatment

        a. receives treatment at home   c. receives treatment at a hospice

        b. requires follow-up care after surgery   d. does not stay overnight in a hospital

_____ 7. **Contraindications** are conditions that suggest

        a. a disease is spreading   c. the patient refuses medication

        b. a drug should not be used   d. the wishes of a diseased person

_____ 8. **Biopsy** refers to the removal of tissue

        a. in the lungs   c. for determining cancer

        b. for transplant to a recipient   d. to use for vaccine therapy

———— 9. A **nurse practitioner** is a nurse who

    a. has received additional training

    b. is only licensed to work in a hospital

    c. does not have a real nursing degree

    d. is studying to become a midwife

———— 10. **Benign** means

    a. cell growth

    b. tumor

    c. noncancerous

    d. abnormal

EXERCISE 8-3   Using Allied Health and Medicine Vocabulary II

Directions: Use words from the list at the beginning of this chapter that complete the meanings of each sentence.

1. Judith was relieved when she learned the tumor on her wrist was _____.

2. Many companies provide health care insurance to their employees by enrolling them in an _____.

3. My mother's cataract surgery was performed at an _____ surgery center.

4. After surgery, the doctor announced the cancer patient's _____ was good.

5. The patient's response to the chemotherapy was _____; she experienced none of the usual symptoms.

6. After knee replacement surgery, my father needed several weeks of _____.

7. The doctor regretfully told his patient that the tumor was _____ and that surgery would be necessary.

8. Vision and hearing tests are _____ procedures.

9. The label on the prescription listed its _____.

10. Everyone exposed to hepatitis should receive an _____.

The following excerpt is taken from *Nutrition: An Applied Approach* by Janice Thompson and Melinda Manore. Read the selection to learn about factors that influence people's choices about eating. Then practice the skills you have learned in Part I of this text by answering the questions that follow.

Why Do We Want to Eat?

1   Food provides us with energy, and the heat our body generates from this energy helps keep our bodies at the temperature required to maintain the proper chemical functions needed for life. Food gives us the **molecular** building blocks we need to manufacture new tissues for growth and repair, thereby keeping us healthy. Considering the importance of food, it makes sense that our bodies would employ a variety of mechanisms to make us want to eat.

Food Stimulates Our Senses

2   You've just finished eating at your favorite Thai restaurant. As you walk back to the block where you parked your car, you pass a bakery window displaying several cakes and pies, each of which looks more enticing than the last, and through the door **wafts** a complex aroma of coffee, cinnamon, and chocolate. You stop. Are you hungry? You must be, because you go inside and buy a slice of chocolate torte and an espresso. Later that night, when the caffeine from the chocolate and espresso keep you awake, you wonder why you succumbed.

3   The answer is that food stimulates our senses. Foods that are artfully prepared, arranged, or ornamented with several different shapes and colors, appeal to our sense of sight. Advertisers know this and spend millions of dollars annually in the United States to promote and package foods in an appealing way. The aromas of foods like freshly brewed coffee and baked goods can also be powerful **stimulants**. Much of our ability to taste foods actually comes from our sense of smell. This is why foods are not as appealing when we are sick with a cold. Interestingly, our sense of smell is so **acute** that newborn babies can distinguish the scent of their own mother's breast milk from that of other mothers. Of all our senses, taste is the most important in determining what foods we choose to eat. Certain tastes, such as for sweet foods, are almost **universally** appealing, while others, such as the **astringent** taste of foods like spinach and kale, are quite individual. Texture is also important in food choices, as it stimulates nerve endings **sensitive** to touch in our mouth and on our tongue: do you prefer mashed potatoes, thick French fries, or rippled potato chips? Even your sense of hearing can be stimulated by foods, from the fizz of cola to the crunch of peanuts to the "snap, crackle, and pop" of Rice Krispies cereal.

Food stimulates our senses. Foods that are artfully arranged or ornamented, like the cakes and pies in this bakery display case, appeal to our sense of sight.

Psychosocial Factors Arouse Appetite

4   If it wasn't hunger that lured you into that bakery, it was probably appetite. Appetite is a **psychological** desire to consume specific foods. It is aroused by environmental cues—such as the sight of chocolate cake or the smell of coffee—and is not usually related to hunger. Appetite is generally related to pleasant sensations associated with food and is often linked to strong cravings for particular foods in the absence of hunger. Hunger is considered a more basic **physiologic sensation**, a drive that prompts us to find food and eat. Although we try to define appetite and hunger as two separate entities, many times they overlap, and symptoms of appetite and hunger are different for many people. Hunger is discussed in more detail in the following section.

5   In addition to environmental cues, our brain's association with certain events like birthday parties or holidays such as Thanksgiving can stimulate our appetite. At these times, society gives us permission to eat more than usual and/or to eat "forbidden" foods. For some people, being in a certain location can trigger appetite, such as at a baseball game or in a movie theater. Others may be triggered by the time of day or by an activity such as watching television or studying. Many people feel an increase in their appetite when they are under stress. Even when we feel full after a large meal, our appetite can **motivate** us to eat a delicious dessert.

6   If you are trying to lose weight or to maintain your present weight, it is important to stay aware, as you go through a day, of whether you are truly hungry or whether you simply have an appetite. If you decide it is your appetite, try to get away from the trigger. For instance, in the previous scenario, you could have simply walked away from the bakery. By the time you'd reached your car, you would probably have forgotten the sights and smells of the bakery and would be aware of how full you felt from your Thai meal. Remember that, because appetite is a psychological mechanism, you can train yourself to stop or ignore its cues when you want to avoid its consequences.

Various Factors Affect Hunger and Satiation

7   A number of factors influence whether we experience feelings of hunger on **satiation**. Signals from our brain, certain chemicals produced by our bodies, and even the amount and type of food we eat **interact** to cause us to feel hungry or full. Let's review these factors now.

Signals from the Brain Cause Hunger and Satiation

8   Because *hunger* is a physiologic sensation that prompts us to find food and eat, it is more often felt as a negative or unpleasant sensation in which the physical drive to eat is very strong. The signal arises from within us, rather than in response to environmental stimuli, and is not typically associated with a specific food. A broad variety of foods appeals to us when we are really hungry.

9   One of the major organs affecting our sensation of hunger is the brain. That's right—it's not our stomachs, but our brains that tell us when we're hungry. The region of brain tissue that is responsible for prompting us to seek food is called the **hypothalamus**. It triggers hunger by **integrating** signals from nerve cells throughout our bodies. One important signal comes from special cells lining the stomach and small intestine that perceive whether these organs are empty or distended by the presence of food. These cells sense changes in pressure and fullness in the stomach and small intestine and send signals to the hypothalamus. For instance, if you have not eaten for many hours and your stomach and small intestine do not contain food, signals are send to the hypothalamus indicating it is "time to eat," which causes you to experience the sensation of hunger.

10   Our blood glucose levels, which reflect our bodies' most readily-available fuel supply, is another primary signal affecting hunger. Falling blood glucose levels are accompanied by a change in insulin and glucagon levels. **Insulin** and glucagon are hormones produced in the pancreas and are responsible for maintaining blood glucose levels. These signals are relayed to the hypothalamus in the brain, where they trigger the sense that we need to eat in order to supply our bodies with more energy. Some people get irritable or feel a little faint when their blood glucose drops to a certain level. The level of blood glucose is related to when we last ate a meal, how active we are, and our individual metabolisms.

11   After we eat, the hypothalamus picks up the sensation of a distended stomach, other signals from the gut, and a rise in blood glucose levels. When it integrates these signals, you have the experience of feeling full, or *satiated*. However, as we saw in our previous scenario, even though our brain sends us clear signals about hunger, most of us become **adept** at ignoring them . . . and eat when we are not truly hungry.

Chemicals Called Hormones Affect Hunger and Satiation

12   A variety of hormones and hormone-like substances signal the hypothalamus to cause us to feel hungry or satiated. **Hormones** are chemical messengers that are secreted into the bloodstream by one of the many *glands* of the body. Hormones exert a regulatory effect on another organ. These glands release their secretions into the bloodstream in response to a signal. Examples of signals include falling or rising fuels within the blood, such as blood glucose, and chemical and nervous signals from the gut and the liver. The level of hormones in the blood then signal the hypothalamus to stimulate hunger or satiation. Examples of hormones and

hormone-like substances that stimulate food intake include neuropeptide Y and galanin, while those that create feelings of satiety include leptin, cholecystokinin, and serotonin (Bell and Rolls 2001).

The Amount and Type of Food We Eat Can Affect Hunger and Satiation

13 Foods containing protein have the highest satiety value (Bell and Rolls 2001). This means that a ham sandwich will cause us to feel satiated for a longer period of time than will a tossed salad and toast, even if both meals have exactly the same number of calories. High fat diets have a higher satiety value than high carbohydrate diets.

Another factor affecting hunger is how **bulky** the meal is—that is, how much fiber and water is within the food. Bulky meals tend to stretch the stomach and small intestine, which sends signals back to the hypothalamus telling us that we are full so we stop eating. Beverages tend to be less satisfying than **semisolid** foods, and semisolid foods have a lower satiety value than solid foods. For example, if you were to eat a bunch of grapes, you would feel a greater sense of fullness than if you drank a glass of grape juice (Zorrilla 1998).

EXERCISE 8-4 **Context Clues and Word Parts**

Directions: Choose the word from the list that best fits into each of the following sentences. If you are unsure of the meaning of a word, use your knowledge of context clues and word parts to figure out its meaning as it is used in the passage. Consult a dictionary if necessary.

wafts (para. 2)	interact (para. 7)
universally (para. 3)	integrating (para. 9)
physiologic (para. 4)	insulin (para. 10)
sensations (para. 4)	adept (para. 11)
motivate (para. 5)	hormones (para. 12)

1. Chimpanzees are skilled with tools, but not as _____ as humans.

2. After he resigned from the White House, former President Richard Nixon was _____ scorned.

3. The _____ of hunger and thirst are caused by our reactions to the sight and smell of food and the responses of our brains to messages from the body.

4. Water vapor and updrafts of air _____ to create clouds.

5. A dandelion spore is released by the plant and _____ through the air until it settles on the ground.

6. When _____ are out of balance, the body may not function properly.

7. Large voter turnout occurs when the issues of an election _____ people to vote.

8. Breathing is an example of a _____ function.

9. _____ helps the body digest glucose.

10. The brain functions like a computer, _____ the many signals it receives in order to make sense of and respond to the environment.

Directions: The following questions are about the words or phrases boldfaced in the passage. Write the letter of the correct answer in the space provided.

_____ 1. If a *molecule* is a tiny particle, then the word **molecular** (para. 1) refers to

a. something divided into sections

b. something made up of small pieces

c. a chemical imbalance

d. unimportant particles

_____ 2. If *stimulate* means "to excite or cause activity," then you know **stimulants** (para. 3) are things that

a. annoy people

b. create smells

c. satisfy hunger

d. motivate people

_____ 3. Using your knowledge or root words, the correct meaning for the word **sensitive** (para. 3) is

a. responsive to feeling

b. able to adapt well

c. likely to cry

d. soft to the touch

_____ 4. The word **acute** (para. 3) means

a. undeveloped

b. sharp and intense

c. small and sweet

d. important

_____ 5. **Astringent** (para. 3) refers to a taste that is

a. sweet   b. popular   c. bitter   d. fibrous

_____ 6. If the root *psych* refers to the mind, **psychological** (para. 4) means

a. related to mental processes

b. related to physical processes

c. being mentally ill

d. being diagnosed with a mental illness

_____ 7. Which word in paragraph 7 provides a contrast clue for the meaning of the word **satiation** (para. 7)?

a. feelings

b. full

c. interest

d. hunger

_____ 8. The **hypothalamus** (para. 9) is

a. a section of your stomach that produces the sensation of hunger

b. the part of your intestine that registers when you are full

c. the part of the brain that triggers the sensation of hunger

d. a gland that processes glucose

_____ 9. An example of a food that is **bulky** (para. 13) would be

a. yogurt

b. iced tea

c. an apple

d. ice cream

_____ 10. A **semisolid** (para. 13) food is something that is

a. partially digested

b. completely solid

c. completely cooked

d. partially solid

9

Education

Learning Core Terms

The following list is representative of the terminology you will be expected to learn in the field of education.

1. **ability grouping** The arrangement of students into classes based on mastery of specific skills, such as reading or math.

2. **accountability** A policy requiring that student progress be measured and teachers be responsible for student progress.

3. **bilingual education** An educational program that teaches a second language (often English) to students whose first language is not English and maintains the students' native language as well.

4. **collaborative learning** A learning situation in which students work together on a project or assignment.

5. **competency testing** The measurement of a student's ability to perform a specific skill (such as multiplication) or achieve a specified level (such as reading at a sixth-grade level).

6. **cultural literacy** The familiarity with a body of knowledge that most educated people in a given society share.

7. **curriculum** A course or program of study.

8. **electronic classroom** A learning environment in which students have access to computers, the Internet, and multimedia sources of information.

9. **gifted and talented program** A program of supplemental instruction designed to stimulate and further the growth of students who exhibit high intelligence or exceptional mastery of skills.

10. **home schooling** A policy that allows qualified parents to educate their children at home.

11. **instructional objectives** Specific learning goals or accomplishments that a school or teacher establishes for students. Objectives identify what a student is to learn.

12. **learning community** An interactive environment in which teachers and students come together to provide respectful and positive feedback for learning.

13. **literacy** The ability to read and write. Math and computer skills are sometimes considered literacy skills as well.

14. **magnet school** A school that offers special, unique programs to attract students from within a school district.

15. **performance assessment** A form of testing that requires students to show what they know by actually doing something, such as performing a specific task.

16. **phonics** A method of teaching reading that emphasizes letters and the sounds associated with them.

17. **school board** A group of elected officials that serves as a governing body of a school district.

18. **standardized test** A formal, usually commercial test that is administered according to specific directions with time limitations. It is often machine scored; results often compare students' abilities to others in the class, the district, the state, or the nation.

19. **tenure** A policy that allows teachers to hold their positions on a permanent basis without periodic contract renewals.

20. **whole language** A method of teaching that integrates reading, writing, speaking, and listening.

 Learn More about Educational Terminology by Visiting the Following Web Site

http://www.learnnc.org/reference/

EXERCISE 9-1 Defining Education Vocabulary

Directions: Write the letters of the correct answers in the spaces provided.

_____ 1. **Cultural literacy** refers to

   a. student improvement

   b. the teaching of values

   c. familiarity with shared knowledge

   d. the separation of high- and low-performing students

_____ 2. **Competency testing** measures students'

    a. skills   c. compatibility

    b. attitudes   d. social awareness

_____ 3. **Home schooling** occurs when

    a. students study at home

    b. teachers consult with parents at home

    c. students and teachers form communities

    d. parents educate their children at home

_____ 4. **Performance assessment** is a form of testing that focuses on

    a. knowing the right answers   c. reacting to the performance of others

    b. thinking critically   d. carrying out a task

_____ 5. A **standardized test** is a

    a. timed oral test   c. timed commercial test

    b. timed essay test   d. untimed informal test

_____ 6. **Whole language**

    a. integrates reading, writing, listening, and speaking

    b. focuses on the child as a whole being

    c. emphasizes setting one's own learning objectives

    d. requires students to interact

_____ 7. **Collaborative learning** involves

    a. planning an evening of study

    b. studying by testing yourself

    c. working with other students

    d. reviewing the work of others

_____ 8. **Ability grouping** is a method of arranging students by

    a. skill level   c. social preference

    b. age   d. size

_____ 9. **Gifted and talented programs** are intended to

    a. stimulate further growth of high-ability students

    b. help all students work together

    c. separate high- and low-achieving students

    d. encourage high-performing students to take school seriously

_____ 10. A **magnet school**

    a. focuses on artistic abilities   c. offers special, unique programs

    b. focuses on basic skills   d. offers traditional instruction

Using Education Vocabulary I

Directions: Use words from the list at the beginning of this chapter that complete the meaning of each sentence.

1. The students were told to work together on a _____ project to complete the course objectives.

2. Maria chose to _____ her children because she had a degree in early childhood education.

3. The new immigrants were able to benefit from a _____ program for adults at the state university.

4. The voters elected their new _____ members in November.

5. The computers in the _____ were upgraded last year.

6. The first-grade teacher used _____ to teach her students how to read.

7. Because the school uses _____, the students are divided up into several different classes according to skill level.

8. Because Eryn excelled in math and science, the school district decided to place her in a _____.

9. The district has several _____ that offer special programs in art and music.

10. Keisha wanted to find a college _____ that included liberal arts courses.

EXERCISE 9-3 Defining Education Vocabulary II

Directions: Write the letters of the correct answers in the spaces provided.

_____ 1. **Tenure** allows teachers to
   a. create their own curriculum
   b. develop individual learning plans for students
   c. hire classroom aides
   d. hold their positions on a permanent basis

_____ 2. **Accountability** is a policy requiring that
   a. teachers fail nonperforming students
   b. teachers keep track of their time
   c. students report incidents of cheating
   d. students' progress be measured

_____ 3. A **curriculum** is a
   a. list of job opportunities
   b. schedule of tests and exams
   c. collection of required readings
   d. course of study

_____ 4. A **learning community** is

    a. a social environment for students

    b. an environment that supports students as learners

    c. a group of students competing for grades

    d. a group of teachers who plan instruction

_____ 5. **Phonics** is a method of teaching

    a. mathematics   c. social studies

    b. reading   d. science

_____ 6. **Bilingual education** is a program that

    a. teaches English to students whose first language is not English

    b. encourages racism among children

    c. teaches a second language to high-ability children

    d. discourages multiculturalism among teachers

_____ 7. An **electronic classroom** is a learning environment primarily involving

    a. computer training

    b. computers and multimedia

    c. technical job training

    d. reading improvement

_____ 8. **Literacy** is the ability to

    a. read and write   c. focus one's attention

    b. work with others   d. succeed academically

_____ 9. The primary job of a **school board** is to

    a. govern the school district   c. meet with parents

    b. select students   d. conduct fund-raising campaigns

_____ 10. **Instructional objectives** identify

    a. what students should learn   c. the methods teachers must use

    b. how much time is spent on each subject   d. how grades are to be determined

Applying Your Skills in Education

This passage is taken from *Charting a Professional Course: Issues and Controversies in Education* by Don Kauchak, Paul Eggen, and Mary D. Burbank. Read the selection to learn about the problems immigrants face in schools. Then practice the skills you have learned in Part I of this text by answering the questions that follow.

The "New" Immigrants

1   The 1965 amendment to the Immigration and Nationality Act has resulted in a large-scale immigration to equal that of the late nineteenth and early twentieth centuries. A more **equitable distribution** of **visas** worldwide has resulted in more than 85 percent of all immigrants arriving from Asia and Latin America. Some areas of the country have been impacted profoundly by these numbers. For example, by the next census, half the population of California will be Asian or Hispanic. Currently, one person in four in California speaks a primary **tongue** other than English. More than one million are classified "limited English proficient" and one in five is an immigrant. Similarly, one-third of the population in New York City is foreign-born, as well as one-third of the [students at] public schools in the city.

2   What are school districts doing to **adapt** to this new population? What challenges are these new students and their teachers facing? Does the assimilation [experience of] European immigrants of the early part of this century reflect the reality of these new immigrants?

3   Many issues confront the new students as well as their teachers. For the students, many adjustment problems emerge. First, new immigrant students have to adjust and understand the new racial labeling and categorization of the United States. For example, students who viewed themselves as simply Chinese, Taiwanese, Korean, or Cambodians are now defined as **Asian**. Similarly, students from varied and culturally distinct Spanish-speaking countries are now considered Hispanics or Latinos. Rarely is the fact that these groups come from different countries with unique histories, cultures, and languages considered. Second, native-born members of these groups are lumped together with the foreign-born. Studies indicate that many American-born members of immigrant groups separate out and make **distinctions** between themselves and the new arrivals. Further, immigrant children, who were born outside of the United States but educated and socialized here—known as the "**1.5 generation**"—are often treated the same as recent immigrant students. The adjustment and experiences of this group differ significantly from those who immigrate at an older age. Youths who migrate as teenagers tend to learn English with an "accent." Younger immigrant children will learn to speak the language as a native and usually without an accent.

4   Many young immigrant students have difficulty with issues of identity and reconciling their home life with their life at school. The lure of America's popular culture and youth culture causes difficulty for many immigrant students from homes that stress standards and expectations of the old country. Teachers should also be aware of the many gender-specific issues that occur in many immigrant families.

5   In an **ethnographic** study of a multiracial high school in California, Laurie Olsen found that to "become an American," immigrant students had to **undergo** the **Americanization** process. This included academic marginalization and separation; speaking English and the necessity of dropping one's native language to participate in the academic and social life of the school; and taking one's place in the racial **hierarchy** of the country.

6   In addition to the above issues, some scholars who are currently analyzing the new immigrants' adjustment to the United States note that because many reside in **multicultural** urban neighborhoods where employment is scarce and schools are **impoverished** poverty may persist from the first to the second generation. This reality **debunks** the prevailing view of previous immigrant straight-line upward mobility, in which their socioeconomic status improved with each generation. Although many European immigrants experienced class and religious discrimination in the early years of their history in the nation, as noted earlier, most did **assimilate** either by choice or **coercion**. However, because of the persistence of racism in the American society, the sociologist Herbert Gans predicts that dark-skinned non-Caucasian immigrants, particularly the men, can expect to suffer more racial discrimination than other immigrants.

Response of School Districts

7   Many urban school districts throughout the nation have responded to the challenges of educating the new immigrant students by establishing special "newcomer" schools. These are currently for high school students believed to have the most difficulty assimilating into a regular high school. Seven such newcomer high school exist in New York City. They function in many ways like the settlement houses of the early part of the century. The newcomer schools helped parents become Americanized and acclimated to the American society. Acculturation programs available to new immigrant families include seminars, speakers, and films.

8   These special schools for newcomers are not without controversy. Many are concerned that these new students, overwhelmingly nonwhite, are being placed on a separate track that will prevent them from entering a regular school. This controversy may well be one of the key civil rights issues of education in the next decade. Many argue that it is important to **mainstream** the newcomer students with the regular students as soon as possible. However, the Olson study revealed that even in mainstream classes and regular schools, newcomer immigrants are not always served well.

9   Despite the often poor and inadequate educational institutions available to many newcomers, there is consistent **documentation** that these students are enthusiastic about school and highly motivated to learn.

10   Despite this enthusiasm, immigrant students who have limited English **proficiency** tend to have much higher dropout rates than those who have English proficiency. Unfortunately, as the younger immigrant students become more Americanized and **susceptible** to the peer pressure of native-born students, their achievement level and educational aspirations tend to mirror those of the general student population.

EXERCISE 9-4   Context Clues and Word Parts

Directions: Match the words taken from the selection on the left with their correct definitions on the right. If you are unsure of the meaning of a word, use your knowledge of context clues and word parts to figure out its meaning as it is used in the passage. Consult a dictionary if necessary.

——— 1. visas (para. 1)   a. experience

——— 2. adapt (para. 2)   b. variety of ethnicities

——— 3. distinctions (para. 3)   c. immigration permits

——— 4. undergo (para. 5)   d. poor

——— 5. hierarchy (para. 5)   e. noted differences

——— 6. multicultural (para. 6)   f. skill

——— 7. impoverished (para. 6)   g. power structure

——— 8. debunks (para. 6)   h. adjust

——— 9. proficiency (para. 10)   i. likely to be influenced by

——— 10. susceptible (para. 10)   j. shows as untrue

EXERCISE 9-5   Using Your Vocabulary Skills

Directions: The following questions are about the words or phrases boldfaced in the passage. Write the letters of the correct answers on the lines provided.

——— 1. The phrase **equitable distribution** (para. 1) is used to refer to
    a. equal rights for immigrants   c. large amounts
    b. an even spread of goods   d. worldwide recognition

——— 2. The word **tongue** (para. 1) usually refers to a part of your mouth, but in this selection it refers to
    a. an accent   c. a country of origin
    b. a version of English   d. a language

——— 3. Although the word **Asian** (para. 3) refers to people who are from or have ancestors from Asia, in this selection the word also has the connotation of
    a. a group not important enough to specifically identify
    b. the dangers of assimilation
    c. people who don't take the time to learn English
    d. immigrants highly skilled in math and sciences

_____ 4. The phrase **1.5 generation** (para. 3) is a newly coined phrase referring to

    a. unborn children

    b. people born in the United States who live in other countries

    c. people born in other countries but raised in the United States

    d. immigrants who have not yet learned to speak English

_____ 5. As used in paragraph 5, the word **ethnographic** refers to

    a. graphs of the numbers of immigrants

    b. the detailed study of numbers

    c. a scientific approach to examining cultures

    d. a way to categorize different religious groups

_____ 6. Which of the following is given as an example of **Americanization** (para. 5)?

    a. speaking English   c. not speaking one's native language

    b. being marginalized   d. all of the above

_____ 7. **Assimilate** (para. 6) means to

    a. react to discrimination   c. remain true to your own culture

    b. be forced to agree   d. conform and fit in

_____ 8. Using a contrast context clue, you can figure out that **coercion** (para. 6) is the opposite of

    a. racism   c. discrimination

    b. choice   d. class

_____ 9. **Mainstream** (para. 8) means to

    a. widen a creek   c. place with the majority

    b. keep a group together   d. protect civil rights

_____ 10. Using your knowledge of word parts, you can determine that the word **documentation** (para. 9) means

    a. documents showing proof   c. translated papers

    b. test results   d. data or information that offers proof

10

Business

Learning Core Terms

The following list is representative of the terminology you will be expected to learn in the field of business.

1. **assets** The resources (properties) a firm owns.

2. **audit** An examination of a company's records to check for accuracy.

3. **CEO (chief executive officer)** The person responsible for managing the day-to-day operations of a company and carrying out the policies established by the board of directors.

4. **deflation** A decrease in the level of prices or an increase in purchasing power due to a reduction in available currency and credit.

5. **deficit** Inadequate or insufficient funds; the amount a sum of money falls short of the required amount, as in a *budget deficit*.

6. **dividend** A distribution of earnings to the stockholders of a company.

7. **depreciation** Loss in value due to age, use, or market worth. In accounting, depreciation refers to an allowance made for loss in value of property.

8. **entrepreneur** A person who initiates and assumes the risks of starting a new business.

9. **equity** The remaining value of a business or property once debts and mortgages are subtracted.

10. **fiscal year** A 12-month period of time in which a business operates and tallies its income and expenses.

11. **franchise** An individually owned business that is associated with a chain of stores and operates under the chain's guidelines.

12. **GNP (gross national product)** The total dollar value of all goods and services produced by all citizens in a country in a given one-year period.

13. **gross income** The total dollar amount of all goods and services sold during a specific period; total income before expenses are deducted.

14. **inflation** A general rise in level of prices or a decline in purchasing power due to the lessening value of the dollar.

15. **liabilities** A firm's debts and financial obligations.

16. **monopoly** An industry in which there is only one company that sells a product or service.

17. **net income** The profit earned by a company or individual after all expenses have been subtracted from total income.

18. **productivity** The average level of output per worker per hour.

19. **recession** Two consecutive three-month periods of decline in a country's gross domestic product (see GDP).

20. **sole proprietorship** A business that is owned and operated by one person.

 Learn More about Business Terminology by Visiting the Following Web Site

http://www.quicken.com/glossary/

EXERCISE 10-1   Using Business Vocabulary I

Directions: Use words from the list at the beginning of the chapter to complete the meaning of each sentence.

1. If you operate a landscaping business alone your business is a _____.

2. A _____ is the 12-month period of time in which a business operates.

3. A company's property and inventory are known as its _____.

4. If you owned a Burger King restaurant, part of a national chain, you would own a _____.

5. Several companies offer day care services and wellness centers to improve worker _____.

6. Your _____ is your total income before expenses are subtracted.

7. A _____ occurs when there has been a consistent decline in a country's gross national product.

8. If only one company provides garbage disposal in your state, it is a _____ .

9. When a company lacks the funds to pay its expenses, a _____ occurs.

10. When a new car ages, its loss of value is known as _____ .

EXERCISE 10-2 Defining Business Vocabulary

Directions: Choose the definitions in column B that best match the words or phrases in column A. Write your answer in the spaces provided.

Column A	Column B
1. _____ fiscal year	a. A distribution of earnings
2. _____ deflation	b. An individually owned business that is associated with a chain of stores
3. _____ liabilities	c. The resources a firm owns
4. _____ sole proprietorship	d. Average level of output per worker per hour
5. _____ assets	e. Examination of a company's records
6. _____ dividend	f. Decrease in level of prices or increase in purchasing power
7. _____ inflation	g. A 12-month period of time in which a business tallies its income and expenses
8. _____ franchise	h. General rise in level of prices or decline in purchasing power
9. _____ audit	i. A company's debts and financial obligations
10. _____ productivity	j. A business owned and operated by one person

---

EXERCISE 10-3 Using Business Vocabulary II

Directions: Use words from the list at the beginning of the chapter to complete the meaning of each sentence.

1. The person responsible for running a company is its _____ .

2. An _____ is a person who initiates or assumes risks in starting a new business.

3. A nation's _____ is the total value of all the goods and services it produces during a one-year period.

4. The value of a company once debts and mortgages are subtracted is its _____ .

5. When prices fall or purchasing power increases _____ occurs.

6. When products, such as clothing, cost more or you can buy fewer items for the same amount of money, _____ has occurred.

7. A company's debts are known as its _____.

8. The distribution of earnings to a company's stockholder is a _____.

9. An _____ of a company may be conducted to discover errors in its financial records.

10. If you owned a carpet cleaning business, your _____ would be your profit after you subtracted costs such as equipment, supplies, and insurance.

MASTERY test

Applying Your Skills in Business

This textbook excerpt was taken from *Consumer Behavior* by Leon G. Schiffman and Leslie Lazar Kanuk. Read the passage to learn about how celebrities are used to sell products. Then practice the skills you have learned in Part I of this text by answering the questions that follow.

Celebrity Sells

1 Within the context of consumer behavior, the concept of reference groups is an extremely important and powerful idea. A **reference group** is any person or group that serves as a **point of comparison** (or reference) for an individual in forming either general or specific values, attitudes, or a specific guide for behavior. This basic concept provides a valuable **perspective** for understanding the impact of other people on an individual's consumption beliefs, attitudes, and behavior. It also provides **insight** into the methods marketers sometimes use to effect desired changes in consumer behavior.

2 From a marketing perspective, *reference groups* are groups that serve as *frames of reference* for individuals in their purchase or consumption decisions. The usefulness of this concept is enhanced by the fact that it places no restrictions on group size or membership, nor does it require that consumers identify with a **tangible** group (i.e., the group can be symbolic such as owners of successful small businesses, leading corporate chief executive officers, rock stars, or golf celebrities).

3 **Appeals** by celebrities and other similar reference groups are used very **effectively** by advertisers to communicate with their markets. Celebrities can be a powerful force in creating interest or actions with regard to purchasing or using selected goods and services. This identification may be based on **admiration** (of an athlete), on **aspiration** (of a celebrity or a way of life), on empathy (with a person or a situation), or on recognition (of a person—real or stereotypical—or of a situation). In some cases, the **prospective** consumer may think, "If she uses it, it must be good. If I use it, I'll be like her." In other cases, the prospective consumer says to himself, "He has the same problems that I have. What worked for him will work for me."

4 Celebrities, particularly movie stars, TV personalities, popular entertainers, and sports **icons**, provide a very common type of reference group appeal. Indeed, it has been estimated that 25 percent of U.S. commercials include celebrity endorsers. To their loyal followers and to much of the general public, celebrities represent an **idealization** of life that most people imagine that they would love to live. Advertisers spend enormous sums of money to have celebrities promote their products, with the expectation that the reading or viewing audience will

react **positively** to the celebrity's association with their products. One discussion about celebrity endorsers noted that "famous people hold the viewer's attention," and this is why the World Chiropractic Alliance recently began a search to find doctors with famous patients and to use such associations in their marketing efforts. Do you remember when Michael Jordan first retired from basketball for about two years? His return to the NBA resulted in the firms whose products he endorses to increase their stock market value by $1 billion, and he is under contract with Nike until the year 2023. But many experts believe that today it is Tiger Woods, and not Michael Jordan, who is the number-one celebrity endorser. His five-year deal with Buick is estimated at $30 million, and his $40 million deal with Nike is expected to double because he has now switched to Nike brand golf balls.

5   Do you or one of your friends own a Microsoft Xbox? When the Xbox was introduced into the Japanese market in February 2002, 50,000 limited edition versions were available. In addition to a black translucent case, the limited edition versions included a silver-plated key chain with the engraved signature of Bill Gates, CEO of Microsoft. It was hoped that this key chain would separate the Xbox from its Sony and Nintendo rivals. And are you aware that the number of Americans who practiced yoga in 1998 represented a 300 percent increase over 1990? This was due in part to celebrities such as actress Gwyneth Paltrow and model Christy Turlington and to Madonna playing a yoga instructor in her film *The Next Best Thing.*

6   A firm that decides to employ a celebrity to promote its product or service has the choice of using the celebrity to give a **testimonial** or an **endorsement** as an actor in a commercial or as a company spokesperson. A testimonial is based on personal usage. A celebrity attests to the quality of the product or service. In an endorsement a celebrity lends his or her name and appears on behalf of a product or service with which he or she may or may not be an expert. A celebrity may appear in a commercial simply as an actor playing the part of a character. A celebrity may also act as a spokesperson, representing the brand or company over an extended period of time. What is **apparent** is that the importance of certain celebrity characteristics varies depending on whether the product being promoted is technical (e.g., PCs) or nontechnical (e.g., jeans) in nature. Specifically, for a product like a PC the "trustworthiness" of a celebrity is considered to be most important, whereas for a clothing item like jeans the "physical attractiveness" of the celebrity is viewed as most important.

7   Of all the benefits that a celebrity might contribute to a firm's advertising program—fame, talent, credibility, or **charisma**—celebrity **credibility** with the consumer audience is the most important. By celebrity credibility we mean the audience's perception of both the celebrity's *expertise* (how much the celebrity knows about the product area) and *trustworthiness* (how honest the celebrity is about what he or she says about the product). To illustrate, when a celebrity endorses only one product consumers are likely to perceive the product in a highly favorable light and indicate a greater intention to purchase it. In contrast, when a celebrity endorses a variety of products, his or her perceived credibility is reduced because of the apparent **economic motivation** underlying the celebrity's efforts. A recent study also found that endorser credibility had its strongest impact with respect to influencing a consumer's attitude toward the ad, but that corporate

credibility (the credibility of the company paying for the advertisement) had a stronger impact on attitude toward the brand.

8   Not all companies feel that using celebrity endorsers is the best way to advertise. Some companies avoid celebrities because they fear that if the celebrity gets involved in some **undesirable** act or event (e.g., an ugly matrimonial problem, a scandal, or a criminal case), the news or press coverage will negatively impact the sale of the endorsed brand. For example, researchers recently complied a list of 48 undesirable events occurring between 1980 and 1994 that involved celebrity endorsers hired by publicly traded companies. The list included such notables as Mike Tyson, Michael Jackson, and Jennifer Capriati.

EXERCISE 10-4   Context Clues and Word Parts

Directions: Use your knowledge of context clues and word parts to figure out the meaning of each of the words or phrases listed below as they are used in the passage. Then, for each word, write a sentence that contains the word and uses it to mean the same as it means in the passage. Consult a dictionary if necessary.

1. point of comparison (para. 1) _____

2. perspective (para. 1) _____

3. insight (para. 1) _____

4. tangible (para. 2) _____

5. effectively (para. 3) _____

6. admiration (para. 3) _____

7. idealization (para. 4) _____

8. positively (para. 4) _____

9. apparent (para. 6) _____

10. undesirable (para. 8) _____

EXERCISE 10-5   Using Your Vocabulary Skills

Directions: The following questions test your knowledge of words or phrases used in the selection. Write the letters of the correct answers on the lines provided.

_____   1. In this selection, the term **reference group** (para. 1) means

a. an internal belief system that controls the choices you make

b. a well-known celebrity's impact on the general public

c. a collection of library books that contain facts and information

d. a group that serves as a point of comparison

_____ 2. The word **appeals** (para. 3) has numerous meanings. Which meaning does it have in this selection?

    a. legal proceedings that bring a case to a higher court for review

    b. an urgent request for help

    c. sincere suggestions or pleas to do something

    d. to be attractive or interesting

_____ 3. Since *to aspire* means to hope or dream something great will happen, **aspiration** (para. 3) means

    a. the act of breathing in   c. a desire for achievement

    b. a lack of action   d. a sense of admiration

_____ 4. Select the synonym that accurately describes the meaning of **prospective** (para. 3) as it used in the selection.

    a. possible   c. visible

    b. positive   d. prohibited

_____ 5. The author uses the word **icons** (para. 4) to connote a feeling of

    a. importance and reverence   c. fear and shame

    b. a sense of negativity   d. commercialization

_____ 6. Based on information in the selection, an **endorsement** (para. 6) differs from a **testimonial** (para. 6) because an endorsement does not involve

    a. the celebrity's name or image   c. making a commercial

    b. personal use by the celebrity   d. an extended period of time

_____ 7. **Charisma** (para. 7) means

    a. being rich and famous   c. personal magnetism

    b. having a beautiful face   d. intellectual achievement

_____ 8. Using your knowledge of word parts, what does the word **credibility** (para. 7) mean?

    a. fame   c. likeability

    b. character   d. trustworthiness

_____ 9. Complete the following analogy: If Tiger Woods's area of **expertise** (para. 7) is golf, then Madonna's area of expertise is

    a. music   c. dancing

    b. painting   d. religion

———— 10. If an economy is a system of exchange of money for goods, then an **economic motivation** (para. 7) is

     a. a legal interest

     b. a financial interest

     c. a market interest

     d. an advertising interest

11

Biology

Learning Core Terms

The following list is representative of the terminology you will be expected to learn in biology.

1. **botany** The scientific study of plant life.

2. **carnivore/herbivore/omnivore** Carnivores are flesh-eating animals; herbivores are animals that feed primarily on plants; omnivores are organisms that consume both plants and animals.

3. **chromosomes** A part of the nucleus of animal and plant cells that carries genes and helps transmit hereditary information.

4. **DNA (deoxyribonucleic acid)** The material of which genes are composed.

5. **fauna/flora** Fauna are the animals of a particular region; flora are the plants of a particular region.

6. **genes** The fundamental hereditary unit, found on chromosomes, that controls the development of hereditary characteristics.

7. **genetics** The branch of biology that studies heredity.

8. **habitat** The natural environment in which a plant or animal lives.

9. **hibernation/estivation** Hibernation refers to passing the winter in a dormant state; estivation refers to spending the summer in a dormant state.

10. **homeostasis** The tendency of an organism to maintain a stable internal environment.

11. **marsupials** Animals such as kangaroos whose newborn live in external pouches where they feed and further develop.

12. **mammals** Warm-blooded vertebrates, including humans, characterized by hair on the skin, and, in the female, milk-producing mammary glands.

13. **metabolism** Chemical reactions that involve the synthesis or breakdown of molecules within a living cell.

14. **mutation** A permanent structural change in a DNA molecule that may result in a new trait or characteristic.

15. **natural selection** The theory that the surviving plants and animals of a particular species are those that are strongest and most adaptable.

16. **taxonomy** The classification of organisms into categories or systems based on shared characteristics.

17. **toxin/antitoxin** A toxin is a poisonous substance produced by an organism; an antitoxin is a substance formed in response to a toxin for the purpose of neutralizing it.

18. **transpiration** The loss of water vapor through the membrane or pore of an organism; usually associated with plants during photosynthesis or cooling.

19. **vertebrate/invertebrate** A vertebrate is an animal that has a backbone or spinal column; an invertebrate does not.

20. **zoology** The scientific study of animals.

 Learn More about Biological Terminology by Visiting the Following Web Site

http://biotech.icmb.utexas.edu/pages/dictionary.html

EXERCISE 11-1 Defining Biology Vocabulary

Directions: Choose the definitions in column B that best match the words or phrases in column A. Write your answers in the spaces provided.

Column A	Column B
1. ——— metabolism	a. The study of plant life
2. ——— homeostasis	b. Flesh-eating animals
3. ——— gene	c. The tendency of the body to maintain a stable internal environment
4. ——— flora	d. A chemical reaction that involves breakdown of molecules within a cell
5. ——— mammals	e. Warm-blooded animals with a spinal column or back-bone who nurse their young

6. —— botany

   f. The plants of a particular region

7. —— transpiration

   g. The study of animals

8. —— marsupials

   h. A unit that controls the development of hereditary characteristics

9. —— carnivores

   i. The loss of water vapor through a pore or membrane

10. —— zoology

   j. Animals whose young live in the mother's external pouch

EXERCISE 11-2   Using Biology Vocabulary I

Directions: Write the letters of the correct answers in the spaces provided.

——   1. **Transpiration** is the loss of water vapor through

   a. the membrane or pore of an organism

   b. the process of heat transfer

   c. a phase change between cells of an organism

   d. the root system

——   2. **Genetics** is the branch of biology that studies

   a. reproduction   c. heredity

   b. plant life   d. mammals

——   3. A **mutation** is a permanent structural change in

   a. a DNA molecule   c. the cell wall

   b. fatty tissue   d. the cell membrane

——   4. **Natural selection** refers to the theory that species that survive

   a. adapt and evolve from one basic organism

   b. are strongest and most adaptable

   c. are more intelligent than other mammals

   d. have evolved more slowly than other mammals

——   5. **Botany** is the scientific study of

   a. animals   c. plant life

   b. insects   d. fish

——   6. **Zoology** is the scientific study of

   a. plants   c. sociology of zoos

   b. zookeeping   d. animals

——   7. **Homeostasis** is

   a. an organism's ability to fight infection or disease

   b. the administration of small doses of a remedy to produce disease-like symptoms

   c. an organism's tendency to maintain a stable internal environment

   d. a state of shock to the central nervous system

_____ 8. **Metabolism** is a chemical reaction that involves

      a. a change in heart rate through exercise

      b. the synthesis of molecules within a living cell

      c. the firing of neurons in brain wave function

      d. a loss of water through perspiration

_____ 9. **Carnivores** are animals that

      a. feed primarily on plants   c. kill for sport

      b. feed on both plants and animals   d. eat flesh

_____ 10. **Vertebrates** are animals that

      a. have no backbone or spinal column   c. have a backbone or spinal column

      b. live on the ocean floor   d. walk upright

EXERCISE 11-3   Using Biology Vocabulary II

Directions: Choose the definitions in column B that best match the words or phrases in column A. Write your answers in the spaces provided.

Column A	Column B
1. _____ chromosomes	a. The theory that the strongest and most adaptable species survive
2. _____ genetics	b. Passing the winter in a dormant state
3. _____ hibernation	c. Parts of the cell nucleus that carry genes
4. _____ natural selection	d. Animals that lack a spinal column
5. _____ taxonomy	e. The natural environment in which a plant or animal lives
6. _____ toxins	f. Poisonous substances
7. _____ DNA	g. The classification of plants or animals into categories
8. _____ invertebrates	h. The material of which genes are composed
9. _____ mutation	i. A change in a molecule that may result in a new trait
10. _____ habitat	j. The study of heredity

MASTERY test

Applying Your Skills in Biology

This textbook excerpt was taken from *Biology Concepts and Connections* by Neil A. Campbell, Jane B. Reece, Martha R. Taylor, and Eric J. Simon. Read the passage to learn about the consequences of spinal cord injuries and to find out whether an injured spinal cord can heal. Then practice the skills you have learned in Part I of this text by answering the questions that follow.

Can an Injured Spinal Cord be Fixed?

1   Protected inside the bony vertebrae of the spine is an inch-thick **gelatinous** bundle of **nervous** issue called the spinal cord. The spinal cord acts as the central communication **conduit** between the brain and the rest of the body. Millions of nerve **fibers** carry **motor** information from the brain to the muscles, while other fibers bring sensory information (about touch, pain, and body position, for example) from the body to the brain. The spinal cord acts like a transcontinental telephone cable jam-packed with wires, each of which carries messages to or from the central hub and an outlying area.

Consequences of Spinal Cord Injuries

2   But what happens if that cable is cut? Signals cannot get through, communication is lost, and the cable must be repaired or replaced. In humans, the spinal cord is rarely severed because the vertebrae provide rigid protection. However, a **traumatic** blow to the spinal column and subsequent bleeding, swelling, and scarring can crush the delicate nerve bundles and prevent signals from passing. The result may be a **debilitating** injury. Such trauma along the back can cause **paraplegia**—paralysis of the lower half of the body. Trauma higher up in the neck can cause **quadriplegia**, which may necessitate permanent breathing assistance from an artificial **respirator**. Such injuries are usually permanent because the spinal cord, unlike other body tissues, cannot repair itself.

3   The late actor Christopher Reeve (best known for playing Superman in several movies) suffered a spinal cord injury during an **equestrian** competition. He was thrown from his horse and landed headfirst. Two vertebrae in his neck were fractured, crushing the spinal cord at the base of his skull and causing quadriplegia. Reeve died of complications related to his injury in 2004.

4   Over 10,000 Americans suffer spinal cord injuries each year. The most common cases are car crashes, violence (usually from gunshots), falls, and sports.

From Neil A. Campbell et al., *Biology: Concepts and Connections*, 5/e, pp. 564–565. Copyright © 2006 Pearson Education, Inc., publishing as Benjamin Cummings. Reprinted by permission.

The late actor Christopher Reeve, an influential advocate for spinal cord research.

Because the majority of spinal cord injuries happen to people younger than 30, the subsequent disabilities often last for decades at great monetary and emotional cost.

Treatments for Spinal Cord Injuries

5 Historically, spinal cord injuries have been considered untreatable. In fact, a 3,700-year-old Egyptian papyrus describes them as "an ailment not to be treated." Recently, however, there has been some minor progress: In 1988, researchers discovered that administering a powerful steroid drug within hours of a spinal cord injury limits its severity. But **reversing** spinal cord damage is a formidable challenge.

6   Some researchers are coaxing damaged nerve cells to **regenerate** by **administering** growth factor proteins or transplanting the cells that produce growth factors to the site of the injury. Other researchers are attempting to block proteins that **inhibit** growth. Still others, believing that damaged nerve cells cannot be fixed, are trying to find ways to replace them with either mature nerve cells from elsewhere in the body or fetal tissue. A recent version of this approach is the attempt to use **embryonic** stem cells—**progenitor** cells capable of developing into all other cell types—or partially **differentiated neural** stem cells to grow new nerve connections. Several recent studies involving combinations of these proposed therapies have shown promise in rats, even partially restoring motor function below the injury. While none of these strategies may ever "cure" a damaged spinal cord, they may still offer benefits of great value, such as regained control of the bladder, bowels, respiration, or a limb. Thanks to the efforts of Reeve and others to raise public awareness, spinal damage is now the subject of much research. The years ahead hold great promise for improving the **prognosis** after spinal cord injuries.

EXERCISE 11-4   Context Clues and Word Parts

Directions: Listed below are ten boldfaced words from the passage. Use your knowledge of context clues and word parts to figure out the meaning of each word as it is used in the passage. Write a definition for each word in the space provided. Consult a dictionary if necessary.

1. nervous (para. 1): _____

2. conduit (para. 1): _____

3. quadriplegia (para. 2): _____

4. regenerate (para. 6): _____

5. inhibit (para. 6): _____

6. embryonic (para. 6): _____

7. progenitor (para. 6): _____

8. differentiated (para. 6): _____

9. neural (para. 6): _____

10. prognosis (para. 6): _____

EXERCISE 11-5   Using Your Vocabulary Skills

Directions: The following questions are about words or phrases used in the passage. Write the letter of the correct answer on the line provided.

_____ 1. The correct pronunciation of the word **gelatinous** (para. 1) is

    a. gə-lăt′-əs   c. jē-lăt′n-əs

    b. jə′-lătn-əs   d. jə-lăt′n-əs

_____ 2. **Fibers** (para. 1) refers to

    a. thread-like blood vessels   c. long thin body tissues

    b. individual cells   d. coarse substances

_____ 3. Read this sentence from paragraph 1; then answer the question that follows.

    The spinal cord acts like a transcontinental telephone cable jam-packed with wires, each of which carries messages to or from the central hub and an outlying area.

    The main purpose of the simile in this sentence is to explain how the

    a. signals from the brain to the body tend to get confused

    b. spinal cord links the brain to other parts of the body

    c. structure of the spinal cord protects the nerves

    d. nerves communicate with each other

_____ 4. The word **traumatic** (para. 2) means

    a. suffering severe emotional shock   c. suffering serious injuries

    b. having a distressing effect   d. having long-term psychological consequences

5. In paragraph 2, the word **debilitating** is explained using

   a. examples
   b. contrasts
   c. definitions
   d. synonyms

6. The type of context clue that helps a reader figure out the meaning of **paraplegia** (para. 2) is

   a. definition
   b. example
   c. synonym
   d. contrast

7. Which word in the sentence provides a context clue that helps readers infer the meaning of the word **respirator** (para. 2)?

   a. trauma
   b. permanent
   c. artificial
   d. breathing

8. Complete the following analogy.
   driver : vehicle :: **equestrian** (para. 3): _____

   a. ride
   b. horse
   c. guide
   d. competition

9. The root of the word **reversing** (para. 5) means

   a. turn
   b. again
   c. send
   d. come

10. **Administering** (para. 6) means

    a. overseeing in a formal way
    b. managing
    c. applying as a remedy
    d. researching

12

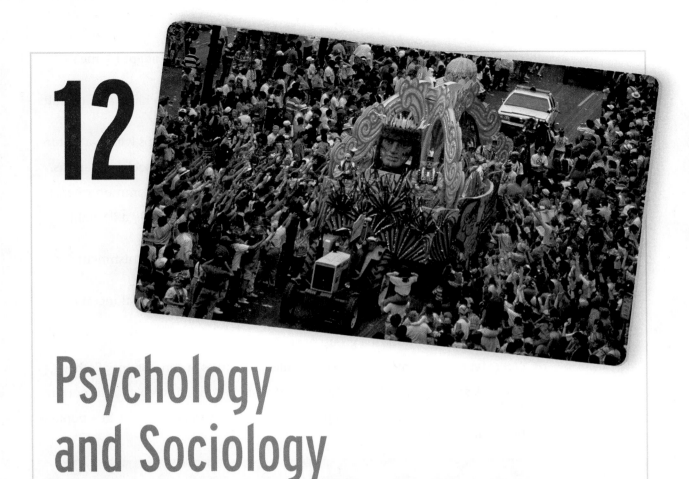

Psychology
and Sociology

Learning Core Terms

The following list is representative of the terminology you will be expected to learn in the fields of psychology and sociology.

1. **case studies** A type of research that involves close, in-depth observation and analysis of individual people.

2. **cognition** A mental process such as thinking, remembering, and understanding.

3. **culture** A system for living that includes objects, values, and characteristics that people acquire as members of a society.

4. **defense mechanism** A method of reducing anxiety by denying or distorting a situation or problem.

5. **empirical** Refers to information obtained from, or that can be verified by, observation or experimentation.

6. **ethnic group** A collection of people who share a cultural heritage.

7. **ethnocentrism** The belief that one's own culture is superior to that of others.

8. **hypothesis** A tentative explanation about how various events are related to one another that can be tested by further experimentation.

9. **intelligence** The capacity to learn from experience and to adapt to one's environment.

10. **learning** A relatively permanent change in knowledge or behavior that results from experience.

11. **multiculturalism** The study of diverse racial and ethnic groups within a culture.

12. **norms** Culturally based rules about appropriate behavior in social situations.

13. **peer group** A group whose members share the same age or common interests.

14. **reinforcement** A reward or the process of giving a reward after a desirable behavior has occurred.

15. **sanction** A reward for conforming to what is expected or a punishment for violating expectations.

16. **social class** A category of people who have approximately equal income, power, and prestige.

17. **status** One's position in a group or society.

18. **stereotypes** Oversimplified, inaccurate mental pictures or conceptions of others.

19. **value** A socially agreed upon idea about what is good, desirable, or important.

20. **variable** A characteristic that changes from person to person within a population being studied.

 Learn More about Psychology and Sociology Terminology by Visiting the Following Web Site

http://www.urich.edu/~allison/glossary.html

EXERCISE 12-1 Defining Psychology and Sociology Vocabulary

Directions: Write the letters of the correct answers in the spaces provided.

————— 1. A **defense mechanism** is a method of

     a. stimulating nonaggressive behavior   c. changing behavior

     b. denying or distorting a situation   d. eliminating fear

————— 2. **Learning** results in a change in

     a. brain structure   c. group behavior

     b. emotions   d. knowledge or behavior

————— 3. **Empirical** evidence can be verified by

     a. comparison with values   c. observation or experimentation

     b. identification of perceptions   d. analysis of emotions

————— 4. A collection of people who share a cultural heritage is called

     a. an ethnic group   c. a peer group

     b. a race   d. a reference group

_____ 5. The attitude that one's own culture is superior is known as

    a. racism   c. prejudice

    b. discrimination   d. ethnocentrism

_____ 6. **Culture** that includes objects, values, and characteristics can best be described as

    a. an undefined lifestyle   c. a political structure

    b. a pattern of economic development   d. a system for living

_____ 7. Within a population, a **variable** is a characteristic that changes

    a. from person to person   c. depending on the researcher

    b. from day to day   d. depending on the source

_____ 8. If you give a child a candy bar as a reward for cleaning his room especially well, the candy bar is a

    a. reinforcement   c. value

    b. stereotype   d. variable

_____ 9. A **hypothesis** is

    a. a conclusion about behavior

    b. an explanation of how events are related

    c. a reason for action

    d. a decision about relationships

_____ 10. The capacity to learn from experience and adapt to one's environment is known as

    a. intelligence   c. multiculturalism

    b. ethnocentrism   d. group interaction

EXERCISE 12-2 Using Psychology and Sociology Vocabulary I

Directions: Use words from the list at the beginning of the chapter to complete the meaning of each sentence.

1. A category of people having approximately the same income, power, and prestige is called a _____.

2. Information that can be verified from an experiment is considered _____.

3. John's _____ shared the same interests in skiing and snowboarding.

4. The researcher conducted detailed _____ on ten different families to decide whether her theory about parent-child interactions was worth pursuing.

5. Luis encountered many _____ about men after he quit his job to stay at home and raise his newborn daughter.

6. A cultural heritage shared by a collection of people is a(n) _____.

7. Because Felicia does not agree that schools should offer religious classes, her _____ are different from those of local priests and rabbis.

8. The teacher uses _____ in her classroom to reward the good behavior of her students.

9. _____ refers to mental processes such as thinking, remembering, or understanding.

10. The social rules that specify how people should behave are called _____.

EXERCISE 12-3   Using Psychology and Sociology Vocabulary II

Directions: Write the letters of the correct answers in the spaces provided.

_____ 1. An oversimplified, inaccurate mental picture or conception of others is referred to as

   a. a stereotype   c. a diversification
   b. an image   d. a sanction

_____ 2. **Cognition** primarily involves

   a. thinking and remembering   c. swimming
   b. painting and drawing   d. cooking

_____ 3. Your position in a group or society is called your

   a. sanction   c. peer group
   b. program   d. status

_____ 4. A **case study** focuses on

   a. a single event   c. an individual person
   b. a group   d. a problem

_____ 5. Having enough money to live comfortably is a commonly agreed upon social

   a. stereotype   c. sanction
   b. variable   d. value

_____ 6. The study of diverse racial and ethnic groups within a culture is known as

   a. environmental studies   c. multiculturalism
   b. ethnocentrism   d. racial diversity

_____ 7. A **norm** is a rule that specifies how people should

   a. behave   c. write
   b. think   d. communicate

_____ 8. A **peer group** shares common

   a. religion   c. age or interests
   b. racial background   d. housing

_____ 9. In society, a punishment for not conforming to what is expected is called a

   a. sanction   c. value
   b. status   d. norm

_____ 10. A category of people who have equal income, power, and prestige is called

   a. an income group   c. a peer group
   b. a social class   d. a value class

MASTERY test

Applying Your Skills in Psychology and Sociology

The following passage is taken from *Sociology: A Down-to-Earth Approach* by James M. Henslin. Read the passage to learn about gender inequality in the workplace. Then practice the skills you have learned in Part I of this text by answering the questions that follow.

Gender Inequality in the Workplace

The Pay Gap

1   One of the chief characteristics of the U.S. work force is a steady growth in the numbers of women who work outside the home for wages. In 1890 about one of every five people in the U.S. paid work force was a woman. By 1940, this **ratio** had grown to one of four; by 1960 to one of three; and today it is almost one of two. Women who work for wages are not evenly distributed throughout the United States. From the Social Map in Figure A on this page, you can see that

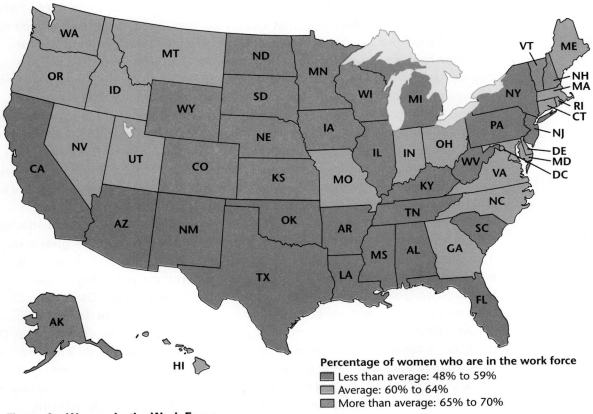

Percentage of women who are in the work force
- Less than average: 48% to 59%
- Average: 60% to 64%
- More than average: 65% to 70%

Figure A   Women in the Work Force

Source: By the author. Based on *Statistical Abstract* 2005: Table 574.

where a woman lives makes a difference in how likely she is to work outside the home. Why is there such a clustering among the states? The geographical patterns evident in this map reflect regional-**subcultural differences** about which we currently have little understanding.

2   After college, you might like to take a few years off, travel a bit, and sit under a palm tree and drink piña coladas. But chances are, you are going to go to work instead. Since you have to work, how would you like to earn an extra $1,100,000 on your job? If this sounds appealing, read on. I'm going to **reveal** how you can make an extra $2,400 a month between the ages of 25 and 65.

3   Is this hard to do? Actually, it is simple for some, but impossible for others. All you have to do is be born a male and graduate from college. If we compare full-time workers, based on current differences in earnings, this is how much more money the *average male* college graduate can expect to earn over the course of his career. Hardly any single factor **pinpoints** gender discrimination better than this total. You can also see that the pay gap shows up at *all* levels of education.

4   The pay gap is so great that U.S. women who work full time average *only 68 percent* of what men are paid. The pay gap used to be even worse. You can also see that the gap closed a bit during the 1980s, but then it grew during the 1990s. Since then, it has held fairly constant, **hovering** between 66 percent and 68 percent. The gender gap in pay occurs not only in the United States but also in *all* industrialized nations.

5   If $1,100,000 additional earnings aren't enough, how would you like to make another $166,000 extra at work? If so, just make sure that you are not only a man but also a *tall* man. Over their lifetimes, men who are over 6 feet tall average $166,000 more than men who are 5 feet 5 inches or less (Judge and Cable 2004). Taller women also make more than shorter women. But even when it comes to height, the gender pay gap **persists**, and tall men make more than tall women.

6   What logic can underlie the gender pay gap? Earlier we saw that college degrees are gender linked, so perhaps this gap is due to career choices. Maybe women are more likely to choose lower-paying jobs, such as teaching grade school, while men are more likely to go into better-paying fields, such as business and engineering. Actually, this is true, and researchers have found that about *half* of the gender pay gap is due to such factors. And the balance? It consists of a combination of gender discrimination (Jacobs 2003; Roth 2003) and what is called the "**child penalty**"—women missing out on work experience while they care for children (Hundley 2001; Chaker and Stout 2004).

7   For college students, the gender gap in pay begins with the first job after graduation. You might know of a particular woman who was offered a higher salary than most men in her class, but she would be an exception. On average, men enjoy a "**testosterone bonus**," and employers start them out at higher salaries than women (Fuller and Schoenberger 1991; Harris et al. 2005). Depending on your sex, then, you will either benefit from the pay gap or be **victimized** by it.

8   As a final indication of the extent of the U.S. gender pay gap, consider this. Of the nation's top 500 corporations (the so-called "**Fortune 500**"), only 8 are headed by women (Jones 2005). And 8 is a record-breaking number! I examined the names of the CEOs of the 350 largest U.S. corporations, and I found that your best chance to reach the top is to be named (in this order) John, Robert, James, William, or Charles. Edward, Lawrence, and Richard are also **advantageous** names.

Amber, Katherine, Leticia, and Maria, however, apparently draw a severe penalty. Naming your baby girl John or Robert might seem a little severe, but it could help her reach the top. (I say this only slightly **tongue-in-cheek**. One of the few women to head a Fortune 500 company—before she was fired and given $21 million **severance** pay–had a man's first name: Carleton Fiorina of Hewlett-Packard.)

The Cracking Glass Ceiling

9   What keeps women from breaking through the **glass ceiling** the mostly **invisible** barrier that keeps women from reaching the executive suite? Researchers have identified a "pipeline" that leads to the top: the marketing, sales, and production positions that directly affect the corporate bottom line (Hymowitz 2004; DeCrow 2005). Men, who dominate the executive suite, **stereotype** women as being less capable of leadership than they are (Heilman 2001). Viewing women as good at "support," they steer women into human resources or public relations. There, successful projects are not appreciated in the same way as those that bring corporate profits—and bonuses for their managers.

10   Another reason the glass ceiling is so powerful is that women lack **mentors**— successful executives who take an interest in them and teach them the ropes. Lack of a mentor is no **trivial** matter, for mentors can provide opportunities to develop **leadership** skills that open the door to the executive suite (Heilman 2001).

11   The glass ceiling is cracking, however (Solomon 2000; Hymowitz 2004). A look at women who have broken through reveals highly motivated individuals with a fierce **competitive** spirit who are willing to give up sleep and recreation for the sake of career advancement. They also learn to play by "men's rules," developing a style that makes men comfortable. Most of these women also have supportive husbands who share household duties and adapt their careers to accommodate the needs of their executive wives (Lublin 1996). In addition, women who began their careers 20 to 30 years ago are running many major divisions within the largest companies: With this background, some of these women will emerge as the new top CEOs (Hymowitz 2004).

12   Then there is the *glass escalator*. Sociologist Christine Williams (1995) interviewed men and women who worked in traditionally female jobs—as nurses, elementary school teachers, librarians, and social workers. Instead of bumping their heads against a glass ceiling, the men in these occupations found themselves aboard a glass escalator. They were given higher-level positions, more desirable work assignments, and higher salaries. The motor that drives the glass escalator is gender—the stereotype that because someone is male he is more capable.

EXERCISE 12-4   Context Clues and Word Parts

Directions: **Part A**   Use your knowledge of context clues and word parts to figure out the meaning of each of the following words or phrases as they are used in the passage. Then write a definition for each word or phrase based on how it is used in the selection. Consult a dictionary if necessary.

1. persists (para. 5) _____

2. advantageous (para. 8) _____

3. severance (para. 8) _____

4. leadership (para. 10) _____

5. competitive (para. 11) _____

Directions: Part B Complete each of the following sentences, so that they provide a context clue for the words in boldface that are taken from the selection. Use your knowledge of context clues to help you determine their meanings as they are used in the reading selection. Consult a dictionary if necessary.

1. The temperature is **hovering** (para. 4), _____, in the mid-eighties.

2. Female executives often experience a **child penalty** (para. 6), which means they _____
   _____.

3. The magazine listed the **Fortune 500** (para. 8), _____, in the United States.

4. A belief that females cannot be successful executives is one example of **stereotype** (para. 9); another example is _____ or _____.

5. The details about when and where U.S. presidents were born was **trivial** (para. 10) compared to the information in the textbook about _____.

| EXERCISE 12-5 | Using Your Vocabulary Skills |

Directions: The following questions test your knowledge of the boldfaced words or phrases used in the selection. Write the letters of the correct answers on the lines provided.

_____ 1. In paragraph 1, the last sentence makes it clear that a **ratio** (para. 1) is

    a. a study of behavior

    b. a characteristic of the work force

    c. an even distribution of gender

    d. a comparison between two numbers or amounts

_____ 2. The word **reveal** (para. 2) is used to mean

    a. repeat important information   c. discover new information

    b. uncover and share hidden information   d. learn something new

_____ 3. **Subcultural differences** (para. 1) are those that occur

    a. beneath or below the primary culture   c. alongside primary cultures

    b. inside primary cultures   d. in opposition to primary cultures

_____ 4. **Pinpoints** (para. 3) is a compound word, so in the context of the selection it means

    a. erases completely   c. locates exactly and precisely

    b. points out in a vague manner   d. makes a small hole

_____ 5. By using the phrase **testosterone bonus** (para. 7) the author is saying that

    a. men who reproduce have more children to support

    b. women who have children have higher incomes

    c. gender is an important factor when deciding who to hire

    d. men get better salaries because they are male

6. In paragraph 7, what word or phrase gives a contrast context clue that suggests the meaning of the word **victimized**?

   a. benefit from

   b. either

   c. depending

   d. or be

7. **Tongue-in-cheek** (para. 8) is an idiom that means

   a. speaking with your tongue in your cheek

   b. speaking with anger and outrage

   c. speaking after careful contemplation

   d. speaking in a humorous manner

8. The author uses the figurative term **glass ceiling** (para. 9) to help readers understand

   a. how office buildings are constructed in a way that is discriminatory to women

   b. the way corporate thinking prevents women from being as successful as men

   c. why some parents give their daughters male names

   d. the ways some women have creatively worked around the gender pay gap

9. Use your knowledge of root words and suffixes to determine that the word **invisible** (para. 9) means

   a. easily seen

   b. magical

   c. not apparent to human eyes

   d. unbreakable

10. **Mentors** (para. 10) are

   a. executives who help employees advance in their careers

   b. bosses who evaluate work performance

   c. instructors in an academic setting

   d. people who are more competitive than others

13

Politics and Government

Learning Core Terms

The following list is representative of the terminology you will be expected to learn in the fields of politics and government.

1. **appropriation** A designated amount of public funds set aside to support a particular project or program.

2. **capitalism** An economic system in which individuals and corporations, not the government, own businesses.

3. **disenfranchise** To deprive an individual of the right of citizenship, especially the right to vote.

4. **conservative** A person who favors state and local government over the federal government's intervention.

5. **electoral college** An electoral body that officially elects the president and vice president of the United States.

6. **entitlement** A law or policy requiring the government to pay money to people or groups meeting a specific set of conditions or criteria.

7. **expenditures** Federal spending of the money the government receives as revenue (income) from sources such as taxes. Major expenditures are medicare, social security, and the military.

8. **impeachment** The process of charging a political official with improper conduct while in office.

9. **incumbent** A person who currently holds a political office.

10. **lame duck** An elected official whose power is reduced because he or she has not been reelected to the position or is not allowed to run for the same office again.

11. **left wing** A liberal or ultraliberal portion of a group.

12. **liberal** A person who favors governmental action to achieve equal opportunity for all.

13. **lobbying** The process of attempting to persuade or influence the decision making of a government official by someone acting on behalf of a person or group.

14. **pacifism** The belief that war and violence are not effective or acceptable means of solving problems or settling disagreements.

15. **patronage** Awarding a job, promotion, or contract for political reasons rather than merit or competence.

16. **revenues** Sources of income of a government; the income tax is a primary source of revenue.

17. **referendum** A state-level process that gives voters the opportunity to approve or disapprove legislation or a constitutional amendment.

18. **right wing** A conservative or ultraconservative portion of a group.

19. **socialism** An economic system in which businesses are owned collectively by the government.

20. **veto** The right of one branch of government to refuse approval of measures proposed by another branch, especially the power of the president to reject a bill proposed by Congress.

 Learn More about Political Science and Government Terminology by Visiting the Following Web Site

http://www.daltonstate.edu/faculty/bguo/p1101/Glossary.htm

EXERCISE 13-1   Defining Politics/Government Vocabulary I

Directions: Choose the definitions in column B that best match the words or phrases in column A. Write your answers in the spaces provided.

Column A	Column B
1. ____ impeachment	a. The radical or liberal portion of a group
2. ____ socialism	b. Public funds designated for a specific purpose
3. ____ left wing	c. Awarding a job contract as a political favor

4. _____ veto

    d. A person who favors governmental action to achieve equality

5. _____ liberal

    e. To deprive an individual of the right to vote

6. _____ appropriations

    f. A body that officially elects the U.S. president and vice president

7. _____ lobbying

    g. The system in which the government controls businesses to maintain equality in society

8. _____ electoral college

    h. An attempt to influence a government official made by an individual or group representative

9. _____ disenfranchise

    i. The power of the U.S. president to reject a bill proposed by Congress

10. _____ patronage

    j. The process of charging an elected official with improper conduct

---

EXERCISE 13-2   Defining Politics/Government Vocabulary II

Directions: Write the letters of the correct answers in the spaces provided.

_____ 1. The word **expenditures** refers to

    a. large expense accounts   c. federal surplus from taxes

    b. the national debt   d. federal spending of taxes

_____ 2. The **left wing** is the part of a group that is

    a. conservative   c. reserved for Republicans

    b. radical or liberal   d. religious or spiritual

_____ 3. **Capitalism** is an economic system in which

    a. individuals and corporations own businesses

    b. corporations and the governments own businesses

    c. corporations are taxed at a higher rate than individuals

    d. corporations are given tax breaks

_____ 4. **Pacifism** is the belief that

    a. voting is a waste of time

    b. war and violence cannot solve problems

    c. wars have always ended a recession

    d. proper legislation will solve all problems

_____ 5. A **veto**, the constitutional power to reject a bill proposed by Congress, can be exercised by the

    a. senate   c. secretary of state

    b. foreign minister   d. president

_____ 6. The term **conservative** refers to a person who

    a. holds a seat in Congress   c. favors state and local government

    b. favors traditional values   d. takes no political sides

_____ 7. The **electoral college** is a body that officially elects

    a. the president and vice president

    b. governors

    c. senators

    d. members of the the House of Representatives

_____ 8. The term **liberal** describes a person who

    a. does not vote

    b. is not tolerant of others

    c. is against organized religion

    d. favors governmental action to achieve equality

_____ 9. **Socialism** is an economic system in which

    a. businesses are not taxed

    b. businesses are owned collectively by the government

    c. each state decides how tax money will be spent

    d. groups of states combine their economic resources

_____ 10. The word **disenfranchise** means to

    a. deprive an individual of the right of citizenship

    b. allow political prisoners to return to their native countries

    c. close a chain store

    d. create government-sponsored funds for businesses

EXERCISE 13-3   Defining Politics/Government Vocabulary III

Directions: Chooses the definitions in column B that best match the words or phrases in column A. Write your answers in the spaces provided.

Column A	Column B
1. ____ expenditures	a. An elected official who has not been, or cannot be, reelected
2. ____ incumbent	b. A person who favors state and local governmental control
3. ____ capitalism	c. Opposition to war and violence
4. ____ revenue	d. Federal spending of money
5. ____ conservative	e. Financial resources of the government

6. —— pacifism

    f. A process that allows voters to approve or disapprove legislation

7. —— lame duck

    g. A system in which individuals and corporations own businesses

8. —— referendum

    h. A person who currently holds an elected office

9. —— entitlement

    i. A law or policy requiring payment of government funds to specific groups

10. —— right wing

    j. Conservative portion of a group

MASTERY test

Applying Your Skills in Politics and Government

This textbook excerpt was taken from *Government in America* by George C. Edwards III, Martin P. Wattenberg, and Robert L. Lineberry. Read the passage to learn about how political polls are conducted, analyzed, and evaluated. Then practice the skills you have learned in Part I of this text by answering the questions that follow.

How Opinion Polls Are Conducted

1   Public opinion polling is a relatively new science. It was first developed by a young man named George Gallup, who initially did some polling for his mother-in-law, a longshot candidate for secretary of state in Iowa in 1932. With the Democratic landslide of that year, she won a stunning victory, thereby further **stimulating** Gallup's interest in politics. From that little acorn the mighty oak of public opinion polling has grown. The firm that Gallup founded spread throughout the democratic world, and in some languages, *Gallup* is actually the word used for an opinion poll.[14]

2   It would be prohibitively expensive and time consuming to ask every citizen his or her opinion on a whole range of issues. Instead, polls rely on a **sample** of the population—a relatively small **proportion** of people who are chosen to represent the whole. Herbert Asher draws an **analogy** to a blood test to illustrate the principle of sampling.[15] Your doctor does not need to drain a gallon of blood from you to determine whether you have mononucleosis, AIDS, or any other disease. Rather, a small sample of blood will reveal its properties.

3   In public opinion polling, a sample of about 1,000 to 1,500 people can accurately represent the "universe" of potential voters. The key to the accuracy of opinion polls is the technique of **random sampling** which **operates** on the principle that everyone should have an equal probability of being selected as part of the sample. Your chance of being asked to be in the poll should therefore be as good as that of anyone else—rich or poor, African American or White, young or old, male or female. If the sample is randomly drawn, about 12 percent of those interviewed will be African American, slightly over 50 percent female, and so forth, matching the population as a whole.

4   Remember that the science of polling involves estimation; a sample can represent the population with only a certain degree of confidence. The level of confidence is known as the **sampling error**, which depends on the size of the sample. The more people interviewed in a poll, the more confident one can be of the results. A typical poll of about 1,500 to 2,000 respondents has a sampling error of ±3 percent. What this means is that 95 percent of the time the poll results are within 3 percent of what the entire population thinks. If 60 percent of the sample say they approve of the job the president is doing, one can be pretty certain that the true figure is between 57 and 63 percent.

5   In order to obtain results that will usually be within sampling error, researchers must follow proper sampling techniques. In perhaps the most **infamous** survey ever, a 1936 *Literary Digest* poll underestimated the vote for President Franklin Roosevelt by 19 percent, **erroneously** predicting a big victory for Republican Alf Landon. The well-established magazine suddenly became a **laughingstock** and soon went out of business. Although the number of responses the magazine obtained for its poll was a **staggering** 2,376,000, its polling methods were badly flawed. Trying to reach as many people as possible, the magazine drew names from the biggest lists they could find: telephone books and motor vehicle records. In the midst of the Great Depression, the people on these lists were above the average income level (only 40 percent of the public had telephones then; fewer still owned cars) and were more likely to vote Republican. The **moral** of the story is this: Accurate representation, not the number of responses, is the most important feature of a public opinion survey. Indeed, as polling techniques have advanced over the last 60 years, typical sample sizes have been getting smaller, not larger.

6   The newest computer and telephone technology has made surveying less expensive and more commonplace. In the early days of polling, pollsters needed a national network of interviewers to **traipse** door-to-door in their **localities** with a clipboard of questions. Now most polling is done on the telephone with samples selected through **random-digit dialing**: Calls are placed to phone numbers within randomly chosen exchanges (for example, 512–471-xxxx) around the country. In this manner, both listed and unlisted numbers are reached at a cost of about one-fifth that of person-to-person interviewing. There are a couple of disadvantages, however. About 7 percent of the population does not have a phone, and people are somewhat less willing to participate over the telephone than in person—it is easier to hang up than to slam the door in someone's face. These are small trade-offs for political candidates running for minor offices, for whom telephone polls are the only affordable method of **gauging** public opinion. However, in this era of cell phones, many pollsters are starting to worry whether this **methodology** will continue to work much longer.

7   From its **modest** beginning with George Gallup's 1932 polls for his mother-in-law in Iowa, polling has become a big business. Public opinion polling is one of those American **innovations** like soft drinks and fast food restaurants, that has spread throughout the world. From Manhattan to Moscow, from Tulsa to Tokyo, people want to know what other people think.

EXERCISE 13-4   Context Clues and Word Parts

Directions: Listed in the first column are ten boldfaced words from the passage. Use your knowledge of context clues and word parts to figure out the meaning of each word as it is used in the passage, and then match the word with its definition in the second column. Consult a dictionary if necessary.

——— 1. stimulating (para. 1)   a. neighborhoods or areas

——— 2. Gallup (para. 1)   b. calls made to numbers selected by chance

——— 3. sample (para. 2)   c. a small group that represents the whole

_____ 4. proportion (para. 2)   d. incorrectly

_____ 5. analogy (para. 2)   e. encouraging

_____ 6. erroneously (para. 5)   f. humble or moderate

_____ 7. staggering (para. 5)   g. an opinion poll

_____ 8. localities (para. 6)   h. percentage, part of a whole

_____ 9. random-digit dialing (para. 6) i. overwhelmingly large

_____ 10. modest (para. 7)   j. a comparison between two similar things

EXERCISE 13-5   Using Your Vocabulary Skills

Directions: The following questions test your knowledge of words or phrases used in the passage. Write the letters of the correct answers on the lines provided.

_____ 1. If you were to create an index card for the term **random sampling** (para. 3), which definition would be the most useful to write on the back of the card?

    a. a way to choose exact samples that relies on highly technical computer models

    b. a process of purposely selecting people based on their individual characteristics and interests

    c. making poll decisions based on opinions that people express, not on actions people take when they vote

    d. a method of choosing participants that gives every part of the population an equal chance of being selected

_____ 2. In the context of the passage, what does the word **operates** (para. 3) mean?

    a. works   c. changes

    b. creates   d. directs

_____ 3. Using context clues from the entire paragraph, what is the meaning of the term **sampling error** (para. 4)?

    a. the percent by which a poll's result are inaccurate

    b. the number of answers poll respondents give

    c. the amount of people the poll failed to question

    d. the quantity of responses that are not relevant to the question being asked

_____ 4. The word *infamy* means "a reputation for being shocking, criminal, or extreme." Using your knowledge of suffixes, what does the word **infamous** (para. 5) mean?

    a. appallingly bad   c. committing a crime

    b. not being famous   d. well-known

_____ 5. From the context of the sentence, you can determine that **laughingstock** (para. 5) means

    a. something intentionally funny   c. a person or thing that needs repair

    b. a person or thing that is made fun of   d. a fun and interesting thing

6. The word **moral** (para. 5) is a homograph. Select the meaning for the word as it is used in this selection.

    a. acting on principles of good and bad behavior

    b. to do with what is right or wrong

    c. the practical lesson behind something

    d. none of the above

7. The word **traipse** (para. 6) has a connotative meaning that words like *walk* or *travel* do not. The writer uses this word in the passage to convey the feeling of

    a. time pressures

    b. exhaustive and repetitive movement

    c. the importance of door-to-door polling

    d. accuracy and carefulness

8. In the context of the passage, what does the word **gauging** (para. 6) mean?

    a. publicizing

    b. measuring

    c. controlling

    d. reducing

9. The suffix *ology* means "the study of," so you know that the word **methodology** (para. 6) refers to

    a. the study of workplaces

    b. the study of changes

    c. the study of institutions

    d. the study of procedures

10. Read the following sentence from paragraph 7 of the selection; then answer the question that follows.

    > Public opinion polling is one of those American **innovations**, like soft drinks and fast food restaurants, that has spread throughout the world.

    The examples in this sentence allow the reader to understand that **innovations** means

    a. unhealthy habits

    b. changes

    c. inventions

    d. historical trends

J.K. Rowling signing copies of one of her bestselling books.

14 Literature

Learning Core Terms

The following list is representative of the terminology you will be expected to learn when studying literature.

1. **allegory** A story in which characters and/or events stand for abstract ideas or forces, so that the story suggests a deeper symbolic meaning.

2. **anthology** A collection of literary works, often by different authors, combined into a single work.

3. **characterization** The methods an author uses to describe and develop characters in a literary work.

4. **classic** A literary work of the highest quality that has long-lasting value and worth.

5. **denouement** The end of a plot (story) in which the final resolution or explanation takes place.

6. **expository writing** A type of writing in which the main purpose is to present information.

7. **fiction** A literary work that is imaginative and not factual.

8. **figurative language** Language that makes a comparison between two unlike things that are similar in one particular way. Metaphors and similes are two common types of figurative language.

9. **flashback** A scene in a play or reference in a story that interrupts the story line to show something that has occurred in the past.

10. **genre** A type or category of literature; common genres include prose, poetry, fiction, and drama.

11. **literary criticism** Works written to interpret and evaluate literary works.

12. **memoir** A narrative or record of events based on personal experience.

13. **mythology** A collection of myths (stories) concerning ancient gods and/or legendary beings.

14. **narrative** A story that relates a series of events, real or imaginary, for the purpose of making a point.

15. **persuasive writing** A type of writing intended to convince readers to accept a particular viewpoint or take a specific action.

16. **plot** The basic story line; the sequence of events and actions through which a story's meaning is expressed.

17. **point of view** The perspective from which a story is told. Two common points of view are first person (I) in which the narrator is telling the story as he or she experiences it, and the third person (he, she, they) in which the story is told by someone who is not a character in the story.

18. **setting** The time, place, and circumstance in which a story occurs.

19. **theme** The central or dominant idea of a story; the main point the author is making about human life or experiences.

20. **tone** How writers convey their feelings or attitudes about the subject to the reader.

Learn More about Literary Terminology by Visiting the Following Web Site

http://www.galegroup.com/free_resources/glossary/index.htm

EXERCISE 14-1   Using Literature Vocabulary

Directions: Use words from the list at the beginning of the chapter to complete the meaning of each sentence.

1. When Derek wrote his first novel, he wrote from the _____ of the first person.

2. The _____ for Angela's story is the Pacific Northwest.

3. Marianne used _____ in her newspaper article to try to convince her readers that the museum needed more money.

4. David studied the gods of ancient Greece in his _____ class.

5. The survey course will be using a(n) _____ that will cover a collection of poetry from the nineteenth century.

6. Miguel used many _____ in his short story so that his readers could understand the history of his characters.

7. Because the sequence of events in her story was very confusing, Yolanda wrote an outline of the _____.

8. The _____ of Nate's story sounded very angry and hostile to the entire class.

9. A story in which characters or events stand for abstract ideas is called a(n) _____.

10. Rosa has decided to write a _____ of her personal experiences during the war.

EXERCISE 14-2   Defining Literary Terms I

Directions: Choose the definitions in column B that best match the words or phrases in column A. Write your answers in the spaces provided.

Column A

1. ——— characterization
2. ——— literary criticism
3. ——— classic
4. ——— allegory
5. ——— genre
6. ——— theme
7. ——— figurative language
8. ——— anthology
9. ——— tone
10. ——— denouement

Column B

a. a high-quality, long-lasting literary work

b. a class or type of literature

c. how a writer conveys feelings to a reader

d. central or dominant idea of a story

e. works that interpret a piece of literature

f. a group of writings by different authors

g. story in which characters or events stand for abstract ideas

h. final resolution of a story

i. language that makes comparisons between two unlike things that are similar in one way

j. methods used to develop main figures in a story

EXERCISE 14-3   Defining Literature Vocabulary II

Directions: Write the letter of the correct definition of each of the following terms on the lines provided.

_____ 1. **setting**
   a. time and place of a story
   b. events in a story
   c. key people in a story
   d. perspective of a story

_____ 2. **persuasive writing**
   a. writing intended to convince
   b. writing intended to inform
   c. writing intended to discuss
   d. writing intended to express feelings

_____ 3. **denouement**
   a. the end of a story
   b. the action in a story
   c. the introduction to a story
   d. the first event in a story

_____ 4. **fiction**

    a. factual story

    b. imaginative story

    c. truthful story

    d. misleading story

_____ 5. **memoir**

    a. story based on interviews

    b. narrative based on personal experience

    c. stories that cannot be verified

    d. historical events

_____ 6. **plot**

    a. time period

    b. key people

    c. important idea

    d. sequence of events

_____ 7. **mythology**

    a. misleading stories about figures in history

    b. stories about ancient gods and goddesses

    c. fictional stories about people

    d. untrue stories about religious figures

_____ 8. **point of view**

    a. actions other characters can view

    b. place where actions occur

    c. perspective from which a story is told

    d. point where the story begins

_____ 9. **narrative**

    a. story without a conclusion

    b. story without a theme

    c. story that persuades

    d. story that makes a point

_____ 10. **theme**

    a. how the writer sounds

    b. most important character

    c. main point of a story

    d. most important event in a story

MASTERY test

Applying Your Skills in Literature

This short story by John Collier was written in the early 1900s in London. Read it, and then practice the skills you have learned in Part I of this text by answering the questions that follow.

The Chaser

1   Alan Austen, as nervous as a kitten, went up certain dark and **creaky** stairs in the neighborhood of Pell Street, and **peered** about for a long time on the dim landing before he found the name he wanted written **obscurely** on one of the doors.

2   He pushed open this door, as he had been told to do, and found himself in a tiny room, which contained no furniture but a plain kitchen table, a rocking-chair, and an ordinary chair. On one of the dirty buff-colored walls were a couple of shelves, containing in all perhaps a dozen bottles and jars.

3   An old man sat in the rocking-chair, reading a newspaper. Alan, without a word, handed him the card he had been given. "Sit down, Mr. Austen," said the man very politely. "I am glad to **make your acquaintance**."

4   "Is it true," asked Alan, "that you have a certain mixture that has—er—quite **extraordinary** effects?"

5   "My dear sir," replied the old man, "my stock in trade is not very large—but I don't deal in laxatives and teething mixtures—but such as it is, it is **varied**. I think nothing I sell has effects which could be **precisely** described as ordinary."

6   "Well, the fact is—" began Alan.

7   "Here, for example," interrupted the old man, reaching for a bottle from the shelf. "Here is a liquid as colorless as water, almost tasteless, quite imperceptible in coffee, milk, wine, or any other beverage. It is also quite **imperceptible** to any known method of **autopsy**."

8   "Do you mean it is a poison?" cried Alan, very much horrified.

9   "Call it a glove-cleaner if you like," said the old man indifferently. "Maybe it will clean gloves. I have never tried. One might call it a life-cleaner. Lives need cleaning sometimes."

10   "I want nothing of that sort," said Alan.

11   "Probably it is just as well," said the old man. "Do you know the price of this? For one teaspoonful, which is **sufficient**, I ask five thousand dollars. Never less. Not a penny less."

12   "I hope all your mixtures are not as expensive," said Alan apprehensively.

13   "Oh dear, no," said the old man. "It would be no good charging that sort of price for a love potion, for example. Young people who need a love potion very **seldom** have five thousand dollars. Otherwise they would not need a love potion."

14   "I am glad to hear that," said Alan.

15   "I look at it like this," said the old man. "Please a customer with one article, and he will come back when he needs another. Even if it is more costly. He will save up for it, if necessary."

16   "So," said Alan, "you really do sell love potions?"

17   "If I did not sell love potions," said the old man, reaching for another bottle, "I should not have mentioned the other matter to you. It is only when one is in a position to **oblige** that one can afford to be so **confidential**."

18   "And these potions," said Alan. "They are not just—just—er—"

19   "Oh, no," said the old man. "Their effects are permanent, and extend far beyond causal impulse. But they include it. **Bountifully**, insistently. Everlastingly."

20   "Dear me!" said Alan, attempting to look of **scientific detachment**. "How very interesting!"

21   "But consider the spiritual side," said the old man.

22   "I do, indeed," said Alan.

23   "For indifference," said the old man, "they substitute **devotion**. For scorn, adoration. Give one tiny measure of this to the young lady—its flavor is impercep-tible in orange juice, soup, or cocktails—and however gay and giddy she is, she will change altogether. She will want nothing but solitude, and you."

24   "I can hardly believe it," said Alan. "She is so fond of parties."

25   "She will not like them any more," said the old man. "She will be afraid of the pretty girls you may meet."

26   "She will actually be jealous?" cried Alan in rapture. "Of me?"

27   "Yes, she will want to be everything to you."

28   "She is, already. Only she doesn't care about it."

29   "She will, when she has taken this. She will care intensely. You will be her sole interest in life."

30   "Wonderful!" cried Alan.

31   "She will want to know all you do," said the old man. "All that has happened to you during the day. Every word of it. She will want to know what you are thinking about, why you smile suddenly, why you are looking sad."

32   "That is love!" cried Alan.

33   "Yes," said the old man. "How carefully she will look after you! She will never allow you to be tired, to sit in a **draught**, to neglect your food. If you are an hour late, she will be terrified. She will think you are killed, or that some **siren** has caught you."

34   "I can hardly imagine Diana like that!" cried Alan, overwhelmed with joy.

35   "You will not have to use your imagination," said the old man. "And, by the way, since there are always sirens, if by any chance you should, later on, slip a little, you need not worry. She will forgive you, in the end. She will be terribly hurt, of course, but she will forgive you—in the end."

36   "That will not happen," said Alan fervently.

37   "Of course not," said the old man. "But, if it did, you need not worry. She would never divorce you. Oh, no! And, of course, she herself will never give you the least, the very least, grounds for—**uneasiness**."

38   "And how much," said Alan, "Is this wonderful mixture?"

39   "It is not as dear," said the old man, "as the glove-cleaner, or life-cleaner, as I sometimes call it. No. That is five thousand dollars, never a penny less. One has to be older than you are, to indulge in that sort of thing. One has to save up for it."

40   "But the love potion?" said Alan.

41   "Oh, that," said the old man, opening the drawer in the kitchen table, and taking out a tiny, rather dirty-looking phial. "That is just a dollar."

42   "I can't tell you how grateful I am," said Alan, watching him fill it.

43   "I like to oblige," said the old man. "Then customers come back, later in life, when they are rather better off, and want more expensive things. Here you are. You will find it very effective."

44   "Thank you again," said Alan. "Good-bye."

45   "**Au revoir.**" said the old man.

EXERCISE 14-4   Context Clues and Word Parts

Directions: Choose the word or phrase from the list that best fits into each of the following sentences. If you are unsure of the meaning of a word, use your knowledge of context clues and word parts to figure our its meaning as it is used in the passage. Consult a dictionary if necessary.

creaky (para. 1)	precisely (para. 5)
peered (para. 1)	sufficient (para. 11)
obscurely (para. 1)	seldom (para. 13)
make your acquaintance (para. 3)	oblige (para. 17)
varied (para. 5)	confidential (para. 17)

1. Because the museum is open only on weekends, we are _____ able to visit it.

2. The suit fit _____ and did not need to be altered.

3. The door was extremely _____ and its hinges needed to be oiled.

4. The notes on the sides of the textbook pages were _____ written and difficult to decipher.

5. The times the library was open over spring break were _____, depending on the day of the week.

6. Therapists are required to keep all patient information _____ and not share it with anyone.

7. The detective gathered _____ evidence to prove that the crime was committed by the butler.

8. As she wrapped presents in the dining room, her son _____ around the corner, trying to see what she was doing.

9. The fan told the famous actor, "It's so exciting to _____."

10. If you accept the invitation, it will _____ you to attend the party.

Directions: The following questions test your knowledge of the meaning of words or phrases used in the selection. Write the letters of the correct answers on the lines provided.

_____ 1. The compound word **extraordinary** (para. 4) means

    a. damaging   c. common

    b. remarkable   d. dangerous

_____ 2. The world **imperceptible** (para. 7) means

    a. sensible to use   c. delicious to taste

    b. not able to be labeled   d. not noticeable

_____ 3. In a television drama, **autopsy** (para. 7) would refer to a medical examination of a dead body, but in this selection, it refers to

    a. inspection or analysis of an item   c. simple or basic facts

    b. unapproved medication   d. things that cannot be proven

_____ 4. The word **bountifully** (para. 19) means

    a. frequently   c. expensively

    b. plentifully   d. sparingly

_____ 5. The phrase **scientific detachment** (para. 20) is used to refer to

    a. unlikely concern   c. unemotional study

    b. separated pieces   d. missing information

_____ 6. A contrast clue for **devotion** (para. 23) is

    a. measure   c. adoration

    b. indifference   d. flavor

_____ 7. **Draught** (para. 33) is an alternate spelling of

    a. daft   c. doubt

    b. drought   d. draft

_____ 8. A **siren** (para. 33) is normally a loud warning sound, but in this selection it is used to mean

    a. a bird of prey   c. a charming or dangerous woman

    b. a sneaky or hidden trap   d. a carefully prepared song

_____ 9. The word **uneasiness** (para. 37) refers to

    a. feeling uncomfortable   c. need to question

    b. a sense of joy   d. hiding emotions

_____ 10. The French phrase **au revoir** (para. 45) means

    a. until we meet again   c. thank you

    b. hello   d. you're welcome

15

Arts

Learning Core Terms

The following lists are representative of the terminology you will be expected to learn in the fields of music and visual arts.

Music

1. **a capella** Vocal music performed without instrumental accompaniment.

2. **consonance** A combination of sounds considered to be pleasing and harmonious.

3. **dissonance** Disagreeable sounds or those lacking harmony.

4. **ensemble** Group of musicians; a musical work performed by two or more musicians or a group of musicians.

5. **maestro** A composer, conductor, or teacher of special importance; master of a particular art.

6. **medley** A musical composition made up of passages selected from different musical works.

7. **rendition** A style or interpretation of a musical piece.

8. **repertoire** A list of musical works a group of musicians is able to perform.

9. **rhythm** A regular pattern of sounds or musical notes created by the variation of the duration and stress of musical notes.

10. **symphony** A musical piece consisting of three or more movements to be played by an orchestra; a large-scale, complex musical piece. Also refers to an orchestra itself.

Visual Arts

1. **aesthetics** The study of the nature, meaning, and expression of beauty, as found in painting, sculpture, and drawing.

2. **collage** A work made by gluing or pasting a variety of materials such as paper, fabric, or photographs on a flat surface.

3. **form** The shape or configuration of an artistic work.

4. **impressionism** A style of painting that is known for short brush strokes to simulate the reflection of light, and for the use of primary colors.

5. **mosaic** An art form in which small squares of marble or other material are laid together to form a pattern or design.

6. **proportion** The relationship between parts with respect to size, quantity, or degree.

7. **realism** A style of painting that intends to show life and objects accurately, as they actually are.

8. **structure** The manner in which the parts of a work are combined.

9. **surrealism** A style of painting that attempts to express the workings of the subconscious mind.

10. **texture** The appearance and feel of the surface of an artistic work.

 **Learn More about Art Terminology by Visiting the Following Web Site**

http://www.theatrecrafts.com/glossary/glossary/shtml

EXERCISE 15-1 Defining Arts Vocabulary

Directions: Choose the definitions in column B that best match the words or phrases in column A. Write your answers in the spaces provided.

Music

Column A	Column B
1. ——— medley	a. Music sung without instrumental accompaniment
2. ——— a capella	b. The regular pattern of sounds created by varying the duration and stress of notes
3. ——— ensemble	c. A selection of passages from different musical works

4. ——— rendition
d. A musical piece consisting of three or more movements for an orchestra

5. ——— rhythm
e. Disagreeable sounds

6. ——— dissonance
f. A musical work for two or more musicians

7. ——— repertoire
g. The list of works a musician performs

8. ——— symphony
h. An important composer or conductor

9. ——— maestro
i. The interpretation of a musical piece

10. ——— consonance
j. Pleasing and agreeable sounds

EXERCISE 15-2   Using Arts Vocabulary I

Directions: Use words from the list at the beginning of the chapter to complete the meaning of each sentence.

1. One painting in the gallery was an interesting _____ made up of sheet music, small gold charms, and flower petals.

2. The artistic school of _____ is known for its use of primary colors and short brush strokes.

3. Although the artist's use of color was impressive, the _____ in the work was off, particularly when you compared the people to their surroundings.

4. The mirror was surrounded by a beautiful _____ of broken pieces of pottery.

5. _____ refers to the manner in which various elements of a work are integrated.

6. The portrait of the racehorse was an excellent example of _____ because it was so lifelike.

7. The _____, or configuration, of the sculpture emphasized the closeness of the two humans.

8. Painters of the school of _____ attempted to express the workings of the subconscious mind.

9. Because the painting depicted a rough and choppy sea, the artist used his brush to lift the paint off the canvas to create a _____ reflecting the disturbance of the water.

10. The study of _____ focuses on meaning and the expression of beauty.

EXERCISE 15-3   Using Arts Vocabulary II

Directions: Write the letter of the correct definition of each of the following terms on the lines provided.

——— 1. **Impressionism** is a style of painting that is known for

    a. long brush strokes to create a smooth surface

    b. short brush strokes and the use of primary colors

    c. stylistic work that is done very quickly

    d. use of mostly dark colors

_____ 2. **Surrealism** attempts to

  a. show only very realistic types of images

  b. encourage the use of primary colors

  c. express the workings of the subconscious mind

  d. create a feeling of immortality for the audience

_____ 3. The term **a capella** means

  a. vocal music performed without instrumental accompaniment

  b. vocal music accompanied by only percussion instruments

  c. a small orchestra

  d. music written for both voice and piano

_____ 4. **Dissonance** is

  a. a small distant sound

  b. a blending of harmonic sound

  c. sounds lacking harmony

  d. the cymbals of the drum set

_____ 5. The term **form** refers to

  a. the layout of a painting

  b. the shape or configuration of an artistic work

  c. the type of clay used in a sculpture

  d. stretching canvas on a frame

_____ 6. A **symphony** is a musical piece consisting of

  a. one movement to be played by an orchestra

  b. music for three to five instruments

  c. music for string quartets that is played very slowly

  d. three or more movements to be played by an orchestra

_____ 7. **Realism** is a style of painting that

  a. was never popular until the twentieth century

  b. uses a lot of texture and color

  c. intends to show life and objects accurately

  d. does not show life and objects accurately

_____ 8. **Consonance** is a combination of sounds

  a. that are atonal

  b. considered to be pleasing and harmonious

  c. played by only string instruments

  d. made up of major thirds and fifths

_____ 9. The term **medley** refers to a musical work

    a. with one dominant sound or tone

    b. consisting of selections from other musical works

    c. made up of several dominant themes

    d. by one composer that repeats a specific theme

_____ 10. A **collage** is a work made by

    a. using many layers of paint to build a thick surface

    b. using only high gloss paints to create a reflective surface

    c. adding extra pigment to enhance paint color

    d. gluing or pasting a variety of materials on a flat surface

MASTERY test

Applying Your Skills in the Arts

This textbook excerpt was taken from *The Art of Seeing* by Paul Zelanski and Mary Pat Fisher. Read the selction to learn about how famous art is being protected. Then practice the skills you have learned in Part I of this text by answering the questions that follow.

Protecting Famous Artworks

1   WHEN TOURISTS FROM around the world visit the Louvre in Paris, seeing Leonardo's *Mona Lisa* at first hand is the most **essential** experience the majority of them are seeking. But **nowadays** the object of their **pilgrimage** can be viewed only in a temperature- and humidity-controlled box through a protective bulletproof shield of 1.52-inch (3.8-cm) thick **nonreflective** glass. They are held at a distance by a wood railing, which also helps to control the crowds as some six million

The Mona Lisa (1503–1506) by Leonardo da Vinci

visitors try to visit the painting every year. They are warned not to photograph the painting, much less try to get closer to it. Within its **hermetically** sealed box, the painting is quite dirty, for the museum **curators** dare not remove its yellowed varnish lest there be a public **outcry**. A twenty-four-hour alarm system is always on alert to prevent damage or theft.

2   With all these protective measures, what is left of the **intimate encounter** between the viewer and the famous artworks? The *Mona Lisa* has become a sacred **icon** of sorts. Museum officials have taken extreme measures to protect the painting precisely because it is so famous.

3   The bulletproof shield is to protect the painting from physical attack. In 1956, a Bolivian tourist threw a rock at it, damaging the left elbow. The ban on photographs is to prevent flashes of bright light, which could turn the varnish even yellower and change the pigments. The climate-control case keeps the painting at 68°F (20°C), with 50–55 percent humidity maintained by boxes of silica gel below, to help preserve the poplar wood panel on which Leonardo painted his famous image. Behind the panel, a series of slats has been added to check its expansion and contraction. Already there is a fine crack descending from the top into the forehead. Monitoring the health of the painting is a precise science, carried out with a sense of **sacred** duty.

4   Paintings are designed to be seen only from the front, so they can be mounted behind glass shields if necessary. To protect sculptures from human damage requires measures that distance the public even farther. Famous statues are often **cordoned** off. After Michelangelo's touching *Pietà* was attacked in 1972 by someone who was out of his senses, a **bulletproof** glass shield was also placed around it. Without such a shield, the foot of Michelangelo's great statue of *David* was attacked in 1991 by a mentally ill person wielding a hammer. He explained that a woman in a painting by Veronese told him to strike the *David*. In a moment of sheer madness, the painstakingly and perfectly sculpted end of a toe was reduced to a pile of marble chips and dust. Museum officials are also trying to find ways to protect the *David* from **corrosive** dirt particles without surrounding it with glass; one solution may be a **curtain** of air jets.

5   The other side of the arguments about protection and **seclusion** from the public is that masterworks are **irreplaceable** and can perhaps never be restored to their original condition once they are damaged. Masters such as Michelangelo and Leonardo are rare in human history. But to truly protect their works for **posterity** would require fully sealing them off from the public in climate-controlled tamper-proof archives. Herein lie the difficulties. What balance should be struck between the desire of people to see famous works of art and the desire to preserve them as long as possible? Who has the right to see them?

6   In 1998, the Hermitage in St. Petersburg again put Rembrandt's *Danaë* on display, but this time behind a barrier, after twelve years of painstaking efforts to restore some of its original beauty, damaged almost beyond **salvation** by an attacker who threw acid on the painting and slashed it with a knife. And in 1995, the Reina Sofia Museum of Modern Art in Madrid chose to remove the protective glass shield with which it had covered Picasso's *Guernica*. Now the great work can be fully seen again, but it is again **vulnerable** to the **unpredictable** passions of the viewing public.

Directions: Listed below are ten boldfaced words from the selection. Use your knowledge of context clues and word parts to match these words with their correct definitions. Consult a dictionary if necessary.

——— 1. essential (para. 1)   a. being saved

——— 2. pilgrimage (para. 1)   b. managers of museum collections

——— 3. curators (para. 1)   c. a long journey with a special purpose

——— 4. sacred (para. 3)   d. isolation

——— 5. cordoned (para. 4)   e. able to be harmed

——— 6. bulletproof (para. 4)   f. necessary

——— 7. corrosive (para. 4)   g. blocked

——— 8. seclusion (para. 5)   h. damaging

——— 9. salvation (para. 6)   i. not able to be shot through

——— 10. vulnerable (para. 6)   j. religious

Directions: The following questions relate to boldfaced words or phrases used in the passage. Write the letters of the correct answers in the spaces provided.

——— 1. **Nowadays** (para. 1) refers to

   a. an uncertain period of time   c. tomorrow

   b. modern times   d. yesterday

——— 2. If the root word *reflect* means "to throw light back," **nonreflective** (para. 1) means

   a. not bulletproof   c. dark and murky

   b. unlikely to allow light through   d. unable to cast back light

——— 3. A jar that is **hermetically** (para. 1) sealed is

   a. airtight   c. isolated

   b. porous   d. guarded

——— 4. A public **outcry** (para. 1) is

   a. a loud cry of sadness   c. a protest against something

   b. a show of support   d. a riot in the streets

——— 5. As used in the selection, an **intimate encounter** (para. 2) means

   a. a first date in a museum   c. a personal connection to an artwork

   b. bumping into something   d. learning a secret about an artwork

6. The word **icon** (para. 2) is used to connote
   a. the artist's great talent
   b. the monetary value of a painting
   c. a duty to preserve art
   d. an item that is highly respected and valued

7. A **curtain** (para. 4) usually means a window hanging, but in this paragraph it means
   a. the covering for a stage
   b. an item that hides something from view
   c. the time a performance begins
   d. a vertical grouping

8. If the word *replace* means to substitute, then **irreplaceable** (para. 5) means
   a. difficult to place
   b. forged
   c. missing
   d. unique

9. The word **posterity** (para. 5) refers to
   a. later study
   b. future generations
   c. archives
   d. forever

10. Use your knowledge of prefixes, roots, and suffixes to select the correct meaning of the word **unpredictable** (para. 6).
    a. unsaid and unspoken
    b. unable to identify in advance
    c. not likely to have an impact
    d. unable to be taught

APPENDIX: Prefixes, Roots, and Suffixes

A. Useful Prefixes

Prefix	Meaning	Sample Word
a-	not	asymmetrical
ab-	away	absent
ad-	toward	adhesive
ante/pre-	before	antecedent/premarital
anthropo-	human being	anthropology, anthropomorphic
anti-	against	antiwar
archaeo-	ancient times	archaeology, archaic
bi/di/du-	two	bimonthly/divorce/duet
bio-	life	biology, biotechnology
centi-	hundred	centigrade
circum/peri-	around	circumference/perimeter
com/col/con-	with, together	compile/collide/convene
contra-	against, opposite	contradict
de-	away, from	depart
deci-	ten	decimal
dia-	through	diameter
dis-	part, away, not	disagree
equi-	equal	equidistant
ex/extra-	from, out of, former	ex-wife/extramarital
geo-	earth	geology, geography
gyneco-	woman	gynecology, gynecopathy
hyper-	over, excessive	hyperactive
in/il/ir/im-	not	incorrect/illogical/irreversible/impossible
inter-	between	interpersonal
intro/intra-	within, into, in	introduction
mal-	bad, wrong	malpractice
micro-	small	microscope
milli-	thousand	milligram
mis-	wrongly	misunderstand
mono/uni-	one	monocle/unicycle
multi/poly-	many	multipurpose/polygon
non-	not	nonfiction
peri-	around	perimeter
post-	after	posttest
pseudo-	false	pseudoscientific

Prefix	Meaning	Sample Word
pysch-	mind	psychology, psychopath
quad-	four	quadrant
quint/pent-	five	quintet/pentagon
re-	back, again	review
retro-	backward	retrospect
semi-	half	semicircle
sub-	under, below	submarine
super-	above, extra	supercharge
tele-	far	telescope
theo-	God or gods	theology, theologian
trans-	across, over	transcontinental
tri-	three	triangle
un-	not	unpopular

B. Useful Roots

Root	Meaning	Example
am	love	amorous
ann	year	annual
aster/astro	star	asteroid, astronaut
aud/audit	hear	audible, audition
bene	good, well	benefit
bio	life	biology
cap	take, hold	capacity
cede	go	exceed
chron(o)	time	chronology
cord	heart	cordial
corp	body	corpse
cred	believe	credible
cur	run	excursion
dent	tooth	dentist
dict	tell, say	dictionary
duc/duct	lead	introduce
fact/fac	make, do	factory
fid	trust	confident
form	shape	transform
geo	earth	geophysics
graph	write	telegraph
ject	throw	reject
lab	work	laborer
liber	free	liberty
log/logo/logy	study, thought	psychology

Root	Meaning	Example
loqu	speak	colloquial
lust	shine	luster
man	hand	manual
mis/mit	send	missile
mort/mor	die, death	immortal
nat	born	native
path	feeling	sympathy
ped	foot	podiatrist
pel	drive	propel
phono	sound, voice	telephone
photo	light	photosensitive
pop	people	populace
port	carry	portable
rupt	break	interrupt
scrib/script	write	inscription
sect	cut	intersection
sen	feel	sensitive
sen/sent	feel	insensitive
spec	look	spectator
sym/syn	same	synonym
tend/tent/tens	stretch or strain	tension
terr/terre	land, earth	territory
theo	god	theology
tract	pull	attraction
vac	empty	vacant
ven/vent	come	convention
ver	turn	inversion
vert/vers	turn	invert
vis/vid	see	invisible/video
voc	call	vocation

C. Useful Suffixes

Suffix	Sample Word
Suffixes that refer to a state, condition, or quality	
-able	touchable
-ance	assistance
-ation	confrontation
-ence	reference
-ible	tangible
-ion	discussion

Suffix	Sample Word
-ity	superiority
-ive	permissive
-ment	amazement
-ness	kindness
-ous	jealous
-ty	loyalty
-y	creamy

Suffixes that mean "one who"

-an	Italian
-ant	participant
-ee	referee
-eer	engineer
-ent	resident
-er	teacher
-ist	activist
-or	advisor

Suffixes that mean "pertaining to" or "referring to"

-al	autumnal
-hood	brotherhood
-ship	friendship
-ward	homeward

Suffixes used to form verbs

-ate	motivate
-ify	quantify
-ize	customize

Suffixes used to form adverbs

-ly	lively
-able, -ible	touchable
-ac, -ic	psychic
-al	minimal
-ant	belligerent
-ary	contrary
-dom	freedom

Suffixes used to form adjectives

-en	brazen
-ful	faithful
-ive	attentive
-like	birdlike
-ous, -ious	anxious
-some	wholesome
-y	cloudy

Suffix	Sample Word

Suffixes used to form nouns

-ac	insomniac
-ance, -ancy	pregnancy
-ary	adversary
-dom	kingdom
-ence	independence
-er	teacher
-hood	parenthood
-ion, -tion	transaction
-ism	tourism
-ist	activist
-ment	employment
-ness	kindness
-ship	friendship
-ure	tenure

CREDITS

Introduction
1: Peter Cade/Getty Images; **2:** Ana Blazic/iStockphoto; **3:** Alexander Denisenko/iStockphoto

Chapter 1
6: Michael Newman/PhotoEdit Inc.; **10:** iStockphoto; **12, top:** Big Stock Photo; **12, bottom:** By permission. From *Merriam-Webster Online* at www.Merriam-Webster. com; **14:** Joseph A. DeVito, *Human Communication: The Basic Course*, 9th Edition, p. 161. Boston: Allyn and Bacon, 2003.

Chapter 2
16: Ken Weingart/Alamy; **17:** Baldur Tryggvason/iStockphoto; **18:** Elmer Parolini/Cartoon Stock; **30, top:** Hulton Archive/ Getty Images; **30, bottom:** DEA/Prima Press/Getty Images; **31:** Chen Chun Wu/iStockphoto; **32:** Alexandr Ozerov/iStockphoto; **35:** John A. Garraty and Mark C. Carnes, *The American Nation*, 10th Edition, p. 267. New York: Longman, 2000.; **36:** Michael Solomon, *Consumer Behavior*, 8th Edition, p. 621. Upper Saddle River, NJ: Pearson Prentice Hall, 2008.; **37:** Joe L. Kincheloe, Patrick Slattery, and Shirley R. Steinberg, *Contextualizing Teaching*, pp. 68–69. New York: Longman, 2000.; **38:** From Baron, Robert A. and Michael J. Kalsher, *Psychology: From Science to Practice*, 1st Edition, pp. 106–111. Published by Allyn and Bacon, Boston, MA. Copyright © 2005 by Pearson Education. Adapted by permission of the publisher.

Chapter 3
44, left: Mark Karass/Corbis; **44, right:** Corbis Premium RF/Alamy; **46:** By permission. From *Merriam-Webster Online* at www.Merriam-Webster.com; **47:** By permission. From *Merriam-Webster Online* at www.Merriam-Webster.com; **48:** Copyright © 2006 by Houghton Mifflin Company. Adapted and reproduced by permission from *The American Heritage Dictionary of the English Language, Fourth Edition.*; **53, top:** Copyright © 2006 by Houghton Mifflin Company. Adapted and reproduced by permission from *The American Heritage Dictionary of the English Language, Fourth Edition.*; **53, bottom:** Randy Glasbergen; **55:** Copyright © 2006 by Houghton Mifflin Company. Adapted and reproduced by permission from *The American Heritage Dictionary of the English Language, Fourth Edition.*; **56:** Copyright © 2006 by Houghton Mifflin Company. Adapted and reproduced bypermission from *The American Heritage Dictionary of the English Language, Fourth Edition.*; **59:** Copyright © 2006 by Houghton Mifflin Company. Adapted and reproduced by permission from *The American Heritage Dictionary of the English Language, Fourth Edition.*; **61, top:** From *Roget's 21st Century Thesaurus*. © 1992, 1993, 1999, 2005 by The Philip Lief Group. Published by Dell Publishing. Reprinted by permission of The Philip Lief Group.; **61, bottom:** Terry Warner/ Cartoon Stock; **64:** From Elaine Marieb, *Essentials of Human Anatomy & Physiology*, 9th Edition, pp. 408–409. Copyright © 2009 Pearson Education, Inc., publishing as Benjamin Cummings. Reprinted by permission.; **66:** From Rebecca J. Donatelle, *Access to Health*, 10th Edition, pp. 74, 91–94, 100–101. Copyright © 2008 Pearson Education, Inc., publishing as Pearson Benjamin Cummings. Reprinted with permission.; **69:** By permission. From *Merriam-Webster's Collegiate® Dictionary, 11th Edition.* © 2007 by Merriam-Webster, Incorporated. (www.Merriam-Webster.com); **70:** By permission. From *Merriam-Webster's Collegiate® Dictionary, 11th Edition.* © 2007 by Merriam-Webster, Incorporated. (www.Merriam-Webster.com)

Chapter 4
71: Words and Meanings/Mark Sykes/Alamy; **74:** Steve Snyder/iStockphoto; **75:** Big Stock Photo; **85-86:** James M. Henslin, *Social Problems*, 6th Edition, pp. 72, 118. Upper Saddle River, NJ: Prentice Hall, 2003.; **86:** Michael D. Johnson, *Human Biology: Concepts and Current Issues*, 2nd Edition, p. 27. San Francisco: Benjamin/ Cummings, 2003. **87:** Dimitry Kalinin/iStockphoto; **96:** Edward F. Bergman and William H. Renwick, *Introduction to Geography*, 2nd Edition, pp. 323, 329, 332. Upper Saddle River, NJ: Prentice Hall, 2002.; **97:** Judy Ledbetter/iStockphoto; **103:** James M. Henslin, *Social Problems*, 6th Edition, pp. 187, 192, 205. Upper Saddle River, NJ: Prentice Hall, 2003.; **106:** Philip G. Zimbardo and Richard J. Gerrig, *Psychology and Life*, 15th Edition, pp. 404–405. New York: Longman, 1999.; **107:** Steven A. Beebe and John T. Masterson, *Communicating in Small Groups*, 6th Edition, pp. 120–122. New York: Longman, 2000.; **109:** From Edward F. Bergman and William H. Renwick, *Introduction to Geography: People, Places and Environment*, 3rd Edition, pp. 91–92. © 2005. Reprinted by permission of Pearson Education, Inc., Upper Saddle River, NJ.

Chapter 5
113: Matt Cardy/Getty Images; **114:** Hedda Gjerpen/iStockphoto; **116:** Craig Barhorst/iStockphoto **121:** iStockphoto; **124:** Halima Ahkdar/Big Stock Photo; **126:** iStockphoto; **128:** James Gately/iStockphoto; **131:** The Menil Collection and Artists Rights Society; **133:** Christy Thompson/iStockphoto; **138, top:** Big Stock Photo; **138, bottom:** Rolf Bodmer/iStockPhoto; **143:** Sylvia Nasar, *A Beautiful Mind: A Biography of John Forbes Nash, Jr., Winner of the Nobel Prize in Economics, 1994.*; New York: Simon & Schuster, 1998.; **144, top:** "New Zoom Paper Describes How to Use Bluetooth® to Move Pictures, Music, and Outlook Contact Names Between a Mobile Phone and a Computer" taken from Marketwire News Releases, 2/4/08. Reprinted by permission of Zoom Technologies, Inc.; **144, bottom:** Annie Proulx, *That Old Ace in the Hole*. London: Fourth Estate, 2002.; **145:** From Vivian, John, *The Media of Mass Communication*, 7/e 2006 Update, pp. 111–113. Published by Allyn and Bacon, Boston, MA. Copyright © 2006 by Pearson Education. Adapted by permission of the publisher.

Chapter 6
150: Jagadeesh/Reuters/Corbis; **154:** From George Beekman and Michael J. Quinn, *Tomorrow's Technology and*

You, 8th Edition, pp. 225–226. © 2008. Reprinted by permission of Pearson Education, Inc., Upper Saddle River, NJ.

Chapter 7
158: Tim Pannell/Corbis; **162:** Sarah Kershaw, "As Shocks Replace Police Bullets, Deaths Drop but Questions Arise," *The New York Times*, March 7, 2004. From The New York Times on the Web, © 2004 The New York Times Company. Reprinted with permission. Graphic "How a Taser Works" © AP/Wide World Photos. Used by permission.; **163:** Courtesy TASER International

Chapter 8
168: David Joel/Getty Images; **172:** From Janice Thompson and Melinda Manore, *Nutrition: An Applied Approach*, My Pyramid Edition, pp. 80–83. Copyright © 2006 Pearson Education, Inc., publishing as Benjamin Cummings. Reprinted by permission.; **173:** Jean-Luc Morales/Getty Images

Chapter 9
177: Comstock/Jupiter Images; **182:** From Linda Perkins, "The New Immigrants and Education: Challenges and Issues," *Educational HORIZONS,* Winter 2000, pp. 116–117. Reprinted by permission of the author.

Chapter 10
186: Charles O'Rear/Corbis; **190:** From Leon G. Schiffman and Leslie Lazar Kanuk, *Consumer Behavior*, 8th Edition, pp. 330, 338–340. © 2004. Reprinted by permission of Pearson Education, Inc., Upper Saddle River, NJ.

Chapter 11
195: Leslie Garland Picture Library/Alamy; **199:** From Neil A. Campbell et al., *Biology: Concepts and Connections*, 5/e, pp. 564–565. Copyright © 2006 Pearson Education, Inc., publishing as Benjamin Cummings. Reprinted by permission.; **200:** Bob Child/AP/Wide World Photos

Chapter 12
203: Ira Block/Getty Images; **207:** From James M. Henslin, *Sociology: A Down-to-Earth Approach*, 8th Edition, pp. 312–316 and Fig 11.6. Published by Allyn and Bacon, Boston, MA. Copyright © 2007 by Pearson Education. Adapted by permission of the publisher.

Chapter 13
212: Chip Somodevilla/Getty Images; **217:** From George C. Edwards III et al., *Government in America: People, Politics, and Policy*, 12th Edition, pp. 188–189. Copyright © by Pearson Education, Inc. Reprinted with permission.

Chapter 14
221: Jeff J. Mitchell/Reuters/Landov; **225:** John Collier, "The Chaser." Originally appeared in *The New Yorker*, 1940. © 1951 by John Collier. Renewed 1978, 2006 by the estate of John Collier. Permission to reprint granted by Harold Matson Co., Inc.

Chapter 15
229: Mark Hill/Alamy; **234:** From Paul Zelanski and Mary Pat Fisher, *The Art of Seeing*, 7th Edition, p. 464. © 2007. Reprinted by permission of Pearson Education, Inc., Upper Saddle River, NJ.; **234:** Reunion des Musees Nationaux/Art Resource, NY

INDEX